HOW TO WRITE THEMES AND TERM PAPERS

THIRD EDITION

by Barbara Lenmark Ellis

Assistant Professor of Technical Journalism, Oregon State University

BARRON'S

New York • London • Toronto • Sydney

All inquiries should be addressed to:

Barron's Educational Series, Inc.
250 Wireless Boulevard
Hauppauge, New York 11788

Library of Congress Catalog Card No. 89-15045
International Standard Book No. 0-8120-4268-9

Library of Congress Cataloging-in-Publication Data

Lenmark-Ellis, Barbara.
  How to write themes and term papers.

  Rev. ed. of: Barron's how to write themes and
term papers. 2nd ed. © 1981.
  Bibliography
  Includes index.
  1. Report writing.   I. Lenmark-Ellis, Barbara.
Barron's how to write themes and terms papers.
II. Title
LB2369.L385   1989   808'.02   89-15045
ISBN 0-8120-4268-9

PRINTED IN THE UNITED STATES OF AMERICA
  1 100 987654

To my hard-working writers
at Maine's Gorham High School,
Oregon's Pacific University,
and Oregon State University.
Barbara Lenmark Ellis

TABLE OF CONTENTS

Section II   THE TERM PAPER

Section **III** WRITING ABOUT COMPLEX
SUBJECTS 198

Section **IV** THE COLLEGE APPLICATION
AUTOBIOGRAPHY

INTRODUCTION

Most students hate theme writing and for some rather solid reasons. Aside from the normal aversion to written work, students rarely have been assigned enough themes to pick up any kind of skill in writing. Most know they are on shaky ground in the spelling, grammar, and mechanics departments. Too, some students may feel that they must come across with the Nobel Prize in literature, junior grade, in composition work, or else! Even if the student could write great prose, if he could put commas in the right spot, if he could organize his thoughts, and if he could clean up the spelling, there's still the problem of making the theme rich in content.

Some canny students decide to cater to the whims of their English instructors, but that method doesn't really teach you how to write well. While most composition teachers have different tastes in composition, they agree that a theme is a good one if it has three qualities: clarity, content, and organization.

The mastery of these three skills will be helpful not only in theme writing, but in doing essay tests, term papers, theses, abstracts, and even contractual bids in business.

This book is not a grammar book. You'll have to use class and homework assignments to conquer your particular grammar problems. You'll have to make those grammar lessons apply to the theme pointers in this book. However, we have included help for those with spelling difficulties—and there are millions of poor spellers around—by a section on a sensible way to curb this problem. There are also chapters on words and usage and on punctuation.

Nor is this book a text in creative writing *per se*. For this reason, the narrative form of theme writing has been excluded so that only the three traditional categories—argumentative, descriptive, and expository (explanatory) —are used. In most high schools and colleges, there are few Hemingways or Melvilles abuilding. There might be those who can write poetically and who give promise of great expectations for a writing future. But too many of these creative writers look at the hard work and financial sacrifices of free lancing as a career and promptly go into selling cars or real estate, or the professions. Since most students will not be using creative writing, they need a book on basic writing skills that anyone will need in ordinary life.

If you do want to write creatively, however, your talents will not suffer if you apply what you learn here to that form of more sophisticated writing.

A word to those in mathematics, engineering, and the science fields: Of all those taking composition, you'll have greater need to know how to write understandable English possibly than any of your friends in other disciplines of study. There was a time when people headed for careers in science, engineering and mathematics shrugged off English composition courses as being of little use in their futures. But the shrugs proved to be expensive in the long run. Many mathematics and science students have had to pay to have someone edit or rewrite (or even write) or organize their reports, abstracts, or theses. Some leaned on friends and probably diminished that relationship considerably. It's better to know how to do it yourself.

There are firms that exist solely because of gaps in writing skills by men and women in the scientific and business communities. One New York research company in Rockefeller Center operates on a seven-figure budget, spending most of its energies "coordinating research" (clarifying often unintelligible reports) from oil and automobile firms. One executive there claimed recently that most engineers seem to write in the James Joyce stream-of-consciousness style. "If they ever learn how to put one word in front of another," the executive said, "we'll be out of business."

Whatever your purpose is in writing, this book will serve as a quick and ready reference on organizing, on theme content, and on style. You will note that it puts a lot of stress on satisfying the reader or at least on consideration of the reader. He is on the receiving end of your writing, after all, and deserves more than to be left in confusion. Whatever you do you *must* keep the reader in mind as you write your theme.

As far as term papers are concerned, the student will discover that the methods explained in this book are easy to understand and are useful for almost any topic or course of study. Moreover, the term-paper techniques can be utilized further. There are the preliminaries to papers for advanced degrees or to reports required in future jobs. Research has to do with careful investigatory work and an intelligibly written report on the findings.

The section on college autobiographies is aimed rather specifically at high school seniors, but its lessons certainly do not stop there. Anyone called upon to write about himself will find the material helpful. Whether one is 18 or nearing his 50s, he will do a résumé about his background for many places of employment in this country.

The writing of themes, term papers, or autobiographies all can be mastered without anguish or confusion and within a short period of time—perhaps a few hours—if the student practices what he reads in this book. What does take time and effort cannot be given in a crash course or 10 easy lessons on composition. That has to do with the reading, the experiences of life, the ability to mull over such information, and to draw some original conclusions.

In instances where the pronouns *he* and *him* appear, they have been used to conform with standard prose. It should be understood that in every case, except where specifically stated, these references apply to both male and female students.

SECTION I

THEMES

CHAPTER 1

THE OUTLINE

Who does not remember the time when his class was told to work up an outline and then to write a theme from it? Someone was bound to do the writing part first and then, to pacify the teacher, scribble an outline that revealed all too clearly what a hash he had made of the organizing. If he was an A student, he probably tore up the first draft and rewrote it in keeping with the organization he should have had in the first place with an outline. If he was pulling "gentlemanly C's" or worse, he probably brazened it out, hoping the teacher would never notice. Invariably she did, of course, and only made him decide to be more devious the next time an outline assignment came up.

No wonder mental blocks have arisen about outlines.

The Jot Outline

If you're to get A's or even B's on your themes, you might as well face the fact that you're going to have to make some kind of outline. It need not be one of those fussy and elaborate jobs with the Roman numerals before main points, the capital letters before subdivisions in thought, the Arabic numbers in sub-subdivisions and the meek little a's and b's in whatever it was that was left over. Indeed, your outline may be nothing more than some cryptic jottings in the paper's margin, or they may look like a series of hentracks to others.

In fact it's called just that, a "jot outline." Should your instructor later demand a formal outline, you will find it relatively easy to convert a jot outline to the formalities of I, A, 1, a, and so forth.

The body, or main part, of all your themes will come from the jot outline if you follow the simple procedures in this book. Students who have used it declare it's easy to learn and vital to any written work. It takes about ten minutes to learn how to do a jot outline and five minutes, when you get in some practice at it, to do when you're writing a theme.

There are two simple parts to such a jot outline. The first part involves jottings. The second part involves the arrangement of those jottings into some kind of order.

In practice it works something like this: When you get the theme topic, jot down *every* thought on the subject that comes into your head. It doesn't matter what it is. Put it down. Despite how mixed up, how disjointed the thoughts may seem or how unrelated they are—in one word or several—the thoughts should be scribbled out. If it's a class theme, put the jottings in the margins of a paper or on a separate piece of paper. If the theme is to be homework, jot down whatever comes into your head when you *first* see the topic. There's a sound psychological reason for the put-it-down-immediately approach. Ideas are fresher and more workable than they will be later.

Remember that these are your own jottings. Nobody else will care about them. Never mind spelling, usage, legibility, or grammatical niceties. The jottings might involve phrases, a single word. You might write only an abbreviation that is meaningful to you. Perhaps even a number means something to you as it concerns the topic. Whatever they are, all jottings should jog your memory about what you're going to put into the theme. To be really helpful, of course, your jottings should include some specific examples. Above all, remember that you don't need Roman numerals or other frills of the formal outline with this method.

Below, you'll find an example of jottings from one such outline. Don't let the topic unnerve you. The students working with this one already had read the two Russian novels on which the topic was based. This is the topic:

Dostoyevsky's *The House of the Dead* and Tolstoy's *Resurrection* both show the punishments in the 1800's given to political and criminal prisoners in Siberia. What do you think of the punishments given to both classes of prisoners in that era?

One student's jottings looked something like this and ran along the top of the first page:

> Dead
> bribes, chains, barges
> 20 murders = only exile
> no books - Bible
> green sticks
> roaches
> 1930 trials
> Koestler + brainwash
> Stalin - liquidations
> 1984
>
> Resur.
> Vera - books
> allow - family - trot; czar
> Larissa (in Dr. Z.)
> food
> 130 no passports
> doctors kind
> bribes, bureaucrats
>
> (Siberia, beautiful, cold, people stay after release)

If that topic still scared you off, watch what one student did with jottings on a well-worn topic that many teachers still give: "What I Did Last Summer." Here is his work on jottings:

To show you just how cryptic you can get, here's one from a girl who wrote on the topic "Patterns I Like in Jazz":

In each outline the jottings made a great deal of sense to the theme writer even though "outsiders," reading them today, can make no sense of them. Each item perhaps provided the meat that made up this or that theme. There's not a Roman numeral, a capital letter, or an Arabic number anywhere. Nor did neatness count.

The next step is to put the jottings quickly in to some kind of order.

This step should be a fast one. All you do is to sort out the jottings. Some you can delete by running a line through them if the jottings are off the subject. Those jottings you want to keep can be put into some kind of order perhaps by numbering them. Or maybe you'll prefer just to circle them. Or maybe checks will work for you. It doesn't matter so long as you find a method of order that takes no more than a minute to do. Remember, however, to put down first the most important things in the theme. You may run out of time to get everything in if you are doing a classroom theme. Even if you're writing the theme out of class, get in the most important things first.

How some students "sorted out" their jottings are shown in the next examples:

> 2 courage - Crane
> 3 coward - Gröss
> 6 suffering - Hasek & Remarque
> 5 friend - Mailer
> 4 enemy - Rem
> 1 amoral - Cross of Iron

One student with a naturally organized mind needed no numbers. All he did on a theme on "Business Ethics" was to circle the three items he wanted to write about first. He did it like this:

> Teapot D   Bobby Baker
>   NHG   Bell Tel.
> Nader   Wythe
>   Sinclair (Jung.)
> Westing. G.E.
> Norris - S.P. - Cyclamates -
>   the movers and F.T.C.

One girl who couldn't shake off completely the old formal outline used the alphabet to sort out the order for a theme on "The Riches Given by Science" in this way:

> B destruct { A-bomb - Hiro   A'comm. (TV, tel. rad)
>   ship - Savannah   A'home { clocks
>   heated water fish   plumb.
>   stove
> A const { Jenner, Lister, Pasteur, Salk B'home (tel. TV)
>   pollution (R. Carson, etc.)
>   Barnard and canibaliz.

There was, to be sure, the student writer who put half of his ideas on one side of the paper, the other half on the other, and then checked them off. Such is the case for this theme on "In Defense of the TV Western" which was outlined like this:

So no matter what your method is—checks, numbers, circles, squares, or letters—indicate some kind of order in which you'll tackle each phase of the theme.

You will notice, by the way, that students here had specific examples to illustrate the points they planned to take up. It is one of the things this book will emphasize, for in good theme writing as in any other kind of writing, you must underpin those statements of yours with some proof.

Here's how to practice the jot outline:

Give yourself a topic. Any one will do, but it helps if it's one interesting to you. Allow yourself 15 minutes on the jottings as they come into your mind concerning the topic. Then begin to put them into some kind of order with numbers or letters or other notations. That should take about 10 minutes for a good reflective job. Add specific examples or even new points as they occur to you. Then, cut your time in half, 7 minutes for the jottings, 5 minutes to put things in order. Cut your time still more until you get the two operations *combined* down to 5 minutes. In classroom themes, 5 minutes spent this way is all you'll be able to allow if you plan to finish by the time the bell sounds at the end of the class.

In the end, no matter what subject is assigned, you'll know what to put into your theme if you use this jot outline technique. You'll present a specific-example-laden composition as well as a well-organized one. Never again will you be that frantic soul who rationalizes his F on themes by complaining: "My mind just went blank, that's all. I couldn't think of a thing to write." Indeed, the only trouble you may have at all is in deciding what to winnow *out* of the theme.

The Quick and Dirty Outline

A speedy variation of the ''jot outline'' is known as the ''quick and dirty outline.'' A quick and dirty outline is just what its name suggests: It can be laid down quickly and neatness does not count.

This is what an outline looks like that describes what will go in a term paper (theme, essay examination). It is based on the jottings, described earlier, that came from the thinking of one student asked to write on the topic "What I Have Learned From Studying Milton."

This kind of outline offers a graphic illustration of what could be a paragraph-by-paragraph structure of a composition. One box could stand for one paragraph. Or it could stand for several.

With a quick and dirty outline, you actually can visualize—immediately—what goes in each paragraph. You quickly can throw down nearly 20 "boxes" of an inch square or larger. (Making the boxes smaller, blocks thinking; it's vital for you to feel you have elbow room when working on the thoughts that will become a fine composition.) It's important that the boxes are large enough and that they contain no more than one word or symbol in each. To put more than one word in a box—or a symbol such as "$" or a letter "M"—means that you're more involved in perfection than using an outline for its fundamental purpose: as a quick reference tool toward writing a composition.

Once you come up with the jottings, you can fill each box with what you want and where you want it. You can see—instantly—which topic grows out of another. Which topic logically follows another. Which topic starts the composition and which ends it. If you change your mind with a quick and dirty outline, you either can erase it or draw an arrow showing where you are shifting material.

For example, in the figure shown, the student decided to deal with diction after imagery and rhyme and meter were to go toward the end of the theme. She put her brief summation of what she would be writing about in the second paragraph, wrapping it up in two sentences.

From there, she took up the first topic she mentioned in that summation and did seven paragraphs on imagery. Then, she took up diction and wrote six paragraphs about it, making a point and then illustrating it with an example. That is the jotting system mentioned earlier in this chapter.

Most writing professionals point out that one of the principal reasons for "writer's block" is not knowing where to go with a piece. With that kind of quandary, a writer gets overwhelmed and then sits immobilized. As a student, you've probably done the same thing. You stare at a piece of paper with a good topic, but you don't know where you're going with it; you don't know what to put where. In the end, you begin fretting about the time that is passing and the class deadline for the theme or paper. Then you give up.

With a "quick and dirty outline" you know exactly where you're going. The question becomes perhaps what to leave out, you have so much to say. Within one or two minutes after your jottings are out of your mind and down on a corner of the paper, you suddenly know what you're going to say in that theme or term paper or report. You can put it at your elbow and type away.

To become proficient at this type of outline, you need to practice for an hour or so on various topics. Do several. Again, do not worry about neatness. This is not an art project. It is a tool to help you write.

meter
Rhyme
① philosophy — theology
imagry
② diction
themes
vowels

open
Paradise
Lost

Summary
① Phil
② dict.
③ P.Skills

phil — theo

Dict.

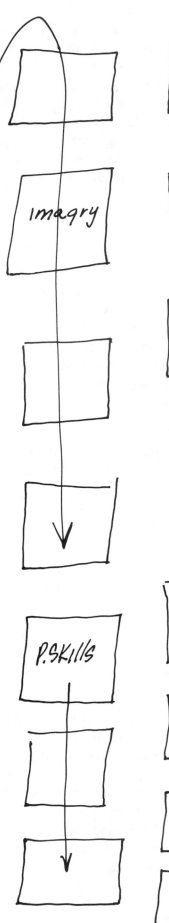

imagry

P.Skills

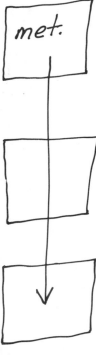

met.

rhyme

vowels

close

CHAPTER

THE THEME'S
BEGINNING

The beginning of a theme is probably the hardest thing to write, as you certainly know already. In that opening paragraph, the student knows he must reveal the subject of the composition and, above all, he must not bore while doing it. Small wonder that professional writers take hours and sometimes days and weeks to do a superb job of that opening. They know they must catch the editors' eyes in that first paragraph of a manuscript.

But you don't have hours, days, and weeks for themes or most writing projects. You might have just the 50-minute class period or overnight, or, at most, two weeks. And no matter what you think, you do not need to come up with an "opener" on themes that is a match for the best of Steinbeck or Victor Hugo.

Once in awhile you may turn out an opener that truly is magnificent, but few authors can do that regularly. This usually does not happen to students who have many compositions to turn in during the year. You can't shine all the time, but you can do a good regular job on openers if you keep reminding yourself that you first want to secure the reader's attention and, second, to supply a brief resumé of the theme.

When to Write the Beginning

You could write the beginning last and mark it for insertion at the beginning of the theme. That way you would have finished the theme and then could present a capsule view of what's in the entire composition. Those adroit at this, however, know that if a theme is being done in class, there is an element of risk in ever getting around to the beginning if it's left until last. What might be left is a body without a head, so to speak.

If you do your beginnings first, as most do, don't agonize over them. Don't spend more than five minutes on them if they are class themes. Themes written outside class shouldn't involve more than 15 to 30 minutes spent on a beginning.

What Goes Into the Beginning?

Basically, the opener should entail one or two paragraphs that tell the reader what he's getting into. Such beginning paragraphs should be short, but intriguing—especially if the subject is a dull one. You want to keep the reader awake. Therefore, the first sentence of the opening paragraph is the most extraordinarily important. To rivet his attention, however, don't include such amateurish starts as "Wow!" or "Good news!" or "Wait until you read this!"

No poll among teachers has ever been taken, but it is almost a certainty they would agree that the following six openers are most likely to exasperate them, so often have these sentences been used by students. These are:

> "I have been assigned to write a theme on . . ."
> "Here I sit, pondering what to write this theme on ."
> "What is fear? Webster's dictionary defines *fear* as . . ."
> "What is love? What is it, indeed? What is hate?"
> "Are you affected by feelings of vengeance, h'mmm?"
> "To be artistic or not to be artistic, that is the question ."

Why Are These Openers Guaranteed to Bore or to Irritate?

No professional writer would start off an article with: "I have been asked by *Sports Illustrated* to write on the subject of . . ." No editorial writer would begin: "The management of this newspaper said I had to write a 350-word editorial on the subject of . . ." In short, never hint at the "assignment" opener or use the word *theme* at any place in the composition.

Aside from the prepositional ending on the second example, few readers really care what mood or what troubles beset the writer. Perhaps they're too dispassionate, but they want the author to get on with the subject and to stop lamenting about his physical or mental problems.

The Webster-dictionary approach in the third example is a stale one used by all too many students stumped for a fresh beginning. They feel a few words from Webster's will pad out a paragraph or more to procrustean lengths.

The "what is love?" lead on the fourth example tells the reader he is about to get snarled in a dispute over the definition of words. He knows such a dispute could go on for pages without coming to grips with the main topic. Writers who back into theme topics in this way not only lose their reader at the end of the first sentence, but also reveal that they, too, are about to find a method to pad out a composition by writing around the subject. It is true that such an opener is very appropriate for a philosophy course where exactness of language is a prime virtue. But in the ordinary high school or college theme, it is not necessary to beat around the semantical bush.

The "you" appeal on the fifth example is offensive to many readers. A first reaction is that of annoyance at a writer who wants to get too familiar. The exception is in explanatory writing, of course, but here few writers get too informal with readers as they instruct. They often employ the "you-understood" form of address and leave out that irksome word *you*. The personal touch of *you* used to be considered effective by hard-sell advertising copywriters, but of late, even these people have toned down this blatant appeal.

The last example of poor openers, the quotation-paraphrase, is an admission the student has so little confidence that he must lean on another's words. Some think they'll be classed with Aristotle or De Tocqueville if they use their names or words in a composition. Or they may feel they'll be thought of as a Shakespearean scholar if they paraphrase or employ direct quotes from his plays often enough. Sadly, this weakness appears all too often in professional writing, particularly editorial columns. It indicates the writer's fear of standing on his own prose, his own opinions. In the case of students, such quotation openers are usually so clumsily done, so inappropriate or so indicative of the "leaning" weakness, as to merit the low grades they rightly should get on such writing. Don't lean. Use your own words.

What kind of beginning sentence should be used then?

If we have selected as taboo your favorite theme openings in the six examples, don't despair. Try to be a little original. Think up openers that will make the reader laugh, or become thoughtful, or be angry, or fascinated. And don't fall into the habit of using the same type of opener on all themes once you do find a satisfactory one.

There are four types of opening sentences you might try for your beginning paragraph in the theme. These are humor, a startling statement or fact, an interesting anecdote, or a *new* metaphor or simile.

The Humorous Opener

To illustrate the humorous openers, here are some examples from student themes:

Does anyone ever stop to think that a horse may have ticklish feet?

Or

There are three things a girl usually looks for in a husband: he must be as boyish as Teddy Kennedy, as rich as the Rockefeller brothers, and as kind as St. Francis of Assisi.

Or

Just because Polonius pocketed Hamlet's love letters to Ophelia is no reason to criticize the mail service at Elsinore or anywhere else.

The Startling Opener

For the startling statement or fact that is to arrest attention from a reader, you'll have to rely on surprising statistics, revelations, or remarks. One such opener on the subject of sports boredom was:

It didn't surprise me to learn that baseball bores 200,000,000 of 280,000,000 Americans.

A college sophomore, countering a popular theory, wrote:

Only the self-satisfied or the selfish can believe the "fullness of life" philosophies of writers Santayana, Dinesen, or Ibañez.

A somewhat heretical approach was contained in this opening sentence:

No matter what the Bible says, vengeance by man is often justified and often sweet.

The Anecdotal Opener

The anecdotal opener has been thought of as the best way to sustain reader interest. Stories *per se* have always carried an especial weight with readers, no matter what their age. Witness the fact that almost anyone can be intrigued with those familiar words: "Once upon a time . . ." With the anecdotal opener, of course, you need not resort to the once-upon-a-time level of writing. But you certainly will use many of the elements of this popular style. On the topic of "Predestination," admittedly a heavy subject, one theme writer began this way:

When I was a boy, I used to sit on the back porch and wonder if God knew before I did that I was going to scratch my toe.

In profiling a neighbor, one girl wrote:

There is a little white-haired lady who digs up crab grass in her yard across from us. One day as I passed, she stood up and hollered at me.

Then there was this interesting anecdote as an opener:

One afternoon, a car drove up in the Square and out stepped Uncle Mike. The car was a 1923 Rolls-Royce, and he informed us he had just bought it for $25 from a man who had only used it to drive to church.

The Metaphorical Opener

The student who wants to use openers involving similes and metaphors must recognize that he is in for a lot of difficulties. Similes and metaphors need a colorful and original comparison of one thing to another. Eyes become limpid pools. Men are Herculean. Machinery sounds like the roar of the sea. Heroines are "like the heavenly angels." Similes and metaphors are designed to summon up a vivid image in quick and emphatic fashion. Sometimes, however, student writers go too far in using such imagery.

This is not to say that you should avoid simile and metaphor openers in the beginning paragraph, but you had better be proficient at it. Incidentally, this is one place where the student who has a bent for creative writing is allowed a somewhat free hand.

This theme on "War" certainly had plenty of mood and imagery:

> War with its rotting corpses, agonized screams of the wounded, acrid smoke of gunpowder, and terrors of the conquered is seen as a necessity by the philosopher Santayana in his essay "Tipperary."

Then there was the metaphorical one:

> The faithlessness shown by an Anna Karenina is the Rorschach ink stain on civilized society.

Another metaphorical opener brought in *Don Quixote*, the Spanish novel, as the author of a theme wrote on the qualities of his future wife:

> A wife should be a Rosinante. Although she was not much on looks or health, the loyal steed required little food, little care, little love, and illustrates the qualities of my prospective mate.

Having seized the reader's attention by one engaging opening sentence or two, you should use the rest of the paragraph to give him the résumé of the theme as a whole. Give him a summation of what you're going to say throughout the composition. If you're writing an explanatory theme, for example, use a sentence or two after the opener to *explain* what you are attempting to *explain*. This sentence may follow the first one in the paragraph, or it may be the first sentence of a second paragraph of the opening.

If you're writing a descriptive theme, you'll have to include a sentence after the opening one on what is to be described. The reader will want to know if he's to be put in the Gobi desert or if he is admiring the view from McMurdo Sound.

For argumentative themes, the reader will be curious about what is to be debated and, certainly, what your position is. Such a sentence or two should be direct and clear. Don't be vague. It might be well to warn you from using satire unless you can use it skillfully. Satire presumes the reader understands that the writer is being sarcastic about his topic. It also presupposes the reader understands that while the theme appears to be supporting something or someone on the surface, it is instead a savage or needling attack on the subject. Newspaper columnist Art Buchwald, in satirizing the Federal Bureau of Investigation, once declared with tongue-in-cheek that there really was no J. Edgar Hoover at the F.B.I. Many people failed to grasp the broad strokes of humor Buchwald traditionally uses. For months afterward, people wrote to their newspapers asking, "You mean there *really* is no J. Edgar Hoover?"

Tying opening sentences to the rest of the beginning paragraph looks something like the following examples. Notice that the first sentence is the intriguing opener of the paragraph, the sentence that is to attract the reader into the rest of the composition. The remaining sentences reveal the gist of the entire theme.

The first sample is in the category of argumentative themes and has a humorous approach to a serious subject:

> Just because Polonius pocketed Hamlet's love letters to Ophelia is no reason to criticize the mail service at Elsinore or anywhere else. A post office is the nerve center of communications in every community and should not be involved in any kind of suppressive act by a governmental leader even when complaints rise about poor service.

Here is the rest of that anecdotal opener which was attached to a descriptive theme:

> There is a little white-haired lady who digs up crab grass in her yard across from us. One day as I passed, she stood up and hollered at me. But then that was Mrs. Smith's way of inviting us to a party.

The explanatory theme that opened with a startling statement or fact had a beginning paragraph put this way:

> No matter what the Bible says, vengeance by man is often justified and often sweet. If this weren't so, there wouldn't be almost a murder a minute in the world, half of which are said to be vendetta killings. States wouldn't have capital punishment either if vengeance weren't in the minds of most of the law-makers and citizens who continue to break the Bible's injunction about vengeance being a province of the Lord.

In each case, the sentences following the openers gave broad hints of the subject matter contained in the themes.

Some theme writers use a second short paragraph to spell out the issues or the terms to be contained in the topic:

> A gerrymander is a slicing of voting areas into districts favorable to one political party.

The second paragraph could be used to explain the need for a reader to know something about the subject:

> Because rabies can strike anyone, people must know how to deal with this disease.

The second paragraph also can point up some recent event that makes the theme topic timely or important:

> Since the Common Market may put Americans out of many jobs eventually, we must know about it.

Or the second paragraph could tell the reader about the limitations, the scope of the theme's subject:

> Only the hidden charges in time payments will be taken up here.

Or it could be a paragraph explaining how the topic will be handled:

> We will move from the Job Corps Program and Head Start to Vista.

The points to be covered may be detailed:

We must look at the financing, the use, the criticism, the praise, and the ultimate goals of the Rural Electrification Administration.

In short, the second paragraph—if you decide to use one for expanding the beginning—completes the résumé of what the theme is about and what may be said in it to aid the reader as he studies your writing. In class themes, there is no need (and probably no time) to stretch out the beginning to more than two paragraphs.

THE ARGUMENTATIVE
THEME

The first type of theme to be taken up is the argumentative one. This usually takes on the aspect of convincing or selling a reader on something. You might write, for example, on why you think Shakespeare's King Lear is not really mad. In so doing, you'd be trying to argue your point of view.

Within the argumentative theme division we have included abstract topics, the most common type of theme subjects given to students. Who doesn't remember the topics "Patriotism," "Friendship," "Humor," "Duty" and the like? We have put abstract topics in the argumentative theme category because experience has shown that student writers can produce more substantial themes if they can argue the pro and con sides of the theme topic. Working through the advantages and disadvantages of, say, "Duty" or "Friendship," a student suddenly will have plenty to say instead of putting down the old platitudes.

General Topics

The general argumentative topic asks you to surrender your beliefs about an aspect of a subject. One such theme topic might be this:

> Critics of the play *Our Town* have called the plot sickeningly sweet and dramatically boring. They have called the characters dull and indistinguishable, comparing them to the weakest characters in other American plays. Do you agree with these critics?

Since the play *Our Town* is rather sacrosanct in many American classrooms, such a topic should make the hackles rise. This is why it's considered an argumentative theme topic. Another topic of this type might treat with a subject in this way:

> There has been much criticism recently about the method of drafting young men into the army. Do you feel this criticism is merited?

Another teacher might shorten up the wording, but the following topic still fits into the argumentative category of theme writing:

> Does the American prison system do its job?

Whether the wording on a topic is long or short or left wide open for interpretation, as is shown above, all the topics are designed to get an argument from you. You should be able to recognize this kind of topic from those given you by your teacher from time to time.

Once you classify the type of topic, go to work on the jot outline. Let's use the *Our Town* topic as an example of how to work up a fast outline. Even if you've no acquaintance with this play, you should be able to follow the instructions.

The theme topic gives you two factors to emphasize: the plot (sickeningly sweet and boring), and the characters (dull and indistinguishable). As you make your jottings, putting down everything that comes into your head, use specific events from *Our Town* or from your own experiences to support every point you'll make in the theme. Or you can jot down specifics from other plays. Movies and television dramas also will qualify as examples.

Once you've drained yourself of ideas for the jottings, go to the job of putting them in some kind of simple order. Remember that any system that works for you—checks, numbering, circles—is the one you'll want to use. You may not use everything you've jotted down. The finished outline for the topic may resemble this sophomore's:

open

Plot
    sweet- (no- like all towns - Winesburg
    boring- (no- drunk, wedding, choir,
                                funeral

char
    dull (who isn't - Emily to Excedrin
    indis . (is about town so not need
            vivid characters - no unity
            if peop. emphasized

end
    critics wrong

A student's jottings on the American prison system and the order he put them into finally looked like this:

One student, working on the draft topic, shaped the jot outline into the following:

As has been said previously, use whatever form of jotting and organizing that works for you.

Don't be surprised if you change your mind on the order or even the items that will go into your theme. There may be new items you overlooked or items you'll want to leave out. With a jot outline, such shifts and switches require only a few corrective strokes with your pen.

Introduction

Your opening sentence may employ humor or the startling statement, but the sentences that follow the first paragraph of the theme must indicate what the subject is and briefly convey your viewpoint. You might include the scope of your theme, telling the reader that you're going to use only the high spots or only one part of a major subject. If you're writing on such gigantic topics as, say, religion, electronics, safety, or war, you'll only be able to handle one or two phases of the subject. Most themes run to four or five pages on the average, don't forget, and nobody can do a thorough job on religion, for example, in that number of pages.

In that opening paragraph you must explain the "who" or the "what" of the topic. Explain also the topical reference or "peg," if there is one, on which the theme topic hangs. Is it based on a book, a play, politics, religion, sociology or what?

How one student handled the beginning on the *Our Town* topic is shown in the next example. In it, he took the first two sentences from the topic itself and attached the opinion that he planned to follow throughout the theme:

> Critics of the play *Our Town* have called the plot sickeningly sweet and dramatically boring. They have called the characters dull and indistinguishable, comparing them to the weakest characters in other American plays. Such critics obviously are unaware of the reasons why this Thornton Wilder drama has been popular for years all over the United States.

A beginning of another sort, this one on the draft, tied up the theme with an anecdotal opener built on a topical peg:

> When Congress passed the first conscription act on March 3, 1863, John Q. Workingclass rioted in New York City, causing no end of destruction to property and to lives. That law didn't specify whether he was a family man or a bachelor, whether he was 20, 30, or 45. He didn't have $300 to stall off service until the next call-up. And he could hardly hire a stand-in as the rich could and did. Every time this country has set up a draft, the same inequities turn up.

Yet another beginning paragraph was written by a student who wanted no reader to have any difficulty understanding the topic:

> The American prison system today may have institutions similar to Arkansas where whipping is permitted, but it also has enlightened institutions such as in California where men may work at downtown jobs and take job training courses. Prisons are not all bad in this country.

Whatever opener you use, don't employ one that assumes the reader already knows the topic:

> No, I don't believe the critics are right about *Our Town*.

A beginning paragraph should be able to stand by itself and not hint it answers a theme topic given as an assignment. It should leave no doubt as to what the topic is and briefly should explain the issues.

What Comes After the First Paragraph

Once you have completed the beginning, put in a short paragraph that summarizes the reasons for your conclusions on the overall topic. Itemize, in other words, the points you are going to take up in subsequent paragraphs.

This is the way the student handled the second paragraph of the theme on the draft:

> When Congress passed the first conscription act on March 3, 1863, John Q. Workingclass rioted in New York City, causing no end of destruction to property and to lives. That law didn't specify whether he was a family man or a bachelor, whether he was 20, 30, or 45. He didn't have $300 to stall off service until the next call-up. And he could hardly hire a stand-in as the rich could and did. Every time this country has set up a draft, the same inequities turn up.

> There are four chief drawbacks to the Selective Service system used in the past. Too many men are exempted from service, in the first place. Secondly, the draft interrupts a man's life at an important stage. The draft has been used as a weapon to silence critics of Administration policies, and it is also said to be a system that is particularly hard on the poor. But each of these charges can be countered.

Notice that all the major items to be used in the theme are listed one by one in what is a second paragraph of a theme. Here is another sample second paragraph that itemizes the theme's main points. It employs even a shorter style:

> Each summer, our community becomes vibrant and violent not about world affairs or even the fees charged for dog licenses. Like so many other towns across the face of America, my town is caught up in the throes of something called the Little League, that baseball circuit for pre-teeny bopper boys.

> Little League does teach the game, prevents delinquency, provides fun, but it can be expensive and exclusive. It also teaches competitiveness at too early an age.

The itemization paragraph is stressed here because it will be your guide for the rest of the theme. You must make certain that when you set up your "case," as you'll be doing in the paragraph after the introduction, that you put the most important points of the topic first. What is important is always a matter of personal opinion, but many times the most telling points of a theme topic are obvious to any reader who certainly will notice those that you fail to include. Aside from this, if you deal with the most important points of a topic first, you'll get them all into the theme.

Now What About the Rest of the Theme

You're ready to begin once you get past the 1) beginning paragraph and 2) the itemization paragraph. From here on, you'll find it relatively easy. Briefly, you'll use one paragraph for each "case point" or argument. If you were to do the Little League topic, based on the points the student used above, you would develop one whole paragraph on the fact that the League teaches the game. The next paragraph would take up the argument that the League prevents delinquency. The next paragraph would deal with the fun this organization offers. After that, there would be a paragraph on the fact that the League is expensive, a paragraph on its exclusiveness, and the last paragraph would deal with the ills of teaching competitiveness at too early an age.

A simple diagram shows how easy it is to construct each paragraph. Bear in mind, of course, that you may use more than one paragraph per case point or argument, but here we're treating the basic set up of the argumentative theme. Embellishments can always be added as you gain speed and ease in this theme method. By paragraphs then, the theme would be constructed like this on the Little League topic:

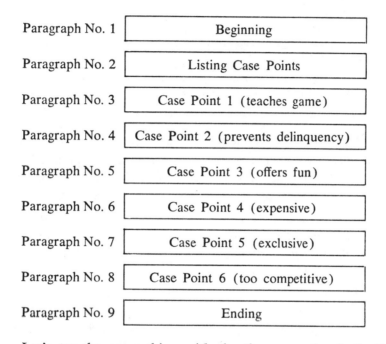

Paragraph No. 1	Beginning
Paragraph No. 2	Listing Case Points
Paragraph No. 3	Case Point 1 (teaches game)
Paragraph No. 4	Case Point 2 (prevents delinquency)
Paragraph No. 5	Case Point 3 (offers fun)
Paragraph No. 6	Case Point 4 (expensive)
Paragraph No. 7	Case Point 5 (exclusive)
Paragraph No. 8	Case Point 6 (too competitive)
Paragraph No. 9	Ending

Let's try the same thing with the theme on the draft. We will take the paragraph where the writer presents the arguments she plans to use and number them. Then we'll set them up for the theme as a whole. Numbering of her arguments, or case points, will be something like this:

There are four chief drawbacks to the Selective Service system used in the past. Too many men are exempted from service, in the first place. Secondly, the draft interrupts a man's life at an important stage. The draft has been used as a weapon to silence critics of Administration policies, and it is also said to be a system that is particularly hard on the poor. But each of these charges can be countered.

The pattern of her theme would be this:

Paragraph No. 1	Beginning
Paragraph No. 2	Listing Case Points
Paragraph No. 3	Case Point 1 (exemptions)
Paragraph No. 4	Case Point 2 (breaks up life)

Paragraph No. 5	Case Point 3 (hard on poor)
Paragraph No. 6	Case Point 4 (used as weapon)
Paragraph No. 7	Case Point 5 (necessary exemptions)
Paragraph No. 8	Case Point 6 (should defend country)
Paragraph No. 9	Case Point 7 (Army gives training)
Paragraph No. 10	Case Point 8 (other systems worse)
Paragraph No. 11	Ending

Once again, this is just a basic one-idea-per-paragraph formula. Most students would probably use two or more paragraphs for each case point.

The setup for the words that go within each paragraph is an easy one to learn. You merely repeat the case point in the first sentence. All other sentences must involve proving that case point statement. That means specific examples, statistics, facts, and the like. A specific example is not made up. It generally involves naming names, dates, places, or the use, as has been said, of statistics and facts. If you were to diagram it, the paragraph would look something like this:

Case Point { The draft system used in the past is hard on the poor, for the most part. The Congressional

Example { committee which did a study on the selective service system reported that 75 per cent of the men drafted between 1962 and 1963 were from families whose total income was less than $3000 a year.

That first sentence of the paragraph where the writer restates the case point can be simple—as it is above—or quite complex. So long as the case point statement is made, it does not matter.

Here is another simple one, followed up by the specific example—also pretty simple:

Case Point { Prisons are cruel sometimes. *The Nation*

Example { magazine recently reported that only about 10 U.S. prisons were without some form of beating of inmates.

And an even simpler one is:

Case Point { Little League teams teach good baseball.

Example { Pitcher Bruce Sutter rates them as best for teaching kids the fundamentals.

A complex one might be this one:

Case Point { The ethics of the business community in this country has never been worse, not even in the Robber Baron stage or when Harding was President.

Example { We have 12 Savings and Loan associations in California accused of bribing a U.S. senator for a favorable vote on a savings-and-loan bill. We have 8 executives from both Westinghouse and G.E. convicted for price rigging on electrical equipment sold to the government. We have 29 oil firms suspected of buying off a federal judge in Tulsa, Oklahoma, so that he would not help to convict them of conspiracy to rig oil prices.

Whatever your style is—simple or complex—the structure to use within these paragraphs is 1) statement, 2) example. Or, if you will, 1) case point, 2) example. And once again, remember that you may take more than one paragraph to finish off a case point. But don't overdo if you expect to cover all the case points you want to cover.

Kind of Examples

A word is necessary here about the kind of examples of use in themes.

Obviously, the example must illustrate the statement or case point. Every reader can spot mistakes in impressive examples even though they don't apply to the case point being made.

While many people will agree with your case point, they may well seize the example you use as inappropriate or exaggerated. They may say the example is a weak one. They may retort with a countering argument that easily undermines your own. That's always the peril of examples.

The writers of exposés and newspaper crusades are among those writers who successfully employ examples that are extreme illustrations of points. In a story on hospital conditions, there's always a writer who finds rats in the kitchen of one hospital for a story on medical conditions around the country even though only one rat was seen in 2000 hospitals. A crusade against police brutality in jail wouldn't be complete unless a writer used an example of how one policeman beat up a handcuffed suspect, despite the fact that everyone else at the stationhouse behaved in an exemplary manner.

The use of extreme examples, called hyperboles, is often effective in calling attention to something. But the thoughtful reader often concludes that one shattering example does not necessarily prove that it represents the total picture. If you yourself plan to use hyperboles, be careful of the ones you select. Your hyperbole may be an obviously isolated case and indicate your poor estimate of issues. You can, of course, use one hyperbole and follow it up with more typical examples to illustrate a case point. That way you would get the reader's attention. Before he can realize it is an atypical example, you can add two more examples that are more representative of the point.

In all examples, be accurate. Don't take quotations out of context from a newspaper story or from someone's speech. Don't twist statistics to suit your position. Don't get the dates wrong or make the facts inaccurate. Don't forget either that some publications you may use as a source aren't holy writ. They make mistakes either intentionally or by accident. All publishers have their own blind spots and prejudices. Statistics on organized labor will be far different in a union paper than they will be in *Fortune* or *Business Week*. "Facts" on civil rights will be different in *Time* than they will be in many Southern newspapers.

Even if you're desperate for an example, don't make up one. You might be proved wrong.

Summary

What about the ending of a general argumentative theme?

Until you develop a store of endings, you'd better stick to one or two methods. One way is to summarize the chief arguments or case points you have covered in the body of the theme. Tell them what you've told them, in other words, but don't use exactly the same words for this "recap." Rephrase your case point statements. Another ending is to make one general statement that sums up your entire position. It's the easier method of the two forms.

Using the *Our Town* topic again, you might handle an ending as this student did, listing the major arguments used in the theme:

> It has been seen, then, that *Our Town* is not sweet or boring so far as plot is concerned because the play echoes life in a small town. The birth-death cycle gives it lots of action. Perhaps the characters were dull and indistinguishable, but ordinary people are usually a little dull anyway. If the playwright had singled out every character for emphasis, he would have had to write a play that would last for weeks. He was trying to portray a to·vn as a whole and this he succeeded in doing.

An ending paragraph that has one general statement that presents all views stipulated in the theme might be:

> The naïve playgoer can't help finding charm and small-town naturalism in *Our Town*. That's why we hicks enjoy it so much.

Handle the ending in as *brief* a form as possible, surely no more than one or two *short* paragraphs.

Don't worry if you don't have time enough to include an ending. Class themes usually use so much time that students are lucky if they can squeeze in an ending. It is not really expected. If the theme is written out of class, that's another story. The ability to end a theme gracefully comes with practice, like anything else, but far more important is the ability to write the material that goes before an ending.

The writing style varies for an argumentative theme. If you use humor, use it wisely. Don't overdo it, particularly on a serious theme topic. The humorous approach demands careful handling if it is to avoid offending or simply falling flat.

Perhaps the best tone to adopt in an argumentative theme of the general sort is one such as is used in the news columns of the papers. When opposing a case point, don't show obvious anger or use sarcasm. Rather, be "concerned" or "disturbed" that "all the facts are not known" by those with opposing views. This makes you seem fair and open-minded. Let your examples speak for themselves and you won't have to shout, to use exclamation points or other outspoken emotions. Borrow a tool from debating and remain cool as you dispute the issues.

It is well to use some choice connective words and "breather" passages, as shown in the section on writing style, when you move from one case point to another. Readers may get lost. Giving them a helping "in addition" or "on the other hand" puts them back on the track.

Abstract Topics

The way for you to tackle some all-encompassing or broad abstract topics such as "Discontent," "Courtesy," and "Laughter," is to argue the pro and con sides. This is the same form as is used by debating teams. You will be organized and you will say something. You will set up your topic, in other words, on the pro (or good) and con (or bad) basis. You will think up the good and bad points about such abstract subjects as "Laughter" (laughter is not *always* a good thing) or "Discontent" (discontent spearheads improvements) and the like.

There are almost always two sides to any subject. On abstract topics, you can use this fact as a means by which to expand a portion of virtually any subject.

On the jot outline for abstract topics, split up your case points or arguments on the "half-and-half" or the "side-by-side" order. In the half-and-half way of doing the theme, half of the composition will take up one side of the topic (perhaps the pro). The other half will take up the opposite view. With the side-by-side set up, you will give one pro case point and follow it up with the con of that case point. You'll go right down your case this way, a pro balanced by a con, a pro balanced by a con, a pro balanced by a con, and so on.

To start out, we recommend you begin with half-and-half structure. This method will keep your thinking straight and is the easiest way to get you started on abstract themes. In a diagram, it would look like this:

Paragraph No. 1	Beginning
Paragraph No. 2	List of Pro Points; List of Con Points
Paragraph No. 3	Con Point No. 1
Paragraph No. 4	Con Point No. 2

Paragraph No. 5	Con Point No. 3
Paragraph No. 6	Con Point No. 4
Paragraph No. 7	Pro Point No. 1
Paragraph No. 8	Pro Point No. 2
Paragraph No. 9	Pro Point No. 3
Paragraph No. 10	Pro Point No. 4
Paragraph No. 11	Ending

If you look closely at the example above, you'll see that the idea is to take four case points and to argue the con side of *each* during the first part of the theme, to argue the pro side during the last portion of the composition. If, for example, we were to take the abstract topic of "Nature," we could set up a case that looks something like this student's jot outline:

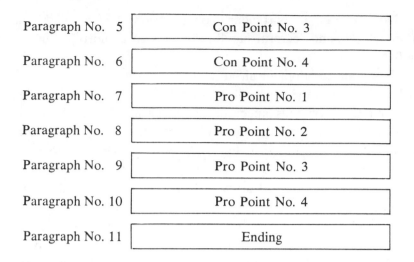

Or you might set up your theme along the lines of this writer who dealt with the abstract topic of "Poverty":

```
disad                           adv.
causes disease (N.Y.)           wealthy sick
  "   discontent (Watts)        doesn't always cause disc. (Denver)
  "   ignorance (Chicago)          "      "     "  ign. (Lincoln)
kills spirit (Watts)             "       "   kill sp. (L.B. Mayer)
  "   morals (drugs, D.C.)       "       "    " morals (Levenson)
lowers tax base (N.Y. LA)       slumlords still pay taxes
```

You will notice that in the outline there are six case points on the con side, five on the pro. But five of the points do match pro with con. One is merely left over.

If you write on "Poverty" in the side-by-side construction of the abstract theme, you will work it up something like this:

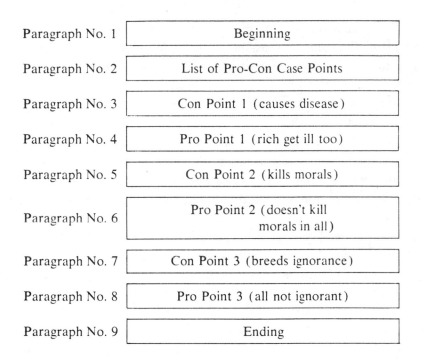

Paragraph No. 1	Beginning
Paragraph No. 2	List of Pro-Con Case Points
Paragraph No. 3	Con Point 1 (causes disease)
Paragraph No. 4	Pro Point 1 (rich get ill too)
Paragraph No. 5	Con Point 2 (kills morals)
Paragraph No. 6	Pro Point 2 (doesn't kill morals in all)
Paragraph No. 7	Con Point 3 (breeds ignorance)
Paragraph No. 8	Pro Point 3 (all not ignorant)
Paragraph No. 9	Ending

In both the half-and-half and side-by-side structures for abstract themes, we have "paired" the case points with pros and cons. That's because most students will find this the easiest and fastest way to write an argumentative composition. With two or three basic contentions, you can get four to six case points simply by taking first the pro and then the con. You don't have to "pair" contentions, however. You can bring up three or four pro case points and follow these with three or four other con points that are not related to the pro. But to do a theme that way, you must stick to the half-and-half structure.

Of the two structures, which is the better?

To decide this, you must again consider the reader. Many psychologists who study readers have found that the average man is forgetful. Even if the first part of what he reads is brilliant, he won't remember too much of it by the time he gets to the end of it. The same thing is true in theme writing. The average reader won't remember much about the first half of it by the time he is caught up in the arguments of the second portion. If, on the other hand, you pair a pro case point with its con, he'll keep most of what you say in mind. He'll remember and find your major arguments quite compelling.

This bit of psychological knowledge is helpful when you're not sure which side of the case to put first, the pro or the con. Since a reader remembers the last thing read, take advantage of this weakness. If you want to convince the reader that the con side is right, put it *after* the pro. If you're supporting the pro side of an issue, ensure that the pro case points come *after* the con.

In this section on abstract themes, we have dealt with the body of the theme. The beginning paragraphs, those for the listing of case points, and the ending are much the same as they are for the general argumentative form of theme writing.

As for the individual paragraphs that carry the pro and con case points, these are set up in the same way as those shown for general argumentative themes. Make the case point statement in the first sentence of the paragraph and then support it with examples.

You will want to follow the advice given on general topics also as it concerns selection of examples, the tone of the language, the use of humor, the use of good connective words and phrases. Again, be sure that you put the most important case point first in writing this kind of theme. It shows you have good, sound judgment and allows, further, for deadline pressures.

There are some other pointers for this type of theme that should be kept in mind.

If you are to argue well, you must *always* anticipate the arguments or case points of the opposing side. Whoever reads your theme (especially if he knows something about the subject) will wonder why you failed to cope with an argument that is so important to the subject. It is far better to come to grips with a damaging argument. Do battle with it by fielding some sizable arguments to the contrary. Remember that there never has been an argument that didn't have at least two sides. It may be that you'll have to do a lot of ruminating to think up a pro argument to a strong con argument, but nothing is impossible for the resourceful student.

Pitfalls to Be Avoided

In both types of argumentative themes—general and abstract forms—there are two pitfalls. One is the use of syllogistic reasoning, and the other pitfall is the use of the "either/or" type of logic. The two shortcomings are closely related.

Don't let the word *syllogism* overpower you. A syllogism is based on a conclusion following a general truth. If the truth is sound, in other words, the conclusion itself *must* be true. For example, one could reason that every virtue is laudable; kindness is a virtue; therefore, kindness is laudable. However, very amusing truths can be proved if you carry this kind of thinking beyond reasonable limits. Dogs like man; man likes television; therefore, dogs like television. Equally, one could say that the world is round; man is part of the world; so man must be round. These are rather obvious examples of exaggerated syllogistic reasoning, but you'd be surprised at the number of student themes that carry this sort of logic.

The either/or type of thinking is more common in student writings, however, than that of false syllogisms. This form of reasoning is sometimes called the black-and-white logic whereby a person refuses to see that there are grays in between. Things are seldom so simple that they can be separated into only two conclusions.

Some samples of students writing in either/or logic are these:

We are either going to have war, or we are going to have peace.

Or

Man must make up his mind that if he is not pursuing capitalism, he is following communism.

Or

If he's not working, he must be playing.

Three decades of coexistence between the United States and Russia have taught us that there is territory between peace and war, that there is ground between capitalism and communism. Sometimes work is play or very near it and *vice versa*. A sure way to avoid this simplistic way of thinking is to beware of sweeping statements or black-and-white generalizations.

CHAPTER **4**

THE DESCRIPTIVE
THEME

When students are assigned a descriptive theme topic, they ordinarily jump into the subject with little organization and leave incomplete pictures by omitting important details.

To keep from such confusion, a jot outline is a must.

True, a descriptive theme allows the creative writer to display poetic command over his prose. But a descriptive theme still requires some kind of order, an organization of features describing the place, the object, or the person.

The key is to work from the most important details to the least important. You can work from the top to bottom of the subject (or *vice versa*), from left to right (or *vice versa*) or from back to front (or *vice versa*). The important thing is to let your reader know exactly where he is supposed to be looking. If you are especially hard put to keep the view in focus, you might jot out a small diagram of the subject. It sometimes helps to have something tangible before you.

We have said that the descriptive theme is a composition that is tailor made for the creative writer. But even if you're not particularly creative, your descriptive phrases can sing a little. Give your thesaurus a workout here, for to describe things means that you'll need imaginative comparisons. It's not enough to say that Aunt Nellie is beautiful. You've got to illustrate Aunt Nellie in words for the reader. You could liken her to something beautiful—a flower, a well-known person, some geographic spectacular—for the benefit of readers who are unacquainted with Aunt Nellie. Lead the reader from the known to the unknown with imagery. Imagery involves similes (Aunt Nellie is *like* a rose) or metaphors (Aunt Nellie *is* a rose). It doesn't matter if you exaggerate a little about Aunt Nellie.

While you're thinking of the colorful descriptive terms, avoid trite figures of speech ("Her eyes were like diamonds," "She is as pretty as a picture"). Most of the trite expressions used in many themes are contained in the writing style section on clichés and bromides. Don't use them.

Another tool for good descriptive themes is good connectives ("Behind the shed . . ." or "Above the mountain . . ." or "To his left . . ." or "It was fronted by . . ."). You'll need words of this sort to move smoothly from one aspect of the object described to another. Abrupt descriptive jumps involving the scene or object will confuse the reader. If you're moving your reader from the outside to the inside of a log cabin, don't suddenly pull him from the bed of daisies bordering the building and place him on a spindle chair inside the cabin. One student, in describing the interior of her home, had her mother appear in the living room to invite a visitor to taste some Finnish bread being served up in the kitchen. This not only provided a smooth transition from one room to another, but it added a human touch as well.

Let's get specific now with the three major types of descriptive themes: those on persons, on places, and on objects.

Description of Places

To describe places, you'll first need to prepare a jot outline or a rough sketch.

The sketch should never take you more than five minutes. If you're the type who loves to dwell on details, you'll run out of time if you're writing in class. You'll run out of paper if you're writing outside class. Just reach the high spots, for few readers savor thousands of words on one small object of an overall scene that is being described. The rough sketch should keep you on the track, for at a glance you can pick out the most important items to be described on a theme that pictures a place. You'll discard the minor things.

One student, who had 50 minutes to describe his home, spent no more than three minutes on this rough sketch:

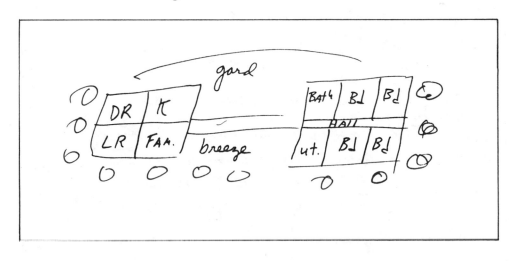

In handling description of the family summer place, another student used this jot sketch:

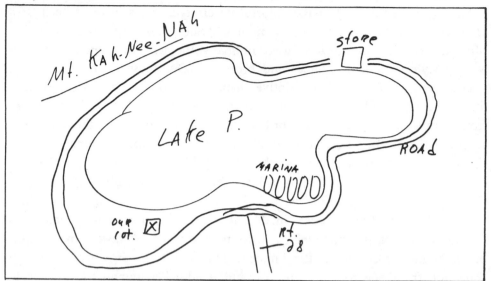

If you'd rather work up a jot outline, do so. In organizing it for the theme, split up the jottings into outside and inside sections for land and buildings. Or divide the place into areas that are near and far if you're dealing with landscape, a city, and the like.

Once you've divided the place, then figure out the areas in each that will warrant the greatest emphasis or number of words. Don't put too much stress on the trivial things. You may neglect the areas that should get the chief focus. Once again, move around the scene in some kind of order, top to bottom, left to right, foreground to background, and the like.

An example of an outline used by one student is this done on a tent located in the mountains:

> ① open (sunrise — whole scene
> ② outside
>   back — mtns. firs
>   front
>   l. river, rapids
>   r. rocks
>   c. pump, car, tent
> ③ ins.
>   B. locker, lantern, cards (on left)
>   guns, rods, canteens (rig)
>   floor rug cots nets - c
>   f. mirror, poles, fabric — tent color
> ④ end pancakes

So much for getting organized.

In the beginning paragraph, as in all other paragraphs of this type of theme, try to work people into your description of places, or animals. Give some evidence of life, even if it's a discarded potato chip bag or a smudge left by small fingers on a wall. Such touches bring warmth and interest to an otherwise static scene.

Beginning Paragraphs

Beginning paragraphs should describe the overall scene or at least hint of the area that will be portrayed. You should reveal the location of the place described in those opening paragraphs. And don't get too detailed ("Turn right at the fourth stoplight") if you can help it. Locations can be indicated by skilful use of the weather, animals, trees (magnolias are not common in Wisconsin), even news stands.

These examples show how some writers opened their compositions describing places:

> The low, undulating Danish landscape was silent and serene, mysteriously wide awake in the hour before sunrise.

Or

> The place where everybody would end up before going home was Barden's Drug Store. It was light, bright and right on the square. A place where a kid could hang out, read a magazine, play the juke box, drown his troubles in Coke floats and buy his mother a birthday card.

Or

> People won't find St. George's avenue on any map of Minneapolis now. As a result of the terrifying things that happened there, the street was changed to Xenwood avenue by the City Council. It is a mean, shabby street of 20 tired houses on either side—none with any lawn but the chipped strip of concrete that posed as a sidewalk.

Or

> You can walk from one end of Old Heidelberg to the other and still never escape the musky smells that seep out of this university town in Germany.

As you write along, touching up the place described with poetic imagery or with picturesque words that lend a human touch to the scene, make sure that any comparisons ("The street is like a corpse" or "Small boys come pouring out like well-trained ants," etc.) are familiar ones to most readers. If you get too exotic with your similes and metaphors, you've spoiled the description for the average reader. He may further conclude that you're showing off. Don't overdo similes, incidentally. A long string of them throughout one composition is very tiring to a lot of readers.

Once you've finished the beginning, how do you go about putting in the items throughout the rest of the theme?

Body of the Theme

Here again, a sketch or outline is a must. One of the first things to decide as you look over the sketch or outline is what item should get the most emphasis or focus. If you're concentrating on a lake, the lake and not trees or wandering animals in the background will get the bulk of the paragraphs in the body of the theme. If you're writing about a village or an entire city, check to see which aspect is the most important in the community. If a house is the subject of your theme, find the part of the home that is the most important and devote most of your paragraphs to it.

In other words, stress something.

It's true that each element in a scene, a home, a city, a person may be of equal worth. But to give exactly the same emphasis to everything means that nothing will stand out. The theme will sound pallid. Good writing has a climax, a high point that makes an impression on a reader. So don't measure out one paragraph of equal length and quality to every aspect of the place you're describing. The chief aspect should get the major share of your paragraphs.

A descriptive theme allows you to put the most important aspect of the place in any position of the theme. Many prefer to place it in the end or the middle. If you wish to do it that way, you'll have to watch your time if you're writing in class.

A paragraph-by-paragraph analysis of one student's theme shows that in his portrayal of New York City he felt the garment district was the most important. He placed it in the middle of his theme as is seen in the following example:

Paragraph No. 1	Beginning
Paragraph No. 2	Board Bus (rapid transit system)
Paragraph No. 3	Upper Bronx Area
Paragraph No. 4	Colleges (CCNY, Columbia, etc.)
Paragraph No. 5	Harlem, Spanish Harlem
Paragraph No. 6	Central Park, Riverside Drive
Paragraph No. 7	Lincoln Center, RCA, Rockefeller, etc.
Paragraph No. 8	Garment District
Paragraph No. 9	Garment District
Paragraph No. 10	Garment District

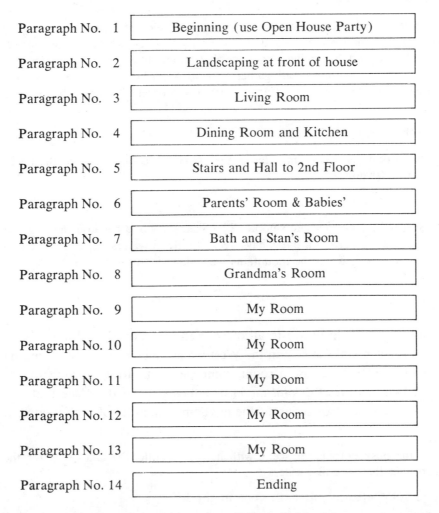

Paragraph No. 11	Garment District
Paragraph No. 12	Garment District
Paragraph No. 13	Garment District
Paragraph No. 14	Theatre District, The Village, etc.
Paragraph No. 15	Shopping District
Paragraph No. 16	Financial District
Paragraph No. 17	Ending

A paragraph-by-paragraph examination of another student's theme, this one on her home, shows that she put her emphasis on the end of her theme in this way:

Paragraph No. 1	Beginning (use Open House Party)
Paragraph No. 2	Landscaping at front of house
Paragraph No. 3	Living Room
Paragraph No. 4	Dining Room and Kitchen
Paragraph No. 5	Stairs and Hall to 2nd Floor
Paragraph No. 6	Parents' Room & Babies'
Paragraph No. 7	Bath and Stan's Room
Paragraph No. 8	Grandma's Room
Paragraph No. 9	My Room
Paragraph No. 10	My Room
Paragraph No. 11	My Room
Paragraph No. 12	My Room
Paragraph No. 13	My Room
Paragraph No. 14	Ending

It should be noted that this writer did not feel it necessary to mention every nook and cranny of her house. She dealt only with the grounds at the front of the house, left out the basement, closets, and other areas that she felt were of no major importance. Her judgment was very sound, for one does not need to include every leaf on the tree in descriptive themes.

In both examples given above, the writers used some unifying element by which to guide their readers through their descriptive themes on places. The first student used a bus ride, the second, an open house party. There are many types of unifying forms that you can use here. We have seen students use trappers arriving on the scene when a camp was being described, a band of Roman soldiers marching through Rome's Forum to depict that portion of that ancient city, an ant traveling through a home, a footsore traveling salesman making his way through a small English village. Not only did the use of a unifying element strengthen the theme, but it also gave life to the place being described.

Some ways of "bringing life" to a place should not be difficult to find. Orange peelings on the floor of a theatre, notches on a tree, a doll carriage left by a well, and the like have livened many a theme. How one student handled it is shown below:

> This part of the living room has suffered and rejoiced from the hardwood floors to the beamed ceiling. It's at the piano by the wall where my two sisters wailed—they called it singing—and warbled when they took singing lessons. And it's where we used to all gather around Saturday nights while Mother played and we sang Christmas Carols when my brother Ben came home from the War.

Or take this example:

> The bathroom is where my dad sings, shaves, reads, and practices those speeches for Kiwanis.

And then there is this one:

> The stones here are flat and smooth. The Sisters say it is because the Pilgrims stooped to kiss the ground, but I have seen the flood waters come to that part of town each spring when the mountains were done with the moisture.

Endings

The ending should do justice to all of your efforts. You should not rely on the old "as-the-sun-sinks-slowly-in-the-West-we-leave-colorful-Tahiti" ending of the travelogue. Instead, use a room, some piece of furniture, a person or some event that captures the *total* mood or atmosphere of the place that you have tried to recreate throughout the theme. Some examples of such treatment are these:

> When the dusk enfolds the scene with its gray mantle, the lakes wait for the moon to light their fire-like waters.

If you're not poetically gifted, this one might do:

> Someday when travelers see the break in the hills, they will plunge into the valley and make what is known only to a few, later known to all men.

And this one had the human touch:

The fire, when it dies, will hide the date of his birth on the wooden chest, the date when Fullerton fled to the house to escape the wrath of the mob.

Description of Objects

To describe objects, follow the same instructions as those given for themes describing places. There are some fine points for writing about objects, however.

In the beginning paragraph(s), describe the object as a whole and include its purpose.

One student did it this way:

A typewriter is a mass of metal that can bring joy, laughter and tears. It is used for letters that inform you that you have just won the Creepies breakfast food jingle contest and have two weeks in South Bend, Indiana for a vacation. It is used for letters from a beau who likes to include funny sayings or observations. It is also used by finance companies who inform you that they're taking away four roomsful of furniture.

Another was a little simpler:

A J-bar tow is shaped like the letter J in steel and when attached to a cable, the tow pulls you to the top of the hill where you can ski down—to get the J-bar tow again.

Once again, inject the human element into the thing described. A staircase, for example, might be worn down by a generation of use. A desk might have significant carvings or scratchings. A jewel might have been cursed and have caused the deaths of several individuals.

Humor may be used to a degree if it is in keeping with the overall use of the object described in your theme. Perhaps a funny incident has been connected with the item's invention or use.

The ending for a theme describing something should avoid the exit that runs something like: "And so now all is known about the sewing machine." You may think of many ending ideas as you gain experience in writing themes, but one of the best has the object being put to use.

One junior had it:

With a whirr, the sleeping IBM computer starts to eat its breakfast of programming.

Another wrote:

The fishing rod is raised and whipped into the stream, poised for another day's catch.

Description of Persons

The descriptive theme on people usually falls into two types. One is that of characterization. The other is that of a profile. We'll take these up separately.

The Characterization

The characterization deals with personality qualities or quirks. When you are asked in themes and essay tests to characterize someone, you emphasize what that person *does* or his traits, not what he looks like or his life history. Characteristics might involve cruelty, carelessness, kindness, lovability, and the like. When you characterize, be sure that the traits cited are fairly common with the person. A selfish person cannot be characterized as kind for a single act of generosity.

The jot outline for characterizations is very simple, as the following one demonstrates on *Everyman*, the leading figure in the medieval morality play by the same name:

```
opener ①
kind = gave money away ⑤
sly — tried stall on D. 4
contrite — sought forgiveness from Conf. 6
happy ← 3
pleasure loving ②
end 7
```

When you are given a topic that asks you to characterize as many as three persons, you could set them up as the student did above, each character receiving a full spectrum of qualities. You'll be pressed for time and space if you have more than one person to characterize, however, so you may not be able to include too many traits.

Another way to do the characterization is to find a common denominator in the people. The persons characterized might have the same traits in common. One student, reporting on several characters from a book the class had been assigned, set up his jot outline like this:

1 Beginning (mention all 3)
2 Cruelty (John, the slaves; George, the girl; Tina, her mother)
3 Greed (John, the rents; George, his life's savings; Tina, insurance)
4 Lovingness (John for Tina; George for Tina; Tina for mother, John, George)
5 Ending

If there are more differences than similarities in the persons being characterized, you can combine the qualities and then add the differences in traits.

Or you might simply organize by going down the roster of everybody's qualities as is shown below:

1 Beginning (mention 9 traits)
2 Cruelty (slaves, Tina, mother)
3 Greed (rents, savings, insurance)
4 Lovingness (Tina-George-John-mother)
5 Kindness (Tina, George's horse)
6 Faithfulness (George to Tina)
7 Jealousy (Tina's mother)
8 Optimism (John for Tina's love)
9 Pessimism (George for Tina's mother)
10 Carelessness (George with matches)
11 Ending

Beginning

What should you put in the beginning paragraph(s) for a characterization? The best method here is to list the *main* qualities of the person. Three traits should be plenty for the average theme. Identify the person being characterized, of course. Here's one from a student using a play in her theme:

> Eliza Doolittle, the heroine of Shaw's *Pygmalion,*was greedy, loving and clever as she climbed in three acts from the Lissom Grove gutters to an embassy garden party.

The writer above has identified the person, has spun out the chief qualities of the girl, and has completed the sketch with a graceful ending in that opening sentence.

Should you have two or more persons to write about, your introduction might resemble this student's:

> Johnson's creation of Bart and Withers in his book *Wilderness* shows two completely different persons to the reader. Bart's basic decency, idealism, and bravery are a sharp contrast to Withers' treachery, pragmatism, and cowardice.

Most teachers would give high marks to a student with that kind of discernment and that kind of organized mind. One becomes organized and discerning with a jot outline.

When the person cannot be characterized by equal contrasts or with equal comparisons, you might find this opener of help:

> When the playwright William Shakespeare wrote *Richard III,* he used the main women characters to be kind, cruel, bossy, and clever. These qualities were shown in his portraits of Anne, Elizabeth, and the Duchess of York.

From all of the previous examples, you'll see that the persons have been properly identified (from books, plays,and the like) as well as artfully sketched for traits. The reader knows who is about to be characterized and what qualities are to be unfolded. And everything is well organized.

Body of the Theme

What about the body of the theme of characterization?

You will notice that in the jot outlines the student writers always included specific examples *after* the traits. This habit is a good one to cultivate, for it is not enough to say someone has the quality of kindness. You must follow up such a statement with a proof or, rather, a specific example of such kindness. Keep this in mind as you follow the next instructions and examples.

After you have completed the introductory paragraph(s), you will use a paragraph per trait if you are writing on one person. You could do more than one, but don't take up a new trait until you've finished all that you want to say about the one on which you're working.

Let us take the characterization of Eliza Doolittle, mentioned in a previous example, and set up the theme's structure by following the order formed by that student writer. He has declared that she was greedy, loving, and clever. We assume that to him her main trait was one of greediness, since he has put it first. Follow that student's lead and be sure that you do put the most important traits *first*. The structure will look like this:

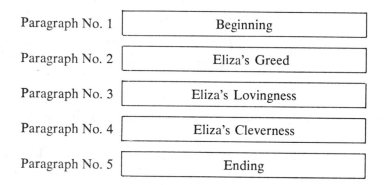

Paragraph No. 1	Beginning
Paragraph No. 2	Eliza's Greed
Paragraph No. 3	Eliza's Lovingness
Paragraph No. 4	Eliza's Cleverness
Paragraph No. 5	Ending

The theme is not just five paragraphs, of course, for it might take two or three to explain greed, perhaps four to deal with her "lovingness." The point is that the qualities are taken up in order. Here's a diagram of one student's theme on the women in *Richard III*:

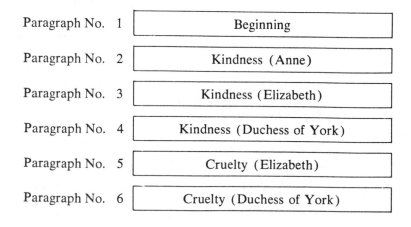

Paragraph No. 1	Beginning
Paragraph No. 2	Kindness (Anne)
Paragraph No. 3	Kindness (Elizabeth)
Paragraph No. 4	Kindness (Duchess of York)
Paragraph No. 5	Cruelty (Elizabeth)
Paragraph No. 6	Cruelty (Duchess of York)

Paragraph No. 7	Bossiness (Elizabeth)
Paragraph No. 8	Bossiness (Duchess of York)
Paragraph No. 9	Cleverness (Anne)
Paragraph No. 10	Cleverness (Elizabeth)
Paragraph No. 11	Cleverness (Duchess of York)
Paragraph No. 12	Ending

Within each paragraph, make the structure that has the statement of the trait as the first sentence. The rest of the sentences in the paragraph(s) should offer proofs or specific examples to illustrate that statement of trait. In other words, 1) the first sentence of the paragraph is a statement of the quality the person had and 2) all other sentences are examples of that statement. Check over the following example to see how this was done:

Statement { The Premier is an extreme egoist. He has flown around in a black flying suit that makes everyone call him Captain Midnight. He has press conferences almost everyday to announce his slightest whim or dictate. Nobody is allowed to contradict him or that person is fired. Four persons alone this month have met this fate.

Example {

Another, somewhat shorter version of the 1) statement, 2) specific example set-up is this one:

Fearlessness is a quality that Lady Macbeth is not lacking. She's not afraid to dream that her husband might be king or afraid to get him to kill the present king so that her dream would come true.

When you come to the ending of a characterization, emphasize either the main point made about the person sketched or else give a short résumé of the many qualities found for the individual. You might use a short sentence pointing out the merits or demerits of the kind of behavior shown by the person being characterized, as this college freshman did:

Ruthlessness and cruelty, sometimes tempered with kindness, were characteristics shown by Richard III. Perhaps these are bad qualities for ordinary people to have, but for rulers with grave responsibilities of a trouble-ridden state, such traits are very necessary.

If one is asked to characterize not people but a state or a city or a group of people as a whole as for, say, an essay test, the same rules set down here for characterizations of persons will still apply.

Use humor with care on these characterizations, by the way. If the person being characterized is humorous himself, use as much humor—in good taste, to be sure—as you like. But if the person is humorless, a light touch may brighten the overall dour cast of his personality. When using comparisons, don't overdo either similes or metaphors. They are tiring to the reader.

The Profile

Popularized by *Time*, *The New Yorker* (which borrowed heavily from the biographer's skills), and other magazines, a profile is a *short* biographical sketch that transforms dry facts and dull statistics about a person into an interesting composition, fascinating even to those who are unfamiliar with that individual. Even unattractive people have come to life if they are portrayed by one skilled at writing profiles.

The profile blends personality traits, physical description, stories of happenings (anecdotes), and pure biographical data into one mold. The person is brought to life on paper by blending his habits, words, and actions within that kind of framework. The construction of a profile, however, is not organized by splitting the theme into those three categories. A far smoother job will be done if you base the theme throughout on the chronological development. As your subject grows from childhood to adulthood, you'll affix the habits, the actions, and the quotations.

A jot outline for this type of theme may be filled with items if it's on someone you know fairly well. But the more jottings you have, the meatier your theme will be. It might look like this student's jot outline on his father:

This student needed no formal outline—just circles—for his jottings, separating the childhood and youth sections from the adult portion of his father's life.

Another student, this one working on a president's profile, put his jot outline in this kind of order:

Boy	Youth	Man
rich $20 mill.	Harvard	PT 109
Mass.	London (S of E)	injuries - pain
thin	'While Eng. Slept	Jackie, C + J-J
sailing	hair bushy	Cuba
	smile	Dallas
	eyes	Senate - Algeria
		Prof in Cour.
		humor - Truman
		friends - "Mafia" - O'Donnel

This student put down everything that came to mind after he had set up the three main categories of the man's life. As he wrote, within time limitations of the class period, he had to discard some of the points as being too detailed in a theme of that short length. He undoubtedly felt the push of a deadline. You will note also the number of specific items (Harvard, sailing, PT109, etc.) that the student used. These are very helpful to substantiate the claims about this president.

Beginning

The profile requires a little more thought and work than the themes describing places, but in many ways it's more challenging. Readers may be hypnotized by a lovely word picture of the city, but it takes some doing to get them interested in your Uncle Charley. To do this, you must have that rousing opening of a beginning paragraph to make the most bored reader alert and interested. Never start with such words as: "The person I picked to profile is . . ." That's far too crude. Your beginning sentence in the first paragraph might involve an anecdote, a blunt statement, or a timely tie-in. The following is a masterly one from a senior:

> The big man came running out of the station's warmth, his friendly hand waving at just another customer who would probably want $2 worth of regular and as many courtesies as the fill-er-up drivers. His hand stopped in mid-wave as he got to the pump banks and he keeled over. My Dad had had his first heart attack.

If you don't want to use the anecdotal type, as that student did, there's always the blunt statement, loaded with revealing details:

> He shambled across the 18th green like a young grizzly bear, his pudgy face

ruddy from the sun, his white cotton shirt soggy with sweat, his cream-colored cap perched on the back of his close-cropped blond head.

Even those who know little and care less about golf might be attracted into such a profile of champion Jack Nicklaus. Moreover, such a leading sentence covers a multitude of things: physique, the way the man walks, what he is doing, his clothes style, and some personal hygiene.

If you want to rivet attention with a shorter one, you might try something like this:

> Just as some people live for the motorcycle, Grandpa Pete lives for the po-tato cycle.

Motorcycle enthusiasts, potato growers and other farmers, and all with grandfathers might be induced to read on. Other readers might like the topical or timely approach:

> The Spaniard with the best chance of unseating the Premier and with the most at stake in the outcome is a six-foot, three-inch blueblood who has not lived in Spain for 31 years.

Here, the physique of the subject, history, and the uncertainty of politics are combined. A topical approach has the disadvantage of losing readers who never pick up a newspaper or who don't care for current events. Gear your first sentence of the introductory paragraph to a general audience.

Once you have the opening sentence written, the next two or three sentences in the beginning paragraph(s) must identify the subject and give some reason why he merits a profile. Such identifications and explanations need not be fancy. Sometimes, just a short sentence or a concise appositive will do just as well as here:

> This dark-haired ex-Miss Maine candidate is currently under fire as the head of the Council.

Once the person is put into focus, you can begin the chronological birth-to-death (or maturity) development.

Organization

The actual organization of the theme, as has been said, follows this chronological development of your subject. You add, as you go, the adornments from childhood, youth, adulthood, and the like. If we were to diagram one such theme, it would look something like this:

Paragraph No. 1	Beginning (plumber's story)
Paragraph No. 2	Boyhood (poverty, newsboy)
Paragraph No. 3	Boyhood (skinny, scrappy, Brusco fight, hospital)

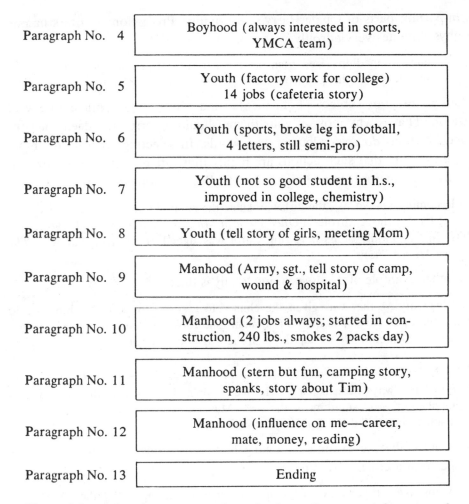

Paragraph No. 4	Boyhood (always interested in sports, YMCA team)
Paragraph No. 5	Youth (factory work for college) 14 jobs (cafeteria story)
Paragraph No. 6	Youth (sports, broke leg in football, 4 letters, still semi-pro)
Paragraph No. 7	Youth (not so good student in h.s., improved in college, chemistry)
Paragraph No. 8	Youth (tell story of girls, meeting Mom)
Paragraph No. 9	Manhood (Army, sgt., tell story of camp, wound & hospital)
Paragraph No. 10	Manhood (2 jobs always; started in construction, 240 lbs., smokes 2 packs day)
Paragraph No. 11	Manhood (stern but fun, camping story, spanks, story about Tim)
Paragraph No. 12	Manhood (influence on me—career, mate, money, reading)
Paragraph No. 13	Ending

You might make your paragraphs quite long. Or you might even take two or three paragraphs where the writer above only used one. When one is writing about something familiar to him, he tends to write at greater length than he ordinarily would. Here, it makes no difference how long or short the paragraphs are. Just don't overwrite on an anecdote or one phase of the subject's life.

Within the paragraphs in the body of the theme, it's not too hard to include those revealing physical and personal details as you move along the person's life cycle. Just remember that such factors should be included in a smooth way and must have a purpose. Use physical description, for example, when it has a *direct* bearing on the point being mentioned or, possibly, when the person is first introduced to the reader. This lets the reader know what the person looks like. Furthermore, physical characteristics have a good deal to do with shaping people's personalities sometimes, as Shakespeare once had Julius Caesar observe. Perhaps a woman's plainness has made her strive to be noticed in other ways. A man's short stature might give him a Napoleon complex. Big hands might have hindered (or helped) the person being described. Nails bitten to the quick are most revealing. But it isn't necessary to include Uncle Harry's hat size or his exact height unless such measurements *are* important parts of Uncle Harry's personality. Professional writers handle the physical notes very adroitly:

> Hastings, a medium-sized man with a springy stride and a lot of energy, maintains that he got his pep from his boyhood in Minneapolis' tough North side.

Actions of your subject—both mental and physical—do much to reveal a person. That is why most of your theme should describe the deeds of your subject. Actions *do* speak louder than words. In selecting such deeds, however, make sure that such actions are highly illustrative of the person or that they involve a major turning point in his life. Ways of doing this are:

> Becoming known as "the girl who sings the song about John Foster Dulles," Carol landed the lead role in *Once Upon a Mattress.* The show and Carol were hits. In the middle of its long run, Carol was signed on as a regular with *The Garry Moore Show.*

Another example of deeds speaking loudly is this:

> When my Mother was given the chance to take a cross-country bus ride to Glendale or to stay at home that summer, she took 15 minutes to pack. Somewhere near Lincoln, Nebraska, the man she was to marry got on.

Or

> Pop has always been a joiner. He likes people, I guess, and that is why he's a member in good standing of the local Masonic temple, the Rotary, the Elks, and something called the Rallyboys Bowling team.

A more elaborate example, showing how deeds reflect the personality, is this one from a college freshman:

> Arabs like Attiyeh have a lot of arrogance in dealing with other Arabs not so high in society. Once in conference with his Arab shop foreman and with his American editor, Attiyeh offered cigarets. The American was handed the pack for his choice. To the Arab foreman, however, Attiyeh yanked out a cigaret from the pack, tossed it at the foreman's feet, and cooly enjoyed the moment as the other Arab groveled around to retrieve it.

Habits, minor personality traits, are close relatives to the deeds of people. They are very revealing of the type of person being profiled. Here, however, don't bluntly say that the subject has this or that habit. Write *what* the subject does. Instead of saying that Cousin Joe is nervous, for example, point up that he chain smokes, or that he drums on tables, or bites his nails. If you can tie those habits into the major deeds of the person, all the better. Here's how one writer did it:

> Don Juan often escapes the formality that has been thrust upon him by birth. At sea, he does his turn on deck with the crew; he normally wears faded dungarees and sneakers ashore in brief stops at foreign ports. At home in Estoril, he goes to nightclubs, chats with friends until the small hours.

Another handled it this way:

> Workdays, Ferkauf gets up before 7 A.M. without an alarm clock, prepares his own breakfast, then washes the dishes using rubber gloves.

Or

> Although he told me he was a devout Catholic, he usually skips Mass for Sunday politicking with those party hacks he calls his friends.

The next most revealing measure of a person is what he says or what others say of him. Sometimes using opinions of others is grossly unfair, yet it is a gossipy technique used through the ages to praise or to damn an individual. It must be remembered that by *directly* quoting the person himself, you indicate his educational level, his background, his philosophies of life. Quoting other people, particularly enemies, gives you new sidelights on your subject. The chances are, however, that in class themes, you'll quote only friends.

The way you use a quotation is important. It's not enough to just include one in any place in the theme. Generally, it has the greatest impact if the quote comes at the end of a buildup or at the close of some point you are making about your subject. The quote highlights the point, in other words. Just how this is done is shown in this example:

> Nicklaus has rarely been rattled since his disastrous experience in that U.S. Amateur. Says his father: "Once, when he was 15, I was driving him to a tournament. I started to encourage him and tell him 'You're good enough to win this.' He told me, 'I know it. Now be quiet.' "

Another example is this one:

> Just because he is the high school principal doesn't mean he has been educated. Over the P.A. it's not out of the ordinary to hear him say: "Now we ain't gonna have no more of this here hand-holding."

And there's another example:

> He and another delivery boy, who were both earning six dollars a week for working afternoons and Saturdays, were asked to work Thursday nights, too, just for supper money. They refused and were fired. Hastings said: "I found out that if there's strength in unity, there's got to be more than two people."

Incidentally, unless you want your subject to appear to be unlettered—sometimes the intent of writers—you may have to fix up the quotations so that they sound more grammatical than they originally did.

Endings

An ending for a profile should leave a good imprint on the reader. It should be short and include an image guaranteed to remain with the reader. You can do it with a quote, a statement about what's in store in future for the person, an anecdote, a remark about the significance of the man. At any rate, it should be the highlight and should also let the reader know he's reached the end of the profile. Here's one:

> Now, in his old age, he is less active. Only his little dog Pete shares with him the adventures of the past.

And this

> With eight dancing years left, she feels she can reach the top of the profession—a spot with the June Taylor group. "I am going to be the best in the business," Anita says.

Or

> Since he himself was once a rag-tailed tramp who made the rounds of the garbage cans in town, he doesn't forget things. One night another tramp popped out of a garbage can and nearly killed him in a struggle for a dried-up ham sandwich. Sullivan never forgets the men of the jungle in the North Side.

Work for lively writing in profile themes. Remember that the reader may not share your enthusiasm for your friend Jim unless you handle the theme in a highly interesting manner.

There is nothing wrong with using humor in profiles, especially since you are out to interest a reader in someone. Wit, lively quotes, or wry stories are never out of place so long as they are in good taste and are illustrative.

The words you use to move from paragraph to paragraph or sentence to sentence—connectives—may be drawn from the list found in the chapter on Writing Style. You'll probably find it necessary to use longer connectives that bridge whole periods of your subject's life, however. Such connectives might be: "*When Simmons was 12*, he entered his first rodeo," or "*Three years after quitting UCLA*, he headed for Manhattan and the Copa," or "*Now, 40 years later*, my father doesn't regret his decision to retire."

CHAPTER **5**

THE EXPOSITORY
THEME

For many reasons, the expository, or explanatory, theme should be the easiest type of composition for students to write. Such a theme requires only two things: *extreme* simplicity and a step-by-step series of instructions on the process being explained.

Simplicity isn't hard to attain if you remember to write as if you were trying to explain something to a 10-year-old who is not particularly a genius. Put away the big words and the confusing, punctuation-pocked structure. Put away all the statements in parentheses and other things that mar clarity. Long paragraphs also are to be avoided. Learning how to do something new is hard enough for readers without their having to tangle with big words and complicated instructions. Take a hint from cookbook writers, manufacturer's instructions, and the like. They use some of the clearest, most direct prose in the English language. These involve simple words, short and simple sentences, and short paragraphs.

For example, study this one from a package of frozen broccoli spears:

1. Place frozen broccoli in ½ cup boiling salted water (¼ teaspoon salt).
2. Cover pan and bring quickly to second boil, turning solid pack with two forks to hasten thawing.
3. When second boil is reached, reduce heat to keep water simmering. Cook, covering, 5 to 8 minutes. DO NOT OVERCOOK. Overcooking impairs flavor, texture, appearance and food value.
4. Drain, season to taste with butter or margarine, salt and pepper. Serve at once.

On a cake mix, the manufacturers also keep instructions simple:

Preheat oven to 350° F. Grease pans generously and dust lightly with flour. Empty mix into large bowl and add all at once: 1⅓ cups water, 2 eggs. Mix three minutes. Bake 35–40 minutes. Cool cakes 10 minutes before removing from pans. Frost when fully cooled.

Instructions from the factory on something vital for ovens are contained here. Again, notice the simple writing:

To relight oven pilot light, turn thermostat full on. Light match. Press in and hold red button in lower left compartment. Light oven burner through lighter hole. After one minute release red button.

It's true that every bit of explanatory writing today is not devoted to igniting pilot lights and to making cakes, but the principles of instructions done by professionals are very useful in your work on compositions. Who knows, perhaps one day you may write an arithmetic or chemistry textbook. If any of your textbooks are difficult to understand, perhaps the writers forgot the elementary composition rules for instructions or explanations.

Since you will be writing in a step-by-step order, it's necessary in the jot outline for you to make sure that you have every step included. Don't assume a thing about your reader. He might not know about the step you consider leaving out. As we have said, write for the 10-year-old mind.

The following example is for a theme on how to change a typewriter ribbon:

2- remove old rib.
   unscrew pins
   lift reel
   detach old rib
   throw away

③ put on new
   new reel on spindle
   unwind to foot of rib
   attach end to empt. reel
   both roll from outside
   put screws back

take top off

thread ④
draw rib thru centerpiece
tighten reels transport
put top on

A student explaining mitosis in a paramecium had this for an outline:

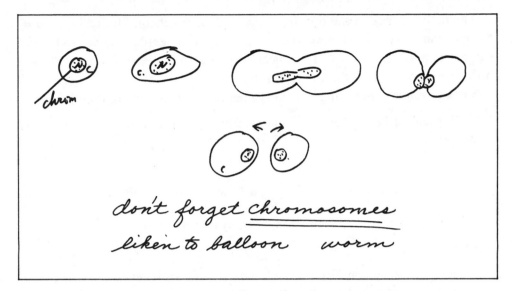

don't forget chromosomes
liken to balloon   worm

Another student's jot outline, this one for how to brand a calf, looked like this:

cut out of head (hand, no horse)
calf on side - use 2 legs throw
sit on side
heated b. iron 30 sec. - haunch
notch ears
vacc. for black leg
castrate some
dehorn (shears or ele. kind)
turn loose — mothers

can use # branding stocks
  1. drive calf into
  2. lock ends, turn
  3. brand, v, d, etc.

Check your jot outline carefully to see that you have *every* single step *in order* as well every step *included*. If you've left something out, you can always add it anywhere. Get in the habit of using care in this portion of theme writing. Omitted material in such books as chemistry manuals or do-it-yourself repair guides can be dangerous, as you know. Just as dangerous is the step that is placed out of order.

Beginning

The first sentence in the opening paragraph of the theme should be inviting to the reader. It should never be: "I am going to explain how open-heart surgery is performed" or "My subject is how a frost heave occurs." Show a little more polish than that, even on dry topics.

Some examples of inviting leads on rather boring subjects are these:

Girls should know that pole vaulting can brighten up a romance that is fast going sour.

Or

It is the last dance of the night, and I am holding my girl close to me. Her heart is beating fast, and I think that her heart must be pumping an awful lot of blood. Let's examine her heart and see why it really beats.

And this one:

Jacks, generally considered a kid's game, is good for relaxation and for developing coordination between eyes and hands.

Or

When the sheik's typists wear out a ribbon, they toss the typewriter into the garbage can and cable to the Remington people for a new one. Since it's too expensive for us to do that, we should know how to change a typewriter ribbon.

The beginning sentence, might be followed by other sentences telling the reader what is to be explained and the need or use of the process. The opener and the sentences that follow might include both of these points. The ways in which some theme writers have done this are shown in these examples:

A horse needs new shoes as much as humans do. If one lets his horse exercise without shoes, the animal may crack or break his hoofs. This, then, is the reason why people have their horses equipped with metal shoes.

Or

Branding calves is a necessary evil among stockmen. Branding hurts the calf for several minutes, but cattlemen have to know what livestock belongs to them so they can take them to market.

Or

Everything in the world is made of atoms. Atoms are little bits of characters, so small that they can't be seen with the most powerful microscope. These atoms are piled one upon another until there are enough of them that one can see the mass, be it a desk, chewing gum, ink or Superman. Without this "piling on," everything we see and touch would fall apart.

Organization

The expository theme is one in which you won't have to put the most important things at the beginning of the composition. As you move from the beginning paragraph(s), you'll still have to keep some balance of material, however. Don't write so much on one step of an operation that you'll have to severely limit another one. In classroom themes, this becomes a very real possibility. If you're writing out of class, however, you should be able to include everything necessary.

You may find it helpful after the beginning to use a paragraph that is a summation of the major steps and tools to be used. This method tells the reader just what he is going to learn and, by including tools, indicates what items will be used throughout the entire operation. Once again, this is a technique used by recipe and do-it-yourself writers who like to include the ingredients before supplying the how-to-do-it steps.

In the body of the theme, write one paragraph per step. If a step involves one or more operations, give *each* operation a paragraph. You do this to keep the reader on the track. Even if it means that some paragraphs will be short, stick to the one-step-one-paragraph formula. You are writing for the utmost in clarity, don't forget.

The way in which you could set up such a theme is shown next in a paragraph-by-paragraph analysis of the theme written on the branding of a calf:

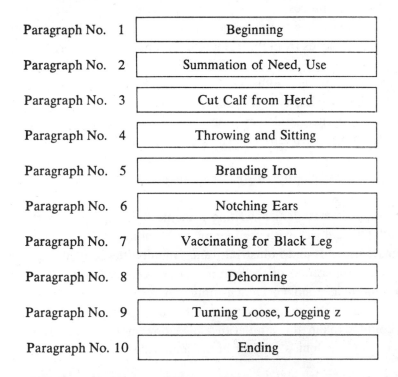

Paragraph No. 1	Beginning
Paragraph No. 2	Summation of Need, Use
Paragraph No. 3	Cut Calf from Herd
Paragraph No. 4	Throwing and Sitting
Paragraph No. 5	Branding Iron
Paragraph No. 6	Notching Ears
Paragraph No. 7	Vaccinating for Black Leg
Paragraph No. 8	Dehorning
Paragraph No. 9	Turning Loose, Logging z
Paragraph No. 10	Ending

A junior, working on "How to Change a Tire" as a topic, had a theme that could be analyzed this way:

Paragraph No. 1	Beginning
Paragraph No. 2	Tools Needed, Safety Tips
Paragraph No. 3	Jacking Car

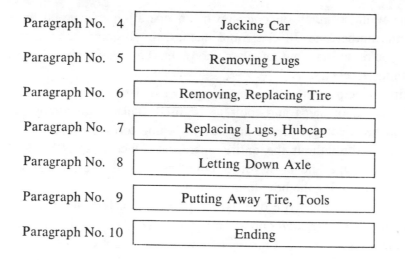

Paragraph No. 4	Jacking Car
Paragraph No. 5	Removing Lugs
Paragraph No. 6	Removing, Replacing Tire
Paragraph No. 7	Replacing Lugs, Hubcap
Paragraph No. 8	Letting Down Axle
Paragraph No. 9	Putting Away Tire, Tools
Paragraph No. 10	Ending

Use of Analogies

In writing first-rate expository themes, you can't assume that the reader knows a thing about the process you're presenting. You'll have to lead him from the things he knows to the things he doesn't know. A device designed for this job is the *analogy*. It leads from the known to the unknown. An arithmetic textbook writer, for example, is forever bringing in apples or oranges for explanations of subtraction and addition. Or he may bring in a pie if he is teaching fractions. The apples, oranges, and pies are known to most youngsters, he reasons as he writes, and they'll be able to understand the abstract principles of arithmetic if he likens the known to the unknown in concrete terms.

Never be afraid to use plently of analogies in explanatory writing. The simpler they are, the better.

For example, suppose a student is writing a theme that explains the stock market. It's a difficult subject with its buying and selling, its references to over-the-counter items, rails and industrials, and commodities. But the writer could liken the whole operation of the market (an *unknown* thing) to some boys running a lemonade stand (a *known* thing). After showing the parallel of the lemonade stand, the theme writer might then go on to purchases of stocks. He could explain the similarities by using more analogies ("If George decides to buy out John's interest in the lemonade stand, he would be doing . . . .").

Here are some sample analogies from student themes on complex topics:

The electrons fly around the nucleus in separate circular paths, much as the planets of the solar system travel around the sun.

(Explaining Half-Life in Physics)

Each octopus has three polka-dot legs out of his normal set of eight legs. Now we want to see how many polka-dot legs the two octopi have, altogether.

(Explaining the Addition of Fractions)

To fix this, one uses a rasp. A rasp is a tool that looks like a file. The only difference is that a rasp has one smooth side and one rough side.

(Explaining How to Shoe a Horse)

If one has followed instructions to this point, the knot should look like a tired spaghetti noodle with its ends overlapping about a half-inch each.

(Explaining How to Tie a Half-Hitch Knot)

Michelangelo's frescoes on the Sistine Chapel are as large as 18 bathtubs put side by side. (Explaining the Sistine Chapel Ceiling)

The average yearly income of a person in Ghana would meet about one car payment on a 36-month plan for a new Ford hardtop.

(Explaining Ghana's Economic Situation)

Another way to help the reader find his way through complex steps is the use of the example. The example brings the known to the unknown if you're adept at selecting one with the general reader in mind. If you're working with an immensely difficult topic, don't be afraid to use more than one example on a complex step. Use three or four if you think that many examples will clear up matters. The use of such words as *for example,* or *in other words* or *putting it another way* are very welcome to readers who are not quite sure they are grasping the step correctly.

As you move from step to step, choose your connective words carefully. A list of them is in the chapter on writing style. Use of words such as *next, first,* and *after this* helps the reader to know where he is in the operation.

Connectives

In addition to connective words and phrases, "breathers" are essential tools in explanatory theme writing. A pause is needed between steps of an operation or process. Remember that in this type of theme a reader does not have pictures or diagrams to help him. All he has is your use of English to "paint" the steps to be followed. Here are a few examples of "breathers":

The next step is easier than the last.

Or

One can take time out for a coffee break, for that's about how long it will take for the glue to dry.

Or

Get the paint stirred. The next step takes only one fast and easy operation.

And last:

At this point, you should find the mixture beginning to thicken.

You will note the use of such psychological words as *easy* and *easier* or *fast* or *simple* in many bits of explanatory writing. Whether the step to come is difficult or not, the use of the word *easy* may make it seem just that way. No one should be facetious with breathers, however (e.g., "If readers have followed me this far, it's a miracle."). This antagonizes many readers who are looking for instructions, not comments on the awkward explanation of the author.

Mathematical and scientific topics need special care. They are usually complex topics with one step dependent on a previous one. A poorly written set of instructions in chemistry, one that leaves something out or does not clarify each step, may cause physical harm to a reader. To write themes in either of these two fields, the student must use short sentences and one paragraph per step. Combining too much material into one sentence or a paragraph may confuse the reader. Make it easy and clear for him.

In mathematical and scientific topics, *overuse* analogies. And make the analogies simple so that an intellectual level of a 10-year-old is kept in mind.

Humor, incidentally, is a great boon to learning, especially on difficult or intricate subjects. Don't overdo humor to the point of bad taste or of burlesque. The idea of good explanations is not to outdo a nightclub comic on one-liner jokes, but to teach a reader how to do something.

Endings

The ending of the expository theme should be brief, surely no more than two sentences and short ones at that. Once you're finished, in short, stop. The graceful ending given here is on addition:

> Once one can add two numbers, he can go on to three or more. It's that simple. It should give you a feeling of confidence, especially when the adding machine breaks down.

Or

> All that remains is to pick up the marbles that have been won and to try to get home before the boy you beat can try to intrigue you into another game.

Or

> Now that the bow has been tied, the man can go to dinner, to the theatre, or to any other formal event.

You might show the process in operation or the effects of the process, as the writer directly above did, for the conclusion. But let the reader know he is at the end of the composition.

CHAPTER 6

THE THEME'S
ENDING

Endings and beginnings are closely related in the composition of any type of theme. The beginning reveals what you're going to *tell* the reader. The ending indicates what you've *told* the reader even though the content in both sections might seem to be almost the same. It's something like the old rule for radio and television writing: tell them what you're going to tell them, tell them, then tell them what you've told them.

Don't be too concerned with an ending when you first begin to write themes. The most important thing then is to worry about how to write the bulk of the theme. The ending is the frosting on the cake, to be added in classroom themes only if time permits. If you're writing a theme for homework, of course, you'll have the time to put in on an ending.

Methods to use for an ending vary with the type theme written. An ending for an argumentative theme might not work too well for an expository theme. And an ending for an expository theme might be out of place in a descriptive composition. This can be seen if you'll go back and read the ending forms in the three sections specifically devoted to particular types of themes (argumentative, descriptive, expository).

Some endings might repeat arguments or points made in the body of the theme to ensure that readers don't forget the basic ideas included. Some endings merely complete the viewpoint that covers all ideas included in the text of the theme. Some endings, on the other hand, are full of poetic imagery, particularly descriptive themes. Other endings rely on an anecdote, a look into the future, or a statement about the importance of the subject.

Whatever you put into the ending, it is not too hard to do if you get some practice at writing this portion of the theme.

Some Basic Principles

There are some basic principles for any ending, whatever type it may be. The most important thing to do is to make that ending short. Also, an ending should clinch all that you've said in the body of the theme. It should leave your reader utterly convinced of the rightness of your arguments, or appreciative of the person or thing described, or enlightened on how to perform some process. It should also tell the reader, in a subtle way, that the theme is at an end.

There is a word of warning here, however. Avoid putting yourself into the ending so that it sounds as if you are crowing in triumph at all the magnificent prose you have mustered in the theme. Intended or not, this writing is certain to irk the reader. Such crude writing usually turns up looking something like this:

> For these three reasons, I have convinced you with certainty that each part of the case should be investigated. I have demonstrated well that the water theory should be discarded. I have shown that Mouton's findings are unnecessary here. And I have proved that some $10,000 will be required to finance the new study.

To circumvent this type of writing, eliminate first the pronoun *I*. The other things should then fall into place in a less boastful ending. Sum up the main points, take out the pronouns involving yourself, and let the facts speak for themselves. Such a presentation could be this ending:

> For these three reasons, it would appear that the matter should be investigated. The public should see that the water theory should be discarded, that Mouton's findings are not needed here, and that some $10,000 will be required to finance the new study.

Many writers make an ending brief and memorable. Such was this one, completing a long expository theme on the function of the lungs:

> Once again, we breathe in. While this air is in our lungs, we change it for waste air. Then, we breathe out and get rid of the bad air we have collected. In this way, our cells are fed and stay safe and healthy.

Here's another, even shorter example:

> All in all, it would seem that many people worked very hard and spent much money to accomplish extremely little.

Not that one must always be that brief. The example from this student involves a good summation of what has gone before in his theme. He writes:

> One can easily see from the preceding examples that Golding's philosophy has much sounder and more substantial evidence to support its case. Shakespeare's philosophy seems to be more theoretical and less applicable to the world of today. As new experiences and historical facts are examined, these ideas may change. However, at the present time, it would seem that Golding has the better grasp of true human nature.

Going into the meaning of it all, was this senior writing on the *carpe diem* philosophy of life. She completed her theme like this:

Regardless of afterlife, ulcers or social clubs, each man has a responsibility that goes far beyond his stomach or an ability to tango. We all owe the world full use of our talents and imagination—not all of us, of course, as Dr. Tom Dooley or the workers at Lambarene; but as thoughtful teachers, social workers, mechanics, and ice-cream vendors. We can't do anything for ourselves if we haven't first done something for everyone else.

Humor, providing it's in good taste, is always a good way to end things. For example:

Wet your thumb, folks. A breeze is rising.

Or

But then we all know what's in those aqua shows: just so much water over a dame.

Finally, picking a good quotation with which to end your theme might provide a good soft-pedaled farewell to the reader. The quote ending is a popular one with students, incidentally. The problem is, however, that they are prone to snatch any quote out of the air—whether it sums up things or not—and put it into the end of their themes. Such quotations must have the air of finality about them. If they don't, avoid them.

Here are two examples:

Martin might have heeded those words from the Bible that "Thou Shalt Love Thy Neighbor As Thyself."

Or

It's no wonder that the Blazer center feels that: "I want to be the best. That should be every athlete's goal if sports are really to be competitive and entertaining."

CHAPTER 7

WRITING STYLE

As you learn how to use content and how to organize your themes, so too, will you develop your own unique writing style. Beyond suggesting a few things that will sharpen your writing abilities, it is not the intention here to turn out students with identical writing patterns. In this chapter, we'll touch on style as well as some tips on paragraphing, use of connectives, clichés, imagery, generalities, idiomatic use, and the like.

General Writing Style

Write primarily so that your themes will be easily understood. Remember that the writings that have remained popular for hundreds of years with the general public and the intelligentsia have become classics because the writing was so clear that the meaning was understandable to everyone. True, each reader might interpret such writings differently, but at least he had a basic understanding of the author's intent. Most of the time, the writing clarity as we find in the classics stems directly from simple, unadorned writing, not the obscure, cryptic ramblings set forth in acrobatic grammatical form or that flossy, flowery gobbledegook favored by the insecure who desperately desire to impress the reader.

Plato and Aristotle are such examples of clear writers. Dickens is another. So is Steinbeck. Even Dr. Spock, that famous baby doctor, is an author whose best-selling work is so simple and clear to understand that his *Baby and Child Care* book at one time nearly outsold the Bible.

How do such writers make themselves clear? There are several basic techniques that they use, techniques that should help you. They have to do with using simple words, short and simple sentences, and short and adequate paragraphs.

Since you are writing themes here and not a complex doctoral dissertation for a graduate committee, why not use simple words? Does a theme with its short length need big words? Is such exactness, such precision in meaning going to be lost if the writer employs a vocabulary that a child can understand?

The same thing is true in the use of foreign phrases—a habit many writers overdo. Often, such phrases are employed by those who feel that English is an imprecise language. It seems to them that a German expression or one in French better encompasses the meaning of what the author is trying to say.

Frankly, this is doubtful.

Granted that English is not so precise in meaning as, say, French, it still can express most thoughts used in themes and other simple bits of oral or written efforts. It is tantalizing for students to use a word or an idiomatic expression that they've picked up in Latin, German, Spanish, or French class, but they should not do it unless the English equivalent *really* lacks the shade of meaning desired. Most of the time, English is adequate.

Moreover, unless you are indeed majoring in philosophy where, as we have observed, disputes go on over the exact definition of such everyday terms as *good* and *truth*, or unless you are writing a doctor's or master's thesis, it would be well for you to keep your vocabulary simple.

Slang and profanity should be eliminated in themes unless such expressions have a definite purpose as, say, when someone is being quoted. Slang is more permissible around English departments than is profanity in student themes, by the way. The writer of slang—if he intends to go into creative writing and wishes world-wide fame—has some difficulties in store for himself. Slang is usually out of date in a month, a year, or a decade and, besides, is hard to translate into foreign languages.

Sentence Style

What about the style for writing sentences?

The length of sentences used in themes should vary. Sentences that continue to be *too* short make for choppy, start-and-stop reading. True, the short sentence that follows other short sentences is handy for writing children's books ("Jump, jump, Sally," said Tommy) or for expressing a lot of action ("He saw the man. He crouched low behind the drums. He took careful aim. He squeezed the trigger."), but this is not the case with themes.

On the other hand, sentences that continue to be *too* long throughout the theme do tend to confuse the reader. He also may wonder if you end up on the same topic on which you started out. Many writers admit they are not quite sure themselves that the ending of their sentences matches the content contained in the beginning. Here is a sample of long-sentence writing that takes more than one reading for comprehension:

Such men will keep you on the way of being contented with yourself, of borrowing nothing of any other but yourself, of restraining and fixing your mind on definite and limited thoughts in which it may take pleasure, and, having recognized the true blessings which men enjoy in proportion as they recognize them, of contenting yourself with them, without desire of prolonging life and name.

There is another reason for shortening such lengthy sentences, a selfish reason too. The longer the sentence, the more punctuating you'll have to do, and the more grammatical errors and misspelled words you are bound to include in the theme.

It is generally recognized by readership-study experts that the reader's eye pauses at each bit of punctuation whether it be a comma, a colon, period, parenthesis, or whatever. In other words, if there is a lot of punctuation in a sentence, there is plenty of pausing. The more pausing that is done, the more tiring it is for readers to absorb what is written on the first reading. You'll make a clearer presentation of your material in a theme if you split up long sentences into shorter ones. This may take some rewriting, but the resulting clarity makes it well worth the surgery.

Try for a balance in sentence lengths.

Other things that interrupt the reader's concentration on your composition are too many parenthetical expressions (*however, by the way, I think, to be sure*, etc.), too many items in too many parentheses, and too many breaks in thought that are set off by dashes. Such writing is hard on the reader. It's probably harder than those tomes that are loaded with footnotes. Reread your theme and use an editing pencil freely to eliminate such expressions if you know that the words are unnecessary. Tighten the material. Perhaps a new sentence would take care of words in parentheses or those between the dashes. Do you really need parenthetical expressions such as *I believe, I think*, and *I feel*? The reader recognizes that you believe the material in the theme to be true.

At first, such editing may be difficult since most people revere words they've put on paper. But with practice and a judicious eye, you'll develop a fine editing skill. No prose is deathless, remember, especially most of that contained in themes. Keats, Whitman, and thousands of other writers did plenty of editing and rewriting.

Variety

Try for variety in the overall construction of sentences. Range beyond the subject-verb, subject-verb, subject-verb sentences which have been called little-red-hen writing style. You know what that is:

> The little red hen looked out the window. The little red hen saw the fox. The little red hen closed the doors and windows. The little red hen locked them. The little red hen began to quiver.

Many students may think they're not writing about little red hens, but they might use the same style such as this:

> The hammer is necessary for this step. The hammer and lock are located

just above the barrel. The barrel carries the bullets. The bullets are shaped in many ways.

As you cast about for new ways in which to form your sentences, avoid the ostentatious, inverted sentence order. Here are **examples:**

Backward ran sentences until reeled the mind.

and

Where it will all end, knows God!

A good way to see how you're progressing in both sentence length and structure is to take two or three of your old themes and do some content analysis. Circle the complete sentences. Once you look them over, you'll be able to see if your writing style involves the too-short or too-long sentence areas. Then mark a big *S* and a big *V* over the subject and the verb of each sentence. If you have too many that follow the subject-verb construction of sentences, you'll be able to begin working yourself out of this habit. To be conscious of your weaknesses is the first step to correction.

What about the tone or mood of a theme?

You'll set up an atmosphere, or slant, matching the subject matter, if you're intelligent about what you're doing. If the topic is a serious one, don't use a humorous style of writing. Likewise, if you're writing on a light subject, don't use a heavy-handed style. This is not to say that some levity or lightness is ruled out altogether for a serious subject if the touch is limited. Or that a serious touch cannot be used sparingly on themes of lighter topics. It's better to conform with the predominant mood throughout the composition.

A minor point that should be kept in mind so far as modifying words are concerned is to keep adjectives and adverbs next to or very near to the words that they modify. This keeps the reader from wondering who is beautiful or just what rock is jagged. As we have said, the average reader is easy to confuse. Dangling modifiers are very familiar and appear often in humor columns. You know them:

While entering the house, the bell rang.

Or

Mother put Dad's shirt into the new washer, which was greasy from hours of working on the car.

There are some basic style rules for writing endings. Custom-made endings for argumentative, descriptive, and expository themes are included in the detailed chapters for each of these forms of compositions.

The Paragraph

No confusion will result in paragraphing if you follow just two simple rules on this subject.

First, if you are writing on a topic that has five aspects each of which is rather simple, allow a paragraph per aspect.

Second, if you are writing on a topic that has five (or more, or less) aspects that are quite complex (with several subdivisions per aspect), allow a paragraph for *each* subdivision.

Knowing how to paragraph involves using common sense. Cluster a group of sentences together in a paragraph if those sentences deal with one aspect of the main topic.

Let's try out the paragraph formula to show you what is meant.

Assume that the theme topic is in the descriptive and involves characterizing Don Quixote and Sancho Panza, two leading characters in Cervantes' *Don Quixote*. Obviously, you'll have to do some paragraphing between the two men if to do nothing more than to fence off one man from the other. Readers have to be able to distinguish where one man's characterization ends and the other's begins. Characterizing, means to show personality traits plus colorful incidents that amply illustrate those qualities. Here is one way you might paragraph such a topic:

Paragraph No. 1	Beginning (2 paragraphs, identify both, give 3 traits each)
Paragraph No. 2	Don Quixote (kindness—to Dorothea)
Paragraph No. 3	Don Quixote (wisdom—advice to Sancho on being a governor)
Paragraph No. 4	Don Quixote (insanity—wineskins, sheep, basin, saw horse, windmills)
Paragraph No. 5	Sancho (practicality—food, shelter, humoring Don Quixote)
Paragraph No. 6	Sancho (wisdom—governor of Barataria)
Paragraph No. 7	Sancho (humor—lashes)
Paragraph No. 8	Ending (sum up 6 traits)

If you feel that each trait is rather complex and has two or three aspects to it, use a paragraph for *each* aspect. In paragraphing, you're helping the reader see where one part of a subject ends and another begins. This is also true for examples. You may wish to give a separate paragraph for each example. Perhaps two or three paragraphs if the example is involved with two or three parts to it.

Once you've done a few of these, you'll also understand that you can do some "instant paragraphing" by merely using the proofreader's mark of ¶. Such a mark is instantly recognizable to any reader and will save you the chore of redoing the entire composition.

Arrangement Within Paragraphs

How do you arrange the material within each paragraph?

There are many ways, but the easiest and quickest one to use is one that involves using the first sentence of the paragraph as the statement. Subsequent sentences in the paragraph offer proof or examples to demonstrate that statement. When you develop skill at writing, you'll probably reverse the procedure, but the statement-proof arrangement is very easy for any reader to understand. No wonder so many writers who are good at explaining complex material do use this arrangement within paragraphs.

If you were writing an expository theme on tennis, the paragraph's content might be handled like this one:

Five pieces of equipment are needed for tennis.	} statement
Players need a racquet, three tennis balls, a net, tennis shoes, and informal clothes.	} example

In an argumentative theme, your paragraph might be written like this sample:

Hitler's generals did not have the matériel or the communications to win the battle.	} statement
In one day alone the Allies pounded the rail center around the area so that the two trains that had ammunition, food, and medical supplies were blown up before they could leave the siding. The highways, over which SS trucks had carried artillery shells for months, were heavily laced with bomb craters and were impassable.	} example

The paragraphs given above are both written with a first sentence that sums up the content of the paragraph. This is followed by sentences that contain examples or evidence supporting that first statement.

This brings us to the short, one-sentence paragraph.

It has been held in past that brief, one-sentence paragraphs were the products of show-off writers. Considering that some novelists write paragraphs with only one word, you might agree with the critics of such paragraphs. These novelists write this way to arrest the reader's attention. Such short paragraphs serve also as useful typographical breaks that provide a rest from the continuous strain of reading moderate to long paragraphs. Readership-study experts also have proclaimed the short paragraph's effectiveness.

Another purpose of the short, one-sentence paragraph is that such a brief unit of words provides a chance for the reader to see if he is keeping up with the presentation of facts and ideas. A short paragraph of this type lets him get his breath for the next portion of the theme.

If you use the short paragraph, make sure it is not to show off or because you're in the mood to use it. Such transition sentences should be used sparingly to get the most emphasis out of them.

The Breather

In connection with the paragraph, there is what we call the "breather" paragraph or sentence. As the name indicates, the breather is a transitional break for the reader. It allows him to think about the material given up to a point in a composition. The reader needs such a pause before going on with the subject, for you cannot give him a great deal of material without a break of some kind if he's to do any kind of thoughtful evaluation of your theme. The mind balks if it is fed too much at once. Also, readers like to know that they are keeping up with the material being presented. Complex subjects, particularly in expository compositions on, say, economics or on nuclear physics almost always require breathers if they are to be digested. Perhaps some breathers are bothersome, but if you want to hold the reader's attention and gain his complete understanding of your point of view, you'll find this device very worth-while.

Sometimes a breather involves an ending as in:

And so, it will be seen how clever Goebbels was as a master propagandist.

Or

These three reasons demonstrate why Johnson is wrong.

Or

Where could such a policy lead?

Equally, a breather might be a token of encouragement, urging a reader not to fall by the wayside as with

The next step is easy.

Or

If you have followed the steps so far, you'll find the rest of the steps simple too.

These short, one-sentence breathers can be included within a paragraph—at the start, the middle, or the end. Or they can be the paragraph itself. Breathers, in short, provide temporary transitions from idea to idea, fact to fact, or serve as a rest stop or a means to sum up a mass of information.

Connectives

In theme writing, you may need a word or phrase to indicate you're moving on to a new aspect or argument of a topic. Or maybe the word you need does reinforce some point you've made or are about to make. Readers are easily confused. They want to know what is happening. Are you, they'll wonder, still on the same phase of the subject, or have you moved on to another? Are you about to provide them with an example? Are you on the final, the second, the sixth point? Are you providing an exception to the point? Is this section opposed to the material you had in an earlier part of the theme? You must lead your readers each step of the way, and the most effective way to do this is with connective words or phrases.

You already know what should go into the content of a paragraph. A connective word or phrase might lead into the first sentence of a paragraph. Or the word might lead into the examples, the illustrations you'll call forth within the paragraph. Such connective words in, say, argumentative writing, might be *on the other hand, however, by contrast, further*, and many others that you will find listed in this section of the book. Whatever connective word(s) you use, you're helping readers to follow the material that you present. If your topic is a complex and heavy one, you'll have to make generous use of connectives to make the subject understood.

There are some pitfalls, however, with connective words.

If you list arguments in your theme, be sure when you say "there are three reasons why" something is so, that there *are* three reasons about to be included. Similarly, if you write *fourth* in listing argumentative points, the point that follows this connective word *fourth* must be the fourth one. If you write *finally,* the material that follows should be of a final nature. Don't be one of the *New Yorker* magazine's Our Forgetful Authors.

On descriptive themes, the words *in the distance* should not involve something that later turns out to be in the foreground. *Consequently* and *as a result* connectives should be followed by the result or consequence of some action. *Equally important* factors should deal with factors that are of equal importance. *To sum up* should concern a summation of material, and *on the other hand* or *on the contrary* requires that something be on the first hand or that something does have a contrary side to it. All connectives need careful use, not just the ones used here.

You'll undoubtedly think up many other connective words in the course of writing themes, taking essay tests and other forms of composition, but here is a list that should help you when you are just beginning. They are divided by theme categories, but are certainly interchangeable:

For Descriptive Themes

above	beyond	on my left
across from	farther	on my right
adjacent to	here	opposite
also	in the distance	to the left
before me	nearby	to the right
behind	next to	to the rear
below		

For Expository Themes

also	for example	on the other hand
another	for instance	otherwise
as a result	for this purpose	second
at last	furthermore	similarly
by contrast	in addition	such
consequently	likewise	then
finally	next	thus
first	on the contrary	too

For Argumentative Themes

accordingly	for example	on the contrary
again	for instance	on the other hand
although	furthermore	otherwise
another	hence	second
as a result	if this be true	such
at the same time	in addition	then, too,
besides	in fact	therefore
by contrast	in short	thus
consequently	moreover	to sum up
equally important	nevertheless	too
finally	obversely	whereas
first		

Clichés and Bromides

Clichés and bromides should be avoided in good writing.

A *bromide* is a trite sentence such as "It's a small world, isn't it?" or "It never rains but it pours." A *cliché* is an expression (not a sentence) that is equally stale ("busy as a bee"). We have assembled a list of the most worn-out clichés and bromides used in themes and ones most cited by the teaching manuals and grammar books. After you write your theme, you'd better check this list and see if any of your favorite expressions are on it. A good way to become familiar with many of them is to sit down and to write a small story using 25 to 50 clichés or bromides. You'll recognize them instantly the next time you begin to use one of them.

They are:

abreast of the times	beggars description
aching void	better half
acid test	better late than never
after all is said and done	bitter end
all in all	blissfully ignorant
all work and no play	blood is thicker than water
a long-felt want	blushing bride
along these lines	bold as brass
among those present	bolt from the blue
ardent admirer	bountiful repast
arms of Morpheus	brave as a lion (tiger)
artistic temperament	breathless silence
as luck would have it	brilliant performance
at a loss for words	briny deep
at one fell swoop	brown as a berry
	budding genius
bathed in tears	busy as a bee
beat a hasty retreat	by leaps and bounds

captains of industry
carrying coals to Newcastle
caught like rats in a trap
center of attraction
checkered career
cheered to the echo
clear as crystal (a bell)
clinging vine
close to nature
cold as ice
consensus of opinion
conspicuous by his absence
course of true love
cute as a bug's ear

Dame Fortune
deadly earnest
defies description
depend upon it
depths of despair
devouring element
discreet silence
doomed to disappointment
downy couch
drastic action
dull, sickening thud

each and every
easier said than done
equal to the occasion
eyes like diamonds (stars)

fair sex
familiar landmark
favor with a selection
festive occasion
few and far between
filthy lucre
flat as a pancake
flavor of the Old South
fold his tent and steal away
fools rush in
footprints on the sands of time
force of circumstances
foreseeable future
from all walks of life

goes without saying
golden tresses (locks)
goodly number
great open spaces
green as grass (with envy)
gridiron warriors (heroes)
grim reaper

happy as a lark (clam)
happy pair
heartfelt thanks
heart's content
heated argument
he-man
he must be cruel to be kind
holy bonds (estate) of matrimony

ignorance is bliss
in great profusion
in the last (first) analysis
iron constitution
irony of fate
it never rains but it pours
it stands to reason

last but not least
last straw
last white line
limped into port
long-felt want
looking for all the world like a

mad as a wet hen (hatter)
mantle of snow
meets the eye
method in his madness
mind over matter
moment of truth
monarch of all he surveys
more in sorrow than in anger
Mother Nature
motley crowd (throng)
myriad of lights

needs no introduction
nipped in the bud

none the worse for wear
no rest for the weary (wicked)
no thinking man

paramount issue
partake of refreshments
pending merger
picturesque scene
pleasing prospect
plot (the) thickens
poor but honest
powers that be
presided at the piano
promising future
proud possessor
psychological moment

quiet as a mouse (tomb)

ran amok
red as a rose
reigns supreme
rendered a selection
replete with interest
rich or poor, young or old
riot of color
ripe old age
rolling in the aisles
ruling passion

sad to relate
sadder but wiser
sea of faces
seething mass of humanity
self-made man
shadow of the goal posts
sharp as a tack
short and sweet
sigh of relief
sign of life
silence reigned supreme
single life
single blessedness
skeleton in the closet
sleep the sleep of the just

snug as a bug in a rug
snow-capped mountains
soul of discretion (honor)
spectacle of humanity
staff of life
sterling character
strong as an ox (lion, bear)
strong, silent type
struggle for existence
sturdy as an oak
sumptuous repast
sweat of his brow
sweet girl graduate

table groaned
take my word for it
take the bitter with the sweet
taken into custody
tall, dark, and handsome
tell it not in Gath
thereby hangs a tale
thick as thieves (mud)
this day and age
thunderous applause
time marches on
time of our lives
tired but happy
too clever by half (for words)
too full for utterance
too funny for words
too much of a good thing

vale of tears
venture a suggestion
view with alarm

watery grave
weaker sex
wee, small hours
wends his way
wheel of fortune
where angels fear to tread
wild and woolly
with bated breath
words fail me (to express)

worked like a Trojan (charm, horse)
worse for wear
wrapped in mystery
wreathed in smiles

wrought havoc
wry countenance (grin)

young or old, rich or poor

Similes and Metaphors

Many of the clichés and bromides listed in this chapter started life as fresh forms of similes and metaphors. When new, they were vivid and most descriptive. Overuse by unoriginal writers and speechmakers, however, turned them into tired expressions of what poets call imagery or word pictures. If your pet expression is among those listed in the cliché and bromide section, you will have to try to think up new similes and metaphors for your themes.

Similes and metaphors have contributed through the ages to what is called good writing. Such expressions, usually short and picturesque, are like code. It takes few words to express an entire situation in vivid form. Such expressions add color to a scene and, probably more important, define the unknown by the use of the known. By definition, strictly speaking, a simile is *like* some object ("Ophelia is *like* a rose"). A metaphor is something that has changed its form ("Ophelia *is* a rose").

Many similes and metaphors are so graphic or descriptive that they instantly bring a picture to our minds or make something else clear. Bear in mind that if your reader is to understand your expressions, he must know the point of reference in the simile or the metaphor. Such a reference is, for example, the beauty of the rose that is used above with Ophelia. She is easily pictured by all who have ever seen this flower.

It's a good idea not to use similes and metaphors that have obscure or cryptic meanings. You'll not be understood by most readers. Similes and metaphors with obscure references rarely become popular. Shakespeare, remember, used nature as his chief reference whenever he employed a simile or metaphor. He reckoned perhaps that nature's objects were familiar to almost everyone. Nature is eternal and because of it, Shakespeare's similes and metaphors are understandable even today.

Here are some spritely bits of imagery offered by students in themes:

He was a walking bacteria culture.
She was a drop of water in a bath tub.
Russia is a whale, ready to swallow us up.
She was an echo in a large cavern.
He was a Richard III.
She was as gossipy as a landlady with 50 apartments.
He was as lonely as an alligator with bad breath.
His thinking was as confusing as a potato growing on a tomato plant.

If you use the metaphor, be sure you don't mix the figures of speech if you include more than one analogy in your writing. The *New Yorker* magazine, in its "Block That Metaphor" section, has printed these gems:

> Mr. Speaker, I smell a rat; I see him forming in the air and darkening in the sky; but I'll nip him in the bud.

Or

> We keep clipping the wool from the goose that lays the golden eggs until we pump her dry.

Or

> He ripped the novel limb from limb, for it didn't hold water at all.

Generalities

The sweeping generality and the questionable statistic are fairly common elements of beginners' themes. It would seem too that the younger or less sophisticated the writer is, the more sweeping the statement, the wilder the statistics. Youth and the inexperienced like things to be simple. It's easier to view the world that way. But as a person grows older, he begins to see that things are not all black and white.

Some of the sweeping generalities spotted in high school and college themes are these:

> Men are no longer so cruel as they were in the time of Genghis Khan.

Or

> The reason the United States fought Germany was to avenge the deaths of six million Jews in concentration camps.

Or

> Women are rather stupid.

Or

> If everyone votes, we'll have true democracy.

Or

> There is no proof that there is a hereafter.

In each one of these instances, the statements would collapse even upon rudimentary research. It is pleasant to be able to sum up some situations with a sweeping statement, but such generalizing is far of the mark when the facts are examined. It may be dangerous to use these expressions, especially in the case of the statement of women being stupid.

If you're going to use statistics or facts, be sure that your data are correct and that you have listed your source. It is easy to mislead with statistics. Polls, for example, are not real indices of how *all* people feel unless *all* people are contacted. Responses vary when given to pollsters before lunch, in the evening, early in the morning, on a good day, or on a bad day. Some authorities also use half-truths or carefully selected facts. These facts may be accurate so far as they go, but there may be much material deliberately omitted that tells a far different story. The listing of a source is therefore helpful to the reader so that he can judge the truth of the matter.

In short, almost everyone has his pet peeves, his blind spots, and his beliefs. It is a rare publication that is truly open-minded. Magazines and books are published by firms headed by people who have particular ideas about things. Many students are far too prone to accept as gospel everything they see on television, hear on the radio, or hear from some adult they respect. Words are not necessarily sacred if they come from ordinary mortals. Is one soap advertised on television truly better than another? Is a radio editorial always true? Is a newspaper or magazine story full of facts and objective?

Doubt material you read or hear from supposedly authoritative sources. The best way to seek the truth is to doubt. If you use some fact from a publication or another individual, credit your source. Identify the place or person who provided the "facts" and let the reader judge the truth.

Even if you quote "fact" and are fair about listing the source, be sure you quote accurately. Your reader might have run into the same source. He might recognize mistakes. Check your sources to be sure you've got things right. Don't pull figures and statements out of the air, of course, either.

If you can't cite a source, but your position on some topic seems to be somewhat sound, drop the statistics and facts. Qualify your statement with such scientific and academic hedges as "it appears" or "it seems" or variations of these remarks. Scientists and other prudent researchers almost always hedge their findings with these expressions, for they know there's nothing certain on this earth but the proverbial death and taxes. Even if evidence is overwhelming and supports their contentions, they still use these devices.

Platitudes

A platitude is kin to a generality. It states the obvious and turns up whenever there seems to be a lull in conversation or a shortage of imagination among writers and speechmakers. Among the platitudes found in many themes are these:

The boys and girls of today are the men and women of tomorrow.

Or

It takes two to make a marriage.

Or

Duty is sacred.

Or

Freedom of speech (or assembly, or religion, or the press) is the cornerstone of liberty.

Or

Our cause is just.

Instead of coming up with these hackneyed expressions, try for something with a little more imagination.

Idioms

An *idiom* is an expression that may be grammatically unsound or figuratively weak, but which has become correct through years and years of use. The following idioms are the ones generally considered to be correctly stated:

accord with	feel free from
according to	frightened by, at
accuse of	was graduated from
acquitted of	identical with
adverse to	in accordance with
aim to prove	in search of
as far as	jealous of
among ourselves	kind of
angry with	listen to
as regards	monopoly of
authority on	oblivious of
blame me for it	in line
cannot help talking	plan to go
comply with	prefer to
conform to, with	prior to
convince that	provided
correspond to	sensitive to
desire to	superior to
desirous of	attend to
die of	at home
different from	treat of
disdain for	try to
dissent from	unequal to
doubt whether	unmindful of
enamored of	vie with

Among the idiomatic expressions used with great frequency are these:

One agrees: *to* a proposal, *on* a plan, *with* a person

One contends: *for* a principle, *with* a person, *against* an obstacle.

One differs: *with* a person, *from* something else, *about* or *over* a question.

One is impatient: *for* something desired, *with* someone else, *of* restraint, *at* someone's conduct.

One is rewarded: *for* something done, *with* a gift, *of* a person.

Interrupters

Check to see if all your interrupters or parenthetical expressions *really* are necessary. Sometimes overuse of these interjections clogs sentences and confuses the meaning of what you're trying to say. Some of the most common to students are *however, nevertheless, naturally, incidentally, of course, by the way, I think, I believe, I feel,* and the like. Readers know that when you state a viewpoint, for example, you are telling them what you believe. If you have the *however* habit, see if you can't delete a few. Not that these expressions *all* should be eliminated from themes, but an overabundance of them would suggest that confusion might result in a composition.

Avoid interrupting your sentences so often with parenthetical interrupters that the reader has a hard time following what is being said.

Pronouns

The misuse of some pronouns—chiefly *it*—has brought out the red marking pencils probably as often as spelling on themes. Readers have particularly short memories, as has been said here. They just may have a difficult time understanding to what *it* refers if there are many nouns going before that pronoun. We can see the reader's dilemma in these examples of pronoun difficulties:

> The students turned the pigs loose on the girls; we had to chase *them* (the girls? the pigs?).

Or

> He gave the books and code to them; *they* were clean of fingerprints (the papers? books? them?).

The correct way to avoid pronouns of faulty reference is *not* to stop using pronouns. You must meet the disease head-on and try to conquer it.

Substitute such confusing pronouns with nouns. In the first example above, you might change the word *them* to the *animals. They*, on the second example, might be converted to *the items*.

Another approach offers a similar amount of success. The student should circle all the pronouns used in the entire theme. He then should read the full sentence to himself to see if there can be any possible misunderstanding. More errors in grammar, particularly faulty pronoun references, have been picked up in this manner than in almost any other editing method.

Redundancies

Once you become proficient at writing, you'll know how to wield the editing pencil like the most critical of editors. One thing you'll eliminate is the redundant expression. Some words are excessive baggage and can be deleted. Such editing actually aids clarity. The following expressions are considered to be the most common redundancies used by students. The words in the parentheses are the correct ones to use. They are

> Whether or not (Whether)
> Tiny little feet (Tiny feet or Little feet)
> Complete monopoly (Monopoly)
> Resume again (Resume)
> Recur again (Recur)

Free gratis (Free)
First beginnings (Beginnings)
Round in form (Round)
Bare essentials (Essentials)
Repeat again (Repeat)
Unusually unique or Very unique (Unique)
On Monday (Monday)
He is a man who (He)
In a hasty manner (Hastily)
Christmas Eve evening (Christmas Eve)

CHAPTER

EDITING SHORTCUTS

If you are writing under a classroom deadline or if you merely want short-cuts in writing, you'll be able to make good use of editors' correction symbols. You may want to add or to subtract material quickly. Or you may want to shift an entire paragraph or two to another part of the theme. Ordinarily, students throw away their false starts and try again. But this isn't necessary. We suggest that you use some editing marks from the publishing field. These marks are understood by most English teachers and wherever a Roman alphabet is printed.

If you are doing a theme in class, such symbols will be godsends for saving time and effort. If you're doing a theme outside of class and find that you are making a great number of editing changes, finish editing the entire theme and then do a perfected form of your theme that includes all changes.

Insertions

An insertion is used in writing when you discover that you've left out something from your composition, or when you want to move material from one part of the theme to another area. Rather than rewrite the entire theme, all you have to do is to take a separate piece of paper and write on it all the material you've omitted. It may involve one sentence, one paragraph, or several paragraphs. The insertion of single words or letters is not handled in this fashion, however. Another method takes care of them.

When you finish writing the material you want to add, enclose it all with large brackets on *both* sides of the complete paragraph(s). Mark *Insert A* outside both of the brackets.

Turn next to the theme and the place where you want to add the new material. Draw a line from the *left* margin of the paper to the area where you want to include the material. At the start of the line in the left margin, write the corresponding term *Insert A*. If you have several insertions to make in different parts of the theme, mark each addition with successive letters of the alphabet (Insert B, Insert C, Insert D, etc.).

If your theme is being written in class, your instructor will know how to interpret these simple instructions on your part. If you are writing the theme as homework, by the mark(s) of insertion you will know where matter is to be included when you begin to write the final draft of the composition.

An insertion looks like the following illustration. The first part shows the original theme draft, marked for inserts. The second section is the one put on a separate piece of paper.

Insert A

The safest way of having no thoughts of one's own is to take up a book every moment one has nothing else to do. Men of learning are those who have done their reading in the pages of a book. Thinkers and men of genius are those who have gone straight to the book of Nature; it is they who have enlightened the world and carried humanity further on its way.

Insert A

Insert

It is this practice which explains why erudition makes most men more stupid and silly than they are by nature, and prevents their writings obtaining any measure of success. They remain, in Pope's words: "For ever reading, never to be read!"

If you want to insert letters or one or two words into your theme, you will use the *caret*, which looks like this: ∧ The correct way to add a letter is:

When in the course of hu∧man events it becomes

To add one or two words, use the caret mark this way:

new form

This ∧ is especially adaptable to ~~examinations~~ tests

Don't use the caret for the insertion of more than a few words or letters. It becomes too hard to follow. You should never write a lot of material to be inserted on the same page where the addition is to be made. Particularly, you should not follow the old stunt of turning the paper sideways and writing inserted material in the margins, circling it.

Deletions

There'll be many times when you'll want to leave out material that you have included in your theme. Throwing away the paper takes time and wastes paper. Besides, what if you change your mind later and want to put back the writing that is now all squashed up in the wastebasket? The journalists—so adept at second thoughts—almost always use the deletion method to get around this problem. It's a good method whether for classroom or homework theme.

The method for deleting, or omitting, a word or two is this one:

It ~~was~~ was on January 2 that ~~Ronald~~ Reagan

If you want to omit material within a paragraph, a sentence or two perhaps, this is the way to do it:

We were further told that we shouldn't try to sell them when we were through with them either. He was writing a new set right then. He asked us if we thought he lived on his salary, and when one boy said he thought so, the professor told us that the third-string quarterback made more money than he did last year alone. Furthermore, we were told to buy eight books that he had written for "outside reading." These weren't available in secondhand stores or even the library.

The way to delete a whole paragraph is this:

A man does not have to match this profile exactly, but it won't help him at all if his line zigs where the chart zags. Take a man who scores considerably higher than the 10th percentile on aesthetic values, for example; such people, Sears, Roebuck notes, "accept artistic beauty and taste as a fundamental standard of life. This is not a factor which makes for executive success. . . . Generally, cultural considerations are not important to Sears executives, and there is little evidence that such interests are detrimental to success." **

If you decide to omit an entire page or pages, you merely run a single arrow from the top, left-hand corner to the bottom, right-hand corner.

Deletions should not be done by scribbling over words or by rolling up the material to be left out and tossing it away. You might change your mind later and want to re-include material you deleted. If it is scribbled out or tossed away, you will have no end of trouble redoing what you wrote.

Let's suppose that you have deleted material from your theme that you later decide to put back in. With the deletion method, you'll write the word *stet* (leave it as it is) on the margins of the omitted material to show that it is to be included. The *stet* markings in operation look like this:

stet   I followed her into the building where the *Minnesota Daily* was published. It was like walking into a movie set. Young men with hats on the backs of their heads and cigarettes dangling from their mouths rushed back and forth screaming "Hold the presses!" or "Leave me to a phone!" Lissom girls sat on desks, chain smoking. Nobody spoke below a shriek or was without a cigarette for a moment.***   *stet*

Other Editing Symbols

Another shortcut in checking your theme and making small changes quickly is to use editing symbols. These can be used in the rough draft you write or to pick off miniscule mistakes in the finished theme. If you have too many corrections in the completed draft, you might just as well do the whole theme over again. Most teachers will accept minor changes usually. The marks shown in this section are in use everywhere the English language is printed. The reason for their universal popularity is rather obvious, of course. They require only a quick use of the editing pencil. Too, they are based on common sense.

*** From Max Shulman's *Barefoot Boy With Cheek*, 1944, Doubleday.

The symbols are these:

Symbol	Explanation	Symbol in Use
⬭	Spell out or abbreviate	N.Y. New York 9 ten
‿	Join separated material	m‿en
/	Separate joined material	old/men
⤳	Insert material	gld Is ∧ in (*Not*)
/	No capital letters	ℓounties
≡	Use capital letters	memphis
∼ ⌐⌐	Transpose words or letters	sold are/firmly/hit
⌒	Delete or carry-over	are ~~always~~ hit
(stet)	Leave it as it is	are ~~always~~ hit (stet)
↳	Join these parts	flaunt. ~~Not in~~ ↳Mercy is always strained
⁋	Paragraph within the text	11 men. ⁋ They
NO ⁋	No paragraph	*NO* ⁋ From all of
⌄	Insert quotation marks	Go! ⌄ he shouted.
⌄	Insert an apostrophe	John⌄s hat
∧	Insert comma	If he is right ∧ he should
⊙	Period	one night ⊙ But there is
⌒	Delete matter	Johnh was ~~going to~~

An example of a theme using many of the editing marks explained in this chapter might be the following:

Let me introduce John Q. Paramecium of (N.Y.)/ He is a happy little fellow, even though he cannot be seen without a microscope. He spends all his time in the water as most tiny one-celled animals do.

When john's body grows so larg‿e that he can ∧ take care of it, he divides in half. This≡ is not as easy as it sounds, however. (*not*)

A ℓaramecium has two main parts. There is the nucleus, which is something like a brain. And then there is the cytoplasm which is like flesh.

Insert A —— Now we have seen what a paramecium ∧ like. The reason why he must/divide is too difficult to go into here ⊙ But it has much to do with john⌄s being overweight. The next step is to see what happens. (*looks*)

When John divides ∧ each half must be the same. There must be a nucl‿es in each half. The chromosomes ⌐must⌐ in each nucleus /also be the same ⊙

(It is not hard to see under a microscope.) ⌒

John's chromosomes unravel as strings would if the ends were not tied. Each chromosome divides into two strings ~~that~~ have spots that are just alike. (*which*)

These halves are pulled apart to each side of the nucleus by a strange force. when these groups get to the sides of the nucleus, they keep on going.

Soon the nucleus is pulled apart into two which are just alike. john, then, has a nucleus at each end. The difficult part is over. John Q. simply divides across the middle between the nucliei.

Each half, then, can go on living without the other.

Insert
A

The nucleus has many little chromosomes. These are like strings with little colored spots on them. Each spot makes some part of the paramecium work as it should. They, also, are nearly the same in every paramecium so that all of John's relatives look and act the same. This is important. If it did not happen, maybe some would end up looking like trees.

Insert
A

CHAPTER

BAFFLING WORDS
AND USAGE

Some words or expressions baffle even the experts. Some insist the last word on any confusing terms is *Webster's Unabridged Dictionary*. Others insist that English is a "living language" and that *real hot* is an acceptable expression in the deep South. In some circles it takes a courageous grammarian to answer the telephone with "This is she." And who has not wondered whether a hyphen always follows *non-, anti-,* or *trans-,* or whether *who* or *whom* is correct, to say nothing of *that, which,* or *who*?

This chapter includes some of the most baffling words and usage problems, listed alphabetically, based on Webster as well as style books from *The New York Times* and the Associated Press, and the famed *Elements of Style* by William Strunk, Jr., and E. B. White.

One helpful observation in all problems involving baffling words and terms is that when you are struggling to keep two things straight, *you need memorize only one of them*; the other term will be mastered in the process. For example, if you are confronted with *emigrate* and *immigrate,* memorize the fact that *em* means "to move out" and you'll know, by process of elimination, that *imm* must therefore mean "to move *into*" a country.

A, An.   *A* goes before a consonant *sound* in the next word: *It was a big game. An* goes before a vowel *sound* in the next word: *She's an only child who had an honored father.*

Abbreviations and Acronyms.   It's *Dr. Melvin Smith, Sen. Steve Johnson, Gen. Gordon Jones,* and *Mr. Phil Anderson,* but *Standard Insurance Co.* and *Irving Story, MA.*

   The first time you mention a group with an acronym (*FBI,* etc.), spell out the name. On the second reference, you may use the acronym: *She was the first woman agent in the Federal Bureau of Investigation, but hardly the last in the FBI. The Atlantic Richfield Corporation was mentioned, but ARCO officials denied the allegation.*

All-.   When *all* is part of a compound adjective, use a hyphen: *all-out effort, all-star game, all-around hero.*

Among, Between.   *Among* involves more than *two* elements, while *between* usually involves *only* two unless there's a *pair* with several elements: *The meeting was between group division's legal and underwriting departments and individual's actuary and policyowner service departments.*

Another.   *Another* doesn't mean *additional.* It's involved with duplicating something mentioned *before: She earned $15 and lost another $10.*

Ante-, Anti-.   Don't use a hyphen with *ante- (antecedent),* but *do* use one with all *anti-* words except these:

antibiotic	antihistamine	antipasto	antiserum
antibody	antiknock	antiperspirant	antithesis
anticlimax	antimatter	antiphon	antitoxin
antidote	antimony	antiphony	antitrust
antifreeze	antiparticle	antiseptic	antitussive
antigen			

Anybody, Any Body, Anyone, Any One.   Use one word (*anyone*) when meaning *nobody* or *no one in particular. Any body* can mean *any corpse* or *any group.* The rule is the same for *everybody, nobody,* and *somebody, someone.* To avoid confusion, however, with two *o*'s, it's *no one.* If you are giving emphasis to part of a group, write *Any one of them may be innocent.*

Arbitrate, Mediate.   An *arbitrator* listens to evidence and decides. A *mediator* listens to evidence, but tries to get quarreling people to make the decision.

As Good or Better than.   Prune for effectiveness: *Smith's view was as good as hers, or better.*

Assassin.   An *assassin* is a *politically* motivated killer.

Average, Mean, Median, Norm.   *Average* is the result obtained when the sum of all the numbers to be added (15+20+30+35= 100) is divided by the total of all the numbers (4; average=25). *Mean* is the middle figure between two extreme numbers. *Median* is the middle number in a series set up by size. *Norm* involves the standard of average performance for a group.

Bad, Badly. *Badly* is an adverb, meaning that it describes something *being described*. *Bad* is an adjective that is correctly used in *I feel bad*. *I feel badly* means that the sense of touch is bad.

Because, Since. *Because* is part of a specific cause-effect situation; one thing led *directly* to another: *He lost his deferment because he was at the Student Union instead of classes. Since* is not *directly* the cause of anything, but an outgrowth of an action: *Since she neither smoked nor drank, he asked her the major questions.*

Bi-. You need no hyphens with *bi-: bilateral, bimonthly, biweekly. Bi-* means twice the period used (*biannual* means *twice a year, biweekly* means *twice a week,* etc.).

Bloc, Block. A *bloc* is a group of people or countries with one goal.

Boycott, Embargo. *Boycott* is an organized movement to stop buying some goods or services. An *embargo* is a law prohibiting trade between countries.

But. *But* is not used after *help* or *doubt. They had no doubt that they would win. Stimson could not help seeing that the nation was ready for war.*

But That, But What. *But* isn't needed in sentences such as *I don't doubt that he'll come.*

By-. *By-* is a prefix that needs no hyphen (*bypass, bylaw*) except for *by-election* and *by-product.*

Co-. You won't need a hyphen in these words, which have outgrown the old rule that a prefix ending in a vowel and linking to a word beginning with the same or another vowel must have a hyphen:

coeducation	coexist	cooperate	coordinate
coessential	coercive	coextensive	coagulate
coalition			

Collective Nouns. Is it *The couple was* or *The couple were, The committee is* or *The committee are*? It depends on whether you're thinking of a *unit* or *individual items*. If you're thinking of a collective noun as a bunch of individual items, the plural verb is correct: *The crowd were slowly finding their places and beginning to be quiet. The old couple were friendless.* If you're thinking of a collective noun as a single unit, use the singular verb: *Humankind is empty. Politics is everyone's business.*

Compared to, Compared with. *Compared to* is used when comparing two or more items that are similar. *Compared with* is used when putting two things side by side to show similarities and differences.

Compose, Comprise, Constitute. *Compose* puts things together. *Comprise* includes or contains. *Constitutes* is considered the best word if *compose* or *comprise* doesn't apply. It may help to know that, strictly speaking, *comprise* means to *embrace*. Men don't comprise (*embrace*) a group; they *constitute* a group.

Composed of, Divided into.   Purists argue that the two are not the same. An apple, if it's cut, can be *divided into* sections; but if uncut, an apple is *composed of* seeds, flesh, and skin.

Conclave.   A secret meeting.

Connote, Denote.   *Connote* suggests something *beyond what's on the surface: That word* tithe *connotes obligation. Denote* deals with what's *on the surface: His conduct denotes treason.*

Convince, Persuade.   People are *convinced* about things, but they have to be *persuaded* to take action. One is an *internal* situation for a person *(convince)*; the other is *external* pressure, applied by others.

Ex-.   Use *ex-* if you mean former *(ex-convict, ex-governor)*. But all other words need no hyphen *(excommunicate, expropriate)*.

Extra-.   Use *extra-* if it's part of a compound adjective *(extra-base hit, extra-large book)*. When *extra-* means *beyond*—as in most such words—don't use a hyphen. The only exception occurs when *extra* is linked to a capitalized word: *extra-Britannic.*

Fewer, Less.   Use *fewer* for individual items and *less* for bulk or quantity: *Fewer than 18 agents turned up. Paul had less than $30 in his account.*

Fore-.   No hyphen is used with *fore-* except for three nautical expressions: *fore-topgallant, fore-topmast,* and *fore-topsail.*

Forego, Forgo.   To *forgo* means to give up something: *I will forgo that pleasure.* To *forego* means to go before something else; a *foregone* conclusion has preceded examination of the question.

Full Time, Full-Time, Part Time, Part-Time.   *Full-time* and *part-time* are compound adjectives *(full-time* or *part-time job)*. Otherwise: *She worked full time, part time.*

Girlfriend, Boyfriend.   One word is now permissible for these terms.

Goodwill.   *Goodwill* as a noun *(Goodwill is part of any purchase price)* or as an adjective *(It was a goodwill gesture)* is spelled as one word.

Half-.   The dictionary is the final arbiter on whether to use a hyphen with *half-.* The rule is to hyphenate any word not listed there. There are combinations such as *half-dollar, half-hour, half-life, half-truth,* and *half-blood.* But there are also *half brother, half note,* and *half tide.* And you'll find *halfback, halfhearted, halftrack.* It is an unruly prefix.

Half-Mast, Half-Staff.   On ships and naval bases, flags are at *half-mast.* Everywhere else, they are at *half-staff.*

Hopefully.   *Hopefully* means having a hopeful attitude. It doesn't stand for *hoped* or *hope.* Say: *It's hoped that we'll finish soon.*

Hydro-. Use no hyphen with this prefix.

Hyper-. Use no hyphen with this prefix.

Imply, Infer. Writers and speakers *imply* things with their words; readers or listeners *infer* things from those words.

In, Into. *In* is concerned with location, but *into* shows locomotion—movement and motion (*came into the house, got into the car*).

In-. This prefix needs no hyphen when it means *not* (*inaccurate, insufferable, inoperable*). A few combinations require a hyphen: *in-depth, in-group, in-house, in-law*. Check the dictionary.

Inter-. In most cases, no hyphen is necessary with this prefix except for *inter-American* and similar terms.

King. Capitalize *King* only when it is used before a monarch's name: *King George VI* on the first reference; *King George* (not *George*) on the second reference. Don't capitalize the word if it stands alone: *The king did not reign.* If you have several kings, use a capital letter: *Kings George, Edward, and Michael.*

Last. Be sure you mean *last* and not *latest*.

Lay, Lie, Laid. *Lie* means *to recline*, *lay* means *to put*, and *laid* is part of the *lay* family.

Like, As. *Like* is a *preposition* comparing nouns and pronouns: *Sallyanne works like crazy. As*, however, is a conjunction that introduces a clause: *Winston tastes good as a cigarette should.*

Like-. Use *like-* when the word means *similar to something* (*like-minded, like-natured*). Omit the hyphen when the words have their own meanings (*likelihood, likeness, likewise*). When *-like* is at the end of a word, use a hyphen only if its omission means three *l*'s: *bill-like, shell-like.*

Magazine Names. Don't capitalize *magazine* unless it's part of the official title (*Harper's Magazine, Time magazine*).

Majority, Plurality. *Majority* means that a candidate or measure got more than *half* of the votes; *plurality* means more than the *next highest number*.

Mass. *Mass* in the religious sense is always capitalized, but not the preceding adjective (*high Mass, requiem Mass*). And a Mass is *celebrated, said, sung.*

May Day, Mayday. *May Day* is the May 1 holiday, but *Mayday* is derived from the French expression *m'aidez* (''help me'').

Mid-. *Mid-* takes no hyphen unless a capitalized word follows it: *mid-Atlantic* and *mid-Africa*, but *midterm* and *midstream*. If *mid-* goes before a number, however, it's *mid-50s*.

Mini-.   No hyphens are used these days with *mini-* *(miniseries, miniconferences, minibus)*.

Mishap, Holocaust.   *Mishap* is an unfortunate but not fatal accident. *Holocaust* is used only where fire is concerned.

Ms.   This is a term for married or unmarried women. If several are mentioned in a series, *Ms.* is used before each name.

Multi-.   This prefix needs no hyphen.

Non-.   *Non-* does not take a hyphen:

nonprofit   nonroutine   nondescript   nonresident

Noncontroversial.   *All* issues are controversial; in fact the word *controversial* is redundant in *controversial issue*.

Nowadays.   The correct word is *nowadays,* not *nowdays*.

Numbers.   Spell out a number at the beginning of a sentence: *Thirty students passed.* Spell out whole numbers below 10; use figures for 10 and above: *There were 10 who signed up, but only two passed.* Spell out *first* through *ninth* when you're showing sequence in time or in location *(third base,* the *third step),* but when you reach *10th,* use figures. In geographic, military, or political designations, use *1st Marines, 7th Ward, 1st Sgt.* If a number is part of a corporate title, be exact: *Big Ten, 20th Century-Fox, The Thirty Club.*

When you have to spell out large numbers, use a hyphen to link a word ending in *y* to another word *(twenty-four, forty-five,* but *one hundred sixty-seven* and *seventy-seven thousand four hundred twenty-two).* Only with years do you start a sentence with numbers: *1976 was a good year.*

Odd.   Use a hyphen with *odd (odd-looking, odd-numbered).*

Off-.   The supreme source is Webster. If the word with *off-* is not found there, use a hyphen. There are too many uses with and without the hyphen *(off-color, off-season, offset, offside,* as well as *blastoff, send-off, playoff,* and *stopoff)* to permit a rule.

One-.   When you're writing fractions, use *one-* for clarity: *one-half, one-fourth,* and so on.

Out-.   *Out-* and *-out* need to be checked in the dictionary since there are many variations. Both should be hyphenated if a particular word is *not* listed.

Over, More than.   *Over* does not mean *more than*; it involves space: *One Flew Over the Cuckoo's Nest. More than* is used with figures: *More than 50 took the MBA degree.*

Over-.   A hyphen is seldom used with *over- (overrated, override,* etc.) as a prefix, but the dictionary is necessary on its use as a suffix *(carry-over, takeover).*

Pan-.   This prefix occurs most often with proper nouns and takes a hyphen as well as capitalization *(Pan-African, Pan-American, Pan-Germanism)*. But aging has dissolved the hyphen in *panhellenic,* and there also are such words as *panchromatic* and *pantheism.*

Pardon, Parole, Probation.   *Pardon* forgives and releases a prisoner from a sentence; a political pardon is *amnesty. Parole* means that a prisoner has been released before sentence has been completed, on condition of good behavior. *Probation* suspends the sentence on condition of good behavior.

Percent.   *Percent* now is one word. It takes a plural verb when a *plural word* completes a prepositional phrase: *Only 10 percent of the employees were on the scene.*

Post-.   Check the dictionary to see whether a particular word is hyphenated. As a general rule, omit the hyphen:

postdate   postscript   postbellum   postmortem

Pre-.   Most *pre-* words are not hyphenated *(prewar, prenatal, preheat, preconvention, predawn, preempt)*.

Prefix Rules.   Two chief rules—with a few exceptions—govern most prefixes. (1) Use a hyphen if the root word is capitalized *(un-American),* and (2) use a hyphen to join double prefixes *(sub-subcommittee)*.

Pro-.   This prefix requires a hyphen when the word indicates supportive conditions: *pro-labor, pro-life, pro-war.*

Raised, Reared.   Only human beings are *reared,* but they also can be *raised.*

Re-.   Use a hyphen if this word is not listed in the dictionary, for there are many exceptions to the rules on prefixes.

Rebut, Refute.   *Rebut* has to do with arguing against a point, but *refute* means winning an argument.

Recur, Reoccur.   Things *recur;* they don't *reoccur.*

Room Numbers.   When a room has a number, write: *Room 211.*

Rosary.   A *rosary* is *recited* or *said,* but never *read.*

Scot, Scots, Scottish, Scotch.   A native of Scotland is a *Scot,* and the plural is *Scots,* not *the Scotch.* The descriptive term is *Scottish.*

Self-.   This prefix is *always* hyphenated except for *selfless.*

Semi-.   This prefix *usually* has no hyphen, but there is an exception or two *(semi-invalid)*.

Shall, Will.   Determination is shown with *shall,* but both *shall* and *will* can be used in other situations.

Should, Would.   *Should* involves duty. *Would* is used in ordinary situations and also is correct when something is conditional: *If Bird had not swung, Lucas would not have been injured.*

Stanch, Staunch.   One *stanches* a flow of blood, and can be a *staunch* believer in Red Cross first-aid training.

Straight-laced, Strait-laced.   A *straight-laced* person holds rigid views. *Strait-laced* has to do with being confined.

Sub-.   This is a prefix that rarely takes a hyphen.

Super-.   This prefix does not need a hyphen unless it is linked to a capitalized word: *Super-Blazer.*

Tenterhooks, Tenderhooks.   The proper term is *tenterhooks.*

That, Which.   The main rule governing *that* and *which* has to do with whether the clause that follows is absolutely *essential* for the sentence to make sense. If it is, use *that;* if not, use *which: A refrigerator that does not run is useless. The refrigerator, which keeps our food cold, is in the shop.*

Both *that* and *which* are used in writing about inanimate objects and animals; *who* and *whom* are for human beings.

Titles.   The principal rule is that a formal title is capitalized if it goes just before the name *(Pope John Paul, King Edward VIII, Mrs. Mary Smith, President Van Buren, Governor Huey Long, Lt. Col. Miles Standish).* If the name is fenced off from the title by commas, don't capitalize the title: *The vice president, Theodore Roosevelt, went to Vermont that summer. Elizabeth II, the current queen, opened Parliament.* When titles are not linked to proper names, don't capitalize them: *The president is expected to speak there. He didn't see the pope.*

If the title is based on a job, don't capitalize it: *movie star Rudolph Valentino, astronaut Buzz Aldrin, superintendent John Ward.*

When someone *has held* or *will hold* a title, don't capitalize the adjective: *former President Nixon, Vice President-designate John Doe, acting Governor Peter Peterson.*

When the title follows the name, separate the proper name from the title with a comma to help the reader: *Max Erntsen, undersecretary for Health, Education, and Welfare.* Also use a comma to separate a lengthy title from the name of the person holding it: *The chairman of the subcommittee on rural schools in Montgomery County, Charles J. Evans.*

Trademarks.   A *trademark* is a term used by a company that has exclusive legal rights to it so that competitors cannot use it. When you use a term like *Levi's, Coke, Kleenex,* or *Xerox,* capitalize the first letter. The Coca-Cola Company has had a reputation for contacting even high school newspaper editors who spell its product as *coke.* The dictionary indicates whether a word is trademarked. A helpful rule is to use a generic equivalent unless the trademark name is essential to the story or theme.

Trans-. In general, this prefix uses no hyphen except when the word linked to it is a proper noun: *trans-Atlantic, trans-Siberian railroad*.

Transpire. *Transpire* means *to escape from secrecy, to leak out*. Its derivation is from *trans* (''across'') and *spirare* (''breathe''). It does *not* mean *to happen* or *occur*.

Trustee, Trusty. A *trustee* manages the property or affairs of people, foundations, corporations, and the like. A *trusty* is a prisoner who has earned special privileges as a trustworthy inmate.

TV. Spell out *television* on the first reference. You may abbreviate the word on the second reference.

U.S., U.N., UNICEF. A rule helpful to readers is to spell out the term (*United States, United Nations Children's Fund, Union of Soviet Socialist Republics*, etc.) on the first reference. On the second reference, use the abbreviation.

Ultra-. This prefix takes no hyphens.

Un-. Unless the word to which *un-* is linked has a capitalized first letter (*un-American*), no hyphen is required (*unnecessary, unneeded*).

Under-. This prefix needs no hyphen.

Under Way. This term takes two words in *every* usage: *The ship was under way. Under way were the first thousand days.*

Up-. When *up-* is a prefix, it needs no hyphen (*upgrade, uptown*). When it's a suffix and not listed in the dictionary, hyphenate it because while there are *checkup* and *lineup*, there are also *walk-up, mock-up, runners-up*.

Vice. Make *vice* a separate word (*vice chairman, vice president*) with no hyphen.

Vital. Since the root of the word *vital* means *life*, make sure that you use it only in a life-or-death context. Something must be truly crucial.

Von, De, Le. This portion of a foreign name is not capitalized when it is used with the full name (*Charles de Gaulle, Ludwig von Beethoven, Martin le Blum*). When the first name is omitted, however, use capitalization: *DeGaulle headed the army. The Red Baron was also called Von Richthofen.*

Well-. This prefix almost always is hyphenated because it is part of a compound adjective: *He is a well-dressed man.* Sometimes it can be part of a noun (*well-wishers, well-being*).

Who, Whom. *Who* is the subject: *Who's there? The man who shot himself left no money. Whom* is the object of a verb or preposition: *Whom did they want to win? The child to whom the money was left became a millionnaire overnight.*

Also, use *who* and *whom* when you're talking about human beings and *that* or *which* for inanimate objects and animals.

Wide-.   When *wide-* is a prefix, it's usually hyphenated except for *widespread*. But when *-wide* is a suffix, it needs no hyphen *(nationwide)*.

-Wise.   This suffix is usually not hyphenated except when it is part of a compound adjective *(street-wise)*.

Words as Words.   When you're singling out words as words *(I would call her* enchanting. *He didn't know the meaning of the word* surrender), underscore them for italics.

Xerox.   *Xerox* is a trademark for a photocopy machine. It is *not* to be used as a verb—yet.

CHAPTER 10

AN EASY GUIDE
TO PROPER PUNCTUATION

We assume that everyone knows the uses of question and exclamation marks as well as the period. The trouble starts when we're faced with deciding, say, whether a comma goes inside or outside a quotation or whether a semicolon is a dead piece of punctuation. And is it *A's* and *the 20's* or *As* and *the 20s,* the *Jones'* or the *Joneses, ifs, ands,* or *but's*? Style experts still war over these points.

Let's start with the easy punctuation—brackets—and leave the most difficult—commas—until last.

Basically, all punctuation is designed to help the reader. A little is good, but more is not necessarily better. Elsewhere in this book, we've said that each time you drop in punctuation, the reader's eye halts. His mind stops to digest what has been said. If you lard sentences with too much punctuation, you'll lose readers. The shorter the sentence, the smaller the problem. The longer the sentence, the more punctuation you'll use.

To prove this point, which example is more inviting?

Letting go runs counter to the prevailing philosophy that "we are the masters of our fates," able to control people and even ice storms.
Or teenagers.
Basketball teams.
Cars.
Plumbing.
The job.
Elevators.
Congress.
Sex.
Computers.
Health.
The vernal equinox.

Letting go runs counter to the prevailing philosophy that ''we are the masters of our fates,'' able to control people and even ice storms. Or teenagers, basketball teams, cars, plumbing, the job, elevators, Congress, sex, computers, health, the vernal equinox.

Eyes tired? Mind wandering? Try this next set:

On the other hand, if we have in view the comprehensibility of a whole of speculative knowledge, which, though wide-ranging, has the coherence that follows from unity of principle, we can say with equal justice that many a book would have been much clearer if it had not made such an effort to be clear.

Either we insist upon dominating the people we know, or we depend upon them far too much. If we lean too heavily on people, they will sooner or later fail us, for they are human, too, and cannot possibly meet our incessant demands.

All of which should not bring us to write as one reporter did when the city room rule was short sentences:

Dead.
That was the condition of Joe Smith yesterday.

Punctuation should not be a crutch for the writer, but, rather, a guidepost for the reader. If you have ''punctuationitis,'' perhaps you just need to recast sentences. Make them simple. Read them aloud if you think they're getting away from you. Ask yourself if a comma is necessary. Would it be better to omit the semicolon and create two separate sentences? Use your common sense.

Brackets

The death knell for the bracket has been tolling for years, particularly in newspapers and magazines. The Associated Press stylebook says, ''Brackets cannot be transmitted over news wires. Use parentheses or recast the material.''

Magazines and newspapers do use brackets, however, when inserting explanatory material within a story. Their function is to clarify or to refute misstatements of fact:

''There were 17 on that committee who did nothing to counteract the $14 million in cost over-runs. Senator Smith said the project would never fly,'' the commissioner said. [On June 14, the committee had only five members. Senator Smith yesterday denied having made such a statement.]

Or

He talked to Thomas [Corcoran] about it.

In the academic world, brackets are still used, as in the examples above, to indicate you are inserting your own comments. Perhaps the source you're using is

ungrammatical or inaccurate. There, you'll use the expression *sic* (from the Latin *so* or *thus*) to show that you know something is incorrect, while faithful to the text:

"He went to skole [sic] when he was seven."

In 1973 [The World Almanac lists it as 1974] the suit was filed in the Court of Domestic Relations.

Parentheses

Parentheses indicate added material that explains the sentence. The material is vital to that sentence, but cannot stand alone, uncovered, unprotected by those curving parental walls. There are writers who overuse parentheses to the point that **their** works look like picket fences. That is cosmetizing words to hide a lack of substance.

To believe your own thought, to believe that what is true for you in your private heart is true for all men—that is genius.

Those are the words of Ralph Waldo Emerson, America's most famous essayist. You will search his writings in vain for many parentheses.

If, like Aristotle's translators, you must use parentheses, be sure to insert the closing mark. Too, don't forget that complete sentences carry periods within the **parentheses:**

So, in another way, nature is the shape and form of things that have a principle of movement in themselves—the form being only theoretically separable from the object in question. (The product of matter and form—man, for instance—is not nature, but does exist by nature.)

A partial sentence doesn't have a period inside the parentheses (as is shown here). (Don't capitalize the first word inside a parentheses unless it is followed by a complete, separate sentence like this one.)

Sometimes parentheses are used to set off a state name, a party affiliation, or a nickname:

She went to Selma (Ala.) High School.
Senator John A. White (D-OR) attended.
Lael E. (Mike) Campbell won the award.

Don't use a comma *before* a parenthesis. Instead, punctuate this way:

Mike Tanner, CLU (Los Angeles), 487-1741, led in disability.

Parentheses are used to define something exactly, as has been said, but also to add information, even humor:

Three long days, from the 25th to the 28th of January of the year 1077, Henry, dressed as a penitent pilgrim (but with a warm sweater underneath his monkish garb), waited outside the gates of the castle of Canossa.

Dashes and Hyphens

Initially, it's well to remember that the hyphen key on the typewriter is used for both hyphens and dashes. To keep them separate, use one hyphen for a hyphen and three or four for the dash. The idea is to distinguish between the two pieces of punctuation.

A *dash* is used to show a sudden thought breaking within a sentence or to emphasize something:

Some perceptions---I think the best---are granted to the single soul.

They have in themselves what they value in their horses---mettle and bottom.

If you have to set off a series of words within a sentence, a dash helps for clarity:

There were several qualities---kindness, thoughtfulness, lovingness, trust---she felt were sucker bait.

Dashes give credit where it belongs, too:

"When you think you're humble, you ain't."---Henry Haupe

A dash goes before certain expressions and abbreviations:

---namely, Smith, Jones, and White---
---viz., smoking, partying, and winning---
---i.e., that they'd never get better---

Dashes give emphasis in a summation:

The wondering, the waiting, the anxieties---all were over.

If a statement has an internal question, handle it this way:

What's all this mean?---you may ask.

Dashes are substitutes for near-anonymous names:

Let's leave this up to George M---.

And they're useful in interrupted speeches:

Ah---Ah---Miss Scarlett, Ah doan know nuthin' 'bout bringin' babies."

"Oh, I know that Ashley is---"

Hyphens join words and keep the reader from confusion:

He'll speak to small-business operators.

Without the hyphen, a reader could conclude the writer was indicating the size of the operator.

Mainly, hyphens combine descriptive words unless the first one ends in *ly* or they have *very* before them:

> He shot a 150-pound elk.
> They sank a well-known ship.
> It was a know-it-all attitude.
> She had a pair of satin-lined boots.
> How did they ever carry a full-time job with a half-a-loaf philosophy into the thick of a four-story building which once was a very lovely edifice with such a jerry-built foundation?

If the descriptive words go *after* a form of the verb *to be* (*is, are, was,* etc.), the hyphen prevents confusion:

> The reporter *was* quick-witted.
> The figure *is* second-rate.
> The well-matched pair *was* not well-knit.

The hyphen is needed when numbers are spelled out:

> One dollar and eighty-seven cents.

Or in what editors call ''suspensive hyphenation'':

> Jackson got a 15- to 30-year sentence.

It's needed when a single letter is linked to a noun:

> I fear the H-bomb.
> Give me a T-square.

And when you're spelling a word or showing syllabication:

> The word was l-o-s-e-r.
> It was pronounced an-thro-po-mor-phism.

We can't include here all words linked with a hyphen. The best authority is a dictionary. That's where you'll learn that it's *Italian-American,* but *French Canadian,* and *semi-independent* and *anti-intellectual,* but *semifinal* and *antitrust.* Historically, such terms usually start as separate words. If used often, they become hyphenated. When they are common, they are written as one word. That's how *co-operate* became *cooperate* and *co-respondent* became *corespondent.* That's why it's *father-in-law,* but *granddaughter* and *stepmother, self-esteem,* but *selfless.*

Ellipses

Ellipses indicate that material, usually unneeded matter, has been left out. Yet to "doctor" sources to suit needs can change the whole meaning of what you're using. Advertisements for films and books are prime offenders in changing original comments. Here's what the film critic said:

> *Little Mary Jones* is an outrageous desecration of one of the main events in the life of labor agitator Joe Hill. To be funny with unforgettable parts of history for the workingman is to assume the public likes what cynics like.

Here's the advertising blurb outside the theatre:

> *Little Mary Jones* is . . . outrageous . . . funny . . . unforgettable . . . what cynics like.

So watch the dishonest cut.

When you leave out part of a sentence, use three periods, as shown in the example above. If you leave out a sentence, use four spaced periods. If entire paragraphs are deleted, put three periods between the passages:

> modern peculiarities of hospitality. So he walked off with the Bishop's candlesticks.
>
> . . .
>
> There are other things that will be stated in other volumes to follow. Don't be alarmed:

Ellipses also indicate unfinished statements or dialogue:

> "If you can't say anything good about me . . ." he interrupted. Nathan fell silent, realizing he was alone, despised, aching. . . .

Colon

Use the colon at the end of a sentence when you're about to cite a series, tabulations, or something lifted from a source:

> Among the agencies involved were the following: Columbia, Hawaii, Siskiyou, Orange, and San Jose.
>
> The figures for utilities that day were:
>
> That key passage from Proverbs (23:29) says: "Who hath woe? Who hath sorrow? Who hath contentions? Who hath wounds without cause? Who hath redness of eyes?"

Don't use the colon for a short quote of less than 20 words. Use it for long ones:

> His simple reply was, "What makes you think that?"

Many harrowing tales were told: She had an enormous foreign news story in careful order on the ledge of a window in the old *Time-Life* building. When the magic moment came to show . . . this action squirted roughly 198 intermediate prints . . . through the open window.

Capitalize the first word after a colon *only* if it's a *proper* noun or if it starts a complete sentence:

We had one thing to hate: Exxon.

Holding up a carrot, she pledged: "I'll never be hungry again."

They worried about three things: money, health, and fun.

A colon lends emphasis:

We feared one thing alone: losing.

It helps dialogue:

JONES: I won't.
SMITH: You will.

And is used for questions and answers:

Q: Mr. President, how will that affect stocks?
A: How should I know!

Also for expressions involving time:

It was 8:30.
He ran it in 2:24:21.

For biblical, legal, or volume/page citations:

Exodus 4:13.
Maryland Code 18: 275-80.
The Nation's Business, 172:30-32.

Don't use a dash with a colon for any reason.

Quotation Marks

Most of the usage of quotation marks for reports is covered in the term paper section. It's applicable to themes as well. There are some other applications, however.

Let's start with the use of single quotes since they're the easiest to understand.

Use single quotes when the person quoted then quotes someone else:

"Listen to this," said Jarvis. "Wilson wrote: 'As we became subjects of King Alcohol, shivering denizens of his mad realm, the chilling vapor that is loneliness settled down.' "

In double quotations, the rules are based mostly on common sense. For example, if you quote several paragraphs, use quotation marks at the beginning of each paragraph. Don't use them at paragraph endings, however, until the last passage comes to an end:

"When in the . . .
"Secondly . . .
"Last . . .

                                . . . I wish you the best."

Quotes are used around words to emphasize irony:

The "riot" consisted of two small boys and a growling dog.

When a word or expression is no longer new, there's no need to give it either quotes or underscoring:

He was spaced out on music.
The machinery was on the fritz.

Quotes are used around the titles of magazine articles, poems, and chapters in books because they generally are *part* of a major work. Titles of books, periodicals, and plays, the names of ships, foreign expressions, and the like are underscored, like this:

"Thither the Blue Collar" was in Newsweek.
Read the "Living Solo" portion of Whither Youth.
It was reported in the "Arsonists' Paradise" story in yesterday's Oregonian.

Libel laws force newsmen and editors to be careful in using quotations, particularly if they haven't the room to print an entire statement. They work to keep the partial quote within the context of what was said:

"I am not a crook," he insisted, telling publishers that the "record looked damning," but that soon extenuating circumstances "would explain everything."

Moreover, before you insist on using a quotation, determine whether you can paraphrase the gist of what the person is saying.
What about using other punctuation with quotes?
The period and comma always go *inside* the quotation marks:

"It is a very hot day in the late eighties," Runyon wrote, "when One-Arm Jack Maddox and his gang come a-cussing and a-shooting into town to hold up the Stockgrowers' National Bank."

However, the dash, semicolon, question mark, and exclamation mark go inside the quotation marks *only when they apply to the quoted matter:*

> The crowd before the palace shouted, ''Assassin! Assassin! Hang the assassin!''

> ''Who are those 'ringleaders'?'' she asked.

> ''Talbot, dey coachman tole me. He wuz shot---''

They go outside when they don't:

> Imagine Woollcott saying ''I like you''!

> Have you read Frost's poem ''Birches''?

> Morgan said, ''That's enough of that''; nevertheless they continued to hound him.

Last, don't forget to close quotation marks—single or double—a common mistake for forgetful writers.

Apostrophe

When letters are omitted—often in this informal society—indicate the omission with an apostrophe:

we've	it's (it is)	don't	ne'er
aren't	you're	can't	who's
won't	'tis	we'll	they'll
they're	ok'd	let's	o'er

The apostrophe is also used when figures are omitted:

> The class of '84.
> The Spirit of '76.
> The '20s.

And in the plural of a *single* letter:

> The B's won the trophy.
> He was good on his p's and q's.

However, when words, two or more letters, or numbers become plural, don't use the apostrophe:

> The company began in the 1920s.
> Temperatures will be in the high 80s.
> There were 14 number 8s.
> Sid gave him five IOUs.
> There were 17 VPs at the dinner.

The classic use of the apostrophe for omitted letters and contractions is seen with writers such as Mark Twain, who ''wrote it as they heard it.'' This example indicates how difficult it is to read words that have been contracted:

''Nuffn never come of it. I couldn' manage to k'leck dat money no way; en Balum he couldn'. I ain' gwyne to len' no mo' money 'dout I see de security. Boun' to git yo' money back a hund'd times, de preacher says!''

The most difficult part of learning to use the apostrophe is in showing possessives. One major step in overcoming worry is to start by knowing that personal pronouns *don't* take apostrophes:

his	hers	its	theirs
yours	whose	ours	

You already know that apostrophes are used to show possession when nouns are singular:

Boyd's book.
The girl's record.
The cat's meow.

When we move into words ending with *s*—whether singular (*Jesus*) or plural (*girls*)—uncertainty begins. And what does one do if a plural word is followed by a word beginning with an *s*? Is *for conscience' sake* or *for conscience's sake* correct?

Start with words ending in *s*, whether singular or plural:

Jones's home	Charles' book	girls' meeting
mathematics' guidelines	United States' armaments	
Kansas' rules of law	Moses' rules	
corps' uniforms		

These all are easy to understand, for they follow logical patterns.

Then there are the illogical rules that confuse even professional writers and editors. Many will recast a sentence before tangling with these uses of the apostrophe. However, a good pair of ears can solve the dilemma. When a word ending in *s* is heavy with the hissing sounds of other *s*'s, the *s* after the apostrophe is usually omitted:

It was Jesus' lot to be first.

Where the word with the apostrophe ordinarily would require a possessive *s* but the next word begins with an *s*, the apostrophe is deleted:

For appearance' sake.

General usage has caused the demise of the apostrophe in some expressions:

St. Elizabeths hospital is famous.

Semicolon

The rise of the short sentence may have been responsible for the phasing out of the semicolon, the favorite piece of punctuation—along with the comma—for the formal writer of yore. In the days of historian Edward Gibbon, when epic events deserved epic sentences, the semicolon flourished:

In this narrow space, the disorderly and affrighted crowd was incapable of resisting on either side a firm and regular attack; the blues signalized the fury of their repentance; and it is computed that above 30,000 persons were slain in the merciless and promiscuous carnage of the day.

The idea was that using a period might make readers think the entire scene or situation had suddenly shifted. This certainly was true in some works, such as the Bible, where one sentence may describe a battle and the next an incident years later.

Punctuation purists insist that the semicolon be used today just as it was in antiquity, but today's periodicals and books prefer the period. There are some compromises between the two positions, however.

A semicolon definitely is needed if a lot of commas have been sprinkled throughout a sentence that has two or more clauses:

They moved close to the walls, listened for footsteps, watched each other for signs of weakness; but even these efforts drained away their energies.

In a series, semicolons keep things clear:

Production leaders for the year were Dan Corrigan, individual life volume; Bill Zimmerman, disability income; and Mike Campbell, paid applications.

My grades were A in French; B, algebra; B, English; C, home economics; B, physical education; and D, American history.

If a clause ends with a quotation, put the semicolon *after* the quotation mark:

He often said his life depended on ''one day at a time''; however, he rarely lived that way.

Comma

Whatever you believe so far about the comma, it is not used to indicate a pause—a common idea among many. There are definite rules.

A comma is used to show a break in thought patterns or sentence structure. It is not a startling interrupter like a dash.

The clearer a writer you become, the fewer commas you'll use. However, this piece of punctuation will be with us always, for it does clarify murky writing.

Let's start with its simplest use, in a series of single words:

Children teach us how little control we really have in those struggles over eating, naps, schoolwork, friends, money, and career goals.

Follow it up with a string of phrases:

Consider that they might be too old to fight, too young to reason, too unfit for regular duty, too muscle-bound to react, too smart to obey, and too dumb to defy orders.

A comma is helpful in a series of descriptive words:

He was tall, dark, and handsome.

The castle was down a winding, brick-lined, dimly lighted, traffic-filled, cold, and clammy street.

A comma stands for an omitted *and,* as has been shown in the foregoing examples. Also, it's used with introductory clauses or phrases if confusion might otherwise result:

When he moved toward me, the willing woman screamed.

But not if the meaning is clear without it:

During the morning I had breakfast.

When sentences become lengthy, overloaded with clauses linked by the conjunctions *and, or, nor, yet, but, for,* chances are that a comma goes *before* those words:

She was glad she moved, for the letters stopped coming.

The three visited Monticello on Thursday, and they planned to return to the track by Saturday.

But if the subject of both clauses is the same, you won't need a comma:

The three visited Monticello on Thursday and returned to the track by Saturday.

Commas used with quotations are easy to understand. You've already read hundreds of books with constructions like this:

Penny said, "Jody, all's been done that was possible."

Or

"I don't mean that," explained Wilson quickly. "I just meant—"

"The piece is known," he concluded lustily, "as 'Vladimir Tostoff's Jazz History of the World.' "

Use a comma when you're talking directly to someone:

You, Sir, are a fraud.
Coach, I'll try it again.
You know I'll get to it, Ma!
How dare you, Middleton, talk to me like that!

A comma goes after weak interrupters too:

Oh, you'll love it!
Why, I never thought you cared.
Well, don't ask.
It could be, say, Philadelphia for two weeks.

And with *yes* and *no*:

Yes, I'm going away.
No, that's not he.

Or when you're giving attribution for something:

The state was the empire and he was the king, according to Huey Long.

Or identifying:

It was July 14, the day the Bastille fell.

He drove the car, a four-door sports number.

The testimony was demanded by Senator Martin, chairman of the subcommittee.

A comma is used with geographical places and with ages:

She was Mary Richard, 18.

They lived in Rye, N.Y.

The class visited Rheims, France, and Heidelberg, West Germany. Although they came from South Bend, Wash., they had read all about those places.

And when two neighboring words are the same:

What the question is, is not the real issue here.

Numbers cannot exist without commas:

> He was awarded a $5,000,000 settlement.
> There was "50,000" on the box.
> July 4, 1776
> Tuesday, September 18, 1913

However, commas can be omitted when numbers do not appear *next* to each other:

> 7 April 1897
> June 1983

The difficulty with commas always seems to arise when they're used with parenthetical expressions, those words that interrupt the flow of the sentence. Here, they're vital for clarity. Let's start with the simplest types of parenthetical interrupters:

> He was, for example, quite mad.
> On the other hand, the problem was difficult.
> The formula is the same, it appears.
> He is, I think, the source of the trouble.
> I think he is the murderer, however.

Words that connect one thought to another also need commas:

> Further, the pay is far too low.
> In addition, he wants to go.
> By contrast, America's role was not defined.

Sometimes parenthetical expressions don't interrupt the smoothness of the sentence:

> They spoke French in addition.
> It seems the problem is small.

Another kind of parenthetical expression comes dressed in Latin abbreviations, or familiar English abbreviations:

> Names, dates, hometowns, etc., were given.
> James Pearcy, Jr., was among the group.
> Louis B. Perry, Ph.D., attended for the company.

Now that you've mastered the small parenthetical expression, you're ready for the long ones—generally clauses. These are easy to understand, for a comma is used only if the clause is *not absolutely essential* to the sentence's meaning. Can the clause be pruned out of the sentence without causing confusion? See what you think of these clauses:

In 1789, *when the town was founded,* both Europe and the Americas were embroiled in war.

That winter, *the season the Blazers won the league title,* New York's budget problems worsened.

The bridge, *which was grimy,* opened to let the cruiser through.

One clue to usage is that clauses starting with *which, when,* and *where* almost always are nonessential (called *nonrestrictive* by grammarians). Other clauses just require judgment on whether they are vital to the sentence's meaning. If they're not, put in a comma.
In the sentence:

His son Marvin was the top scorer.

no comma is used because he may have more than one son. In this example:

The play *Waiting for Lefty* won the award.

the same logic applies. However, the following needs commas:

His wife, Darlene, looked haggard.

Last, a comma is used in sentences with contrasting elements, which are usually linked by *not* or *but:*

I feel she should get praise, not blame.
The team was down, not out.

CHAPTER 11

SPELLING HELPS

Ever since you've been in school, you've probably been told that you can learn to spell by mastering a few rules or by sounding out the syllables. You even might have memorized a little jingle to help you over the more difficult words ("*I* before *e* except after *c* and when sounded as *a* as in *neighbor* and *weigh*").

The trouble with learning how to spell by rules is that there are far too many exceptions to those rules. Upon discovering that rules do not apply in many instances, it's no wonder that many students turn their back on them. The syllabication rule, for example, works well if the student is dealing with Italian, Latin, or Spanish where each letter and syllable is sounded, but in English—that potpourri of so many languages—what does one do on syllabication with such words as *through, subpoena,* and *suite,* to say nothing of *subtle*? There are too many exceptions for pronunciation to be of singular help. The little jingle on *i* before *e* is fine until the student runs into the words *weird* and *seize*. There are no *c*'s in these words, and they certainly do not sound like *neighbor* and *weigh*.

To spell correctly in English, you must really think about each word individually. This is probably why those people with photographic memories do so well without the aid of a dictionary.

But if you're a poor speller—and many English-speaking people are—there are a number of ways to help yourself without rules, jingles, or a photographic memory. The best way to overcome spelling problems is to be utterly dependent upon the dictionary. Buy one of those low-priced paperback dictionaries for class work and carry it with you wherever writing is to be done. Get a larger dictionary for use outside class. And consult it without feeling that you are not quite bright. Since you always will have access to a dictionary once you leave school, this habit is a good one to cultivate.

If you want to master as many widely used words as possible, remember that it takes a good memory to spell things correctly in English. In addition to a good memory, there is the method of knowing the foreign derivative of a word, the mnemonic (word association) device, and, last, the "looks-wrong" approach.

If none of these methods work, join the Spellers Anonymous Association, explained later in this chapter.

You will have to improve your spelling to do well in theme work. You may be at the top of your class, you may have a 799 SAT verbal skill score, you may be Phi Beta Kappa material, but if you cannot spell properly, you'll not do any writing well. Misspellings, to many people, indicate a slovenly mind that is unable to cope with detail work.

Foreign Derivatives

With the foreign derivative method, you'll need a dictionary that after the word gives in italics the history of the word's development. It should give the country where the word originated and the changes made as the word took its present form. English is the repository of thousands upon thousands of foreign words. It is not a "pure" language. It has been generalized that the English language is 50 per cent French, 35 per cent Latin, and 15 per cent of everything else. This is a great exaggeration, but you might make this thought work for you in learning to spell. Those who do well in foreign languages will find this "derivative" method very useful. Even if you have no such talents, you may find some assistance for troublesome words you just cannot seem to master.

Let's take a few "demon" words to demonstrate how knowing the foreign derivation can help in spelling:

> *kindergarten* (German. *kinder* = children; *garten* = garden).
> *mortgage* (French. *mort* = death; *gage* = pledge).
> *disastrous* (French-Latin. *astro* = star)
> *cigarette* (Spanish-French. *cigarro* = cigar; *ette* = little)
> *lieutenant* (French. *lieu* = place; *tenant* = tenant)
> *vaccine* (French. *vacca* = cow)
> *manual* (French. *manus* = hand)

Even knowing a minor thing, such as the Greek *e*, can help you with some of the more difficult words that trip misspellers. With *y*, or the Greek *e*, the sound is either as in *creep* or in *tried*. This is a great help when you come to spell such Greek-rooted words as *psychology, physique* and *physics.*

Mnemonic Devices

There's also another method.

Learning to spell by mnemonic devices (word associations) appears to be an easy method for many students with spelling problems. It involves memory work, the word mnemonic coming from the Greek *mnemonikos* (mindful).

You merely associate something with the word you have trouble spelling. For example, some students have figured out a mnemonic device for the word *cemetery*. Since there are three *e*'s in the word and since cemeteries are rather frightening places after dark for many people, one might well shriek "eeeeeee!" when thinking about how to spell *cemetery*. You'll be aware of the *e*'s in the word that way. Another word mastered by mnemonic method is *niece*. Many who have missed it even with the *i*-before -*e* jingle have no trouble spelling it when they remember that a n*iec*e is often n*ic*e. Similarly, the word *yacht* has been remembered by the mnemonic phrase, "*Ach*! He can afford a y*ach*t!" *Elegant* is surmounted by misspellers who remember that *gant* is French for *glove* and that wearing gloves is considered an elegant manner of dress.

The use of mnemonic devices is entirely personal, for what will jog one person's memory might not do for another. Perhaps you will remember how to spell a word by associating with your Aunt Jane or an outing when you were 10. Once you have begun thinking up such memory associations with troublesome words, the process will develop into an easy one. Many have found that the mnemonic device method enabled them to spell far more troublesome words than any other technique.

Appearance of Words

Another spelling method is the most unorthodox to English instructors, and yet to proofreaders, editors and voracious readers the device has been a quick and useful one to conquer misspelled words. This is called the "looks-wrong" technique. In it, the user sees a word and instantly knows it is misspelled. He follows up his suspicions with a dictionary. If he has seen the word spelled correctly a number of times or if he has had to correct it in many instances, he will make the change without consulting a dictionary. Doing that, however, involves the same kind of supreme self-assurance as is the case with the person who does crossword puzzles in ink.

To be successful with this method requires a background of reading. As mentioned, it is used successfully and unconsciously by those whose livelihoods revolve around reading and in catching errors in word usage as well as errors in facts. Such readers immediately see that *acommodate* needs to be changed to *accommodate*, or that *acknowledgement* and *judgement* must be corrected to the American form of English of *acknowledgment* and *judgment*. Asked how they know that these words are misspelled, they seldom recite syllabication and pronunciation rules, jingles, or even foreign derivations. "It just looks wrong," they'll explain.

Review

Yet another method to catch troublesome words is to go back over past themes and see which words gave you the most difficulty. Each person seems to misspell different words. You will soon learn that a definite pattern does seem to crop up in your mistakes in spelling. Some people have trouble with suffixes (word endings) and begin to spot this difficulty if they study past themes (is it *ent, ant* or *int*? Is it *ence* or *ance*?). Some people have problems with prefixes (is it *pre* or *per*?). At least if you recognize your problem, you will check a dictionary whenever you use troublesome words in future.

Some students circle every word they're not sure of. When they finish a theme, they look up the words in a dictionary. In any case, your dictionary is your best friend in coping with spelling problems. Don't be too proud to use it. Nobody but a spelling bee champion has that much confidence. And how many of them are there?

All of the methods suggested here will help you if you combine them. Some devices may prove to be of more use to you on some words than other methods. But when you recognize that no one, single method can solve *all* spelling problems, you will have come a long way in conquering this age-old weakness in English composition.

If you're beyond this, you might join the loose-knit organization started in a Maine school—Spellers Anonymous. To join requires no dues, just the recognition that you need help and are willing to make the effort to help yourself. It involves far too much work for those who are casual in improving their spelling. If your case seems to be hopeless and you do want to conquer misspellings, read the next section of this chapter carefully.

The Spellers Anonymous Method

The Spellers Anonymous method stems from checking techniques used partly by *Time, Incorporated* researchers and reporters and partly by professional writers.

Basically, you check your spelling by starting with the last word of your theme. Working backward word by word, put a dot over each word that you are certain is spelled correctly. For those words that are doubtful, check a dictionary.

This is how a checked sentence should look. Remember, you work from the *last* word to the first. It's like this:

There are ways in which every policeman can do his duty without relying on force.

This method sounds peculiar at first, but there are several sound psychological principles involved that have helped students averaging 15 to 25 misspelled words per theme to move to few errors.

By working backward, you detach yourself from the forward flow of the theme, the meaning and trend of a composition. You are concentrating on each individual word. This is a variation on a technique used by professional writers who check a finished manuscript from the last page to the first. They work by pages, not by words, but then they are not working on themes where every word does count. At *Time, Incorporated* the researchers and reporters are trained to use the dot method to ensure that each word is spelled correctly, is used correctly in terms of grammar, and is factually correct. *Time* publications put a premium on accuracy with their staffs since letter writers love to catch magazines in errors. This method has been found to be the best way to attain such exactness. Therefore, you might as well borrow the technique. You might circle those words you are not sure of as you move from backward word to word. When you are finished with the "backward check," then look up the circled words.

The first two times students use the Spellers Anonymous checking method, they usually eliminate almost all of their errors. The next few times, they are so overconfident that they miss very common words. Each theme must represent a separate challenge if you're going to avoid regressions in spelling. Also, it is well to know that when you are working on a theme topic you like, you tend to make many more mistakes than you would on a topic that doesn't interest you. You do this because you get carried away with what you're saying.

There is nothing easy about the Spellers Anonymous checking method. It is an onerous and irksome process, taking much time to complete. But for those who *really* want to clean up their bad spelling, the 20 to 30 minutes required for the average two to four-page theme will be well worth the effort. The method *does* work.

Spelling Demons

Don't feel you're not quite bright because some words always cause you difficulty. Chances are there is a pattern to your problems. Many, for example, have had trouble with suffixes—word endings. Once you identify your particular shortcoming, it should set off an alert for the dictionary. Despite the fact that English includes thousands of words and few people have photographic memories, pride or overconfidence often keeps people from the dictionary.

Editors, those who make their living with words, are never too proud to look up correct spellings. If they can, so can you. Almost every newspaper stylebook has a list of "spelling demons," often used and easily confused words that trip up many. Here's a list of the most commonly misspelled words, plus some words everyone seems to be using:

absence	acquired
accept (verb)	across
except (exclusive of)	actually
access	adolescence
accidentally	advice (noun)
accommodate	advise (verb)
accompanying	aesthetic
accustom	affect (to influence)
ache	effect (a result)
achieve	aficionado
acknowledgment	aggravate
acquaint	aggression

aide (helper)
  aid (verb)
aisle (passage)
  isle (island)
a la carte
alcohol
allege
all right
allusion (reference)
  illusion (fantasy)
alma mater
already
altar (church)
  alter (change)
although
altogether
aluminum
amateur
analysis
analyze
anesthesiologist
anesthetic
aneurysm
angel (heaven)
  angle (math)
announcer
annual
anonymous
answer
anxiety
apology
appall
apparatus
apparent
appear
appearance
appreciate
archbishop
arctic
argue
aroused
ascent (rise)
  assent (agree)
assassin
association

athlete
attaché
attack
attendance
attitude
attorney
auger (tool)
  augur (fortune)
awestruck
awhile
axe

bachelor
balance
ballot (vote)
  ballet (dance)
bar mitzvah
basis
  bases (baseball)
battalion
battlefield
bazaar (shop)
  bizarre (strange)
beginning
believe
bellboy
beneficial
benefited
berth (bed)
  birth (born)
besiege
better
  bettor (gambler)
biased
bibliography
bicycle
billet doux
bird's-eye
bivouac
blasé
blitzkrieg
blond (male)
  blonde (female)
bloodthirsty
blueprint

bogey (golf)
  bogy or bogie (ghost)
bona fide
bookcase
bookkeeper
bookstore
bouquet
boutonniere
box office
brand-new
breadth
breath (noun)
  breathe (verb)
breakdown
bric-a-brac
bridal (bride)
  bridle (horse)
briefcase
brilliant
Britain (nation)
  Briton (citizen)
brouhaha
buccaneer
bull's-eye
bureau
bus (vehicle)
  buss (kiss)
business
  busyness (activity)

cafe
calendar
caliber
Calvary (Golgotha)
  cavalry (horses)
camaraderie
canceled
cancellation
candidate
candlelight
cannot
canvas (cloth)
  canvass (solicit)
capital (money, city)
  capitol (building)

captain
carat (weight)
  caret (mark)
  carrot (vegetable)
carburetor
careful
cargoes
carload
carte blanche
caster (wheel)
  castor (oil)
casualties
catalogue
catcall
categories
caveat emptor
cave-in
ceiling
cemetery
certainly
challenge
champagne
changeable
chaperon
characteristic
chargé d'affaires
chassis
chateau
chatterbox
chieftain
chinaware
chit-chat
choirmaster
chord (music)
  cord (vocal)
choose (present)
  chose (past)
chute (inclined passage)
  shoot (gun)
cigarette
classmate
clean-cut
clean-up (noun)
  clean up (verb)
clear-cut

cliché
clientele
clockwise
close-up (noun)
   close up (verb)
clue
coconut
cognizance
cold-blooded
collectible
collegiate
colonel (officer)
   colonial
color
colossal
column
combated
comedy
commitment
committee
common sense
communiqué
comparative
comparison
compelling
competitor
complaint
complement (augment)
   compliment (praise)
comptroller (expenditures)
   controller (manager)
concede
conceive
concerto
concessionnaire
condemn
confidant (close friend)
   confident (sure)
connoisseur
conqueror
conscience
conscientious
conscious
consensus
consistent

consul (diplomat)
   counsel (advice)
   counselor (adviser)
   council (group)
contemptible
continuous
controversy
convenient
convertible
coolly
cooperative
cornerstone
corralled
corps (unit)
   corpse (dead)
corespondent (divorce)
   correspondent (writer)
cortege
coup d'état
coupe (car)
courteous
   curtsy (bow)
courthouse
court-martial
couturier
creditor
crept
crisis
criteria (plural)
criticize (verb)
   criticism (noun)
crystalize
cue
cul-de-sac
cure-all
curious
currant (berry)
   current (recent)
curricular
curtain
customer
cutoff (noun)
   cut off (verb)
cutthroat
cylindrical

dairy (milk)
  diary (book)
damned
darkroom
data (plural)
daylight
deadline
deaf-mute
dealt
debacle
debater
debris
debut
debutante
deceased
deceive
decent (good)
  descent (down)
décor
deductible
defendant
defense
defensible
definite
demagogy
demarcation
demigod
denouement
dependable
dependence
  dependent
de rigueur
descendant
describe
desert (leave, sand)
  dessert (ice cream)
desirability
detector
develop
devotee
dexterous
diaphragm
diarrhea
die, dying (death)
  dye, dyeing (color)

diesel
die-hard (noun)
dietitian
different
dilapidated
dilettante
dinghy (boat)
  dingy (dirty)
diphtheria
disappearance
disappointment
director
disastrous
discordant
discretion
diseased
dispatch
dissipate
distributor
disturbance
divide
divine
dog days
dominant
dormitory
double-cross
draft
drought
dry, drier
dual (two)
  duel (fight)
  duo (two)
duchess
dynamo

earnest
easy-going
ebullient
echo
ecstasy
efficient
eligible
elite

embarrassment
embryo
emigrate (leave)
   immigrate (enter)
emigré
emissary
empathy
emphasize
employee
empty-handed
encircle
enclose
enclosure
encumber
encyclopedia
endorse
enforce
energetic
enrollment
en route
entree
entrench
entrust
envelope (noun)
   envelop (verb)
environment
equaled
equipment
erroneous
esophagus
especially
esprit de corps
evacuee
everybody
evildoer
exaggerate
examine
exceed
excellence
excitable
exercise (muscles)
   exorcise (expel)
exhausted
exhilarating
exhort
expeditionary

expense
experience
experiment
expose
extracurricular
extraterritorial
extravagant
extremely
exuberance
eyewitness

facade
facsimile
fact-finding
faker (cheat)
   fakir (religion)
fallacy
familiar
fantasy
far-fetched
farmhouse
farther (distance)
   further (in addition)
fascinate
faultfinder
faux pas
favorite
February
fiancé (male)
   fiancée (female)
fiber
fictitious
field marshal
fiery
finally
financially
financier
fingerprint
firearms
flagpole
fleur-de-lis
flier, flyer
flimflam
fluorescent
fluoride
focused

follow-up (noun)
   follow up (verb)
foodstuffs
foolhardy
forbear (shun)
  forebear (ancestor)
forehead
foreign
forfeit
formally
  formerly (before)
forth (go)
  fourth (4th)
frame-up
frantically
fraternities
freelance
friend
fulfill
fundamentally
furniture
furor
fusillade

gaiety
gaily
gauntlet
garçon
gauge
gelatin
get-away (noun)
  get away (verb)
ghost
gibe (jeer)
  jib (sail)
  jibe (shift)
gilt-edge
give-away (noun)
  give away (verb)
gladiolus
glamorous
  glamour
go-between (noun)
  go between (verb)
godfather
good-by

goodwill
gorilla (animal)
  guerrilla (soldier)
gothic
government
governor
grammar
granddaughter
grandstand
gray
great-grandson
grief
grown-up (adjective)
grueling
gruesome
guarantee
guardian
guidance
guide
gunfire
gypsy

habitué
half-nelson
halfway
halo
hammer
handball
hangar (airplanes)
  hanger (clothes)
hanger-on
happiness
hara-kiri
harass
hard-bitten
harebrained
headdress
headmaster
head wind
hear (ears)
  here (place)
heartbroken
heavyweight
height
helter-skelter
hemorrhage

herculean
heretofore
hero
hideout (noun)
  hide out (verb)
hideous
highball
highbrow
high-handed
hijack
hillside
hindrance
hippopotamus
hit-and-run (adjective)
hoard (keep)
  horde (people)
hoarse (throat)
  horse (animal)
hold-up (noun)
  hold up (verb)
hole-in-one
home rule
home run
homestretch
horizontal
hors d'oeuvre
horseplay
horsepower
horse race
hot-blooded
houseboat
human (man)
  humane (kind)
humorous
hungrily
hurly-burly
hurriedly
hygiene
hypnosis
hypnotic
hypnotize
hypocrisy
hypocrite
hysterical

iceberg
ice water
ideé fixe
ignorance
illogical
imagine
immediate
imminent (close)
  eminent (prominent)
impanel
impasse
implement
impromptu
impugn
inadequate
inasmuch
incessantly
incidentally
incommunicado
incredible
independent
indictment
indispensable
influence
influential
ingenious (smart)
  ingenuous (artless)
ingenue
inimitable
initiation
innocuous
innuendo
inoculate
inquire
insignia
insofar
insomuch
install
installation
instill
instructor
insure
intellectual
intelligent
  intelligentsia

intercollegiate

interest

intern (confine, doctor)

interrupt

interstate

intolerance

inventor

ironclad

irrelevant

irreligious

irreparable

irresistible

irreverent

irrevocable

it's (it is)

jailer

jalopy

jaywalker

jollity

journeyman

judgment

jump-off (noun)

  jump off (verb)

junta

jury

keyboard

khaki

kidnap

kidnapped

kilowatt

kimono

kindergarten

kindergartners

kitchenette

kneecap

knockdown

knowledge

knowledgeable

labeled

laboratory

laborer

laboriously

laissez-faire

lamp-post

landfall

languor

lasso

later (time)

  latter (last)

laughingstock

laurel

law-abiding

layoff

laxative

lazybones

lead (present)

  led (past)

lean-to

leatherneck

leave-taking

left-handed

legacy

legionnaire

legitimate

  illegitimate

leisurely

length

lese majeste

letterhead

letter-perfect

liable (likely)

  libel (law)

liaison

liar

liberal

librarian

license

lieutenant

lifeboat

lifestyle

lightening

  lightning (storm)

light-hearted

likable

likelihood

likewise

lily of the valley

linage (lines)
   lineage (family)
liqueur (after meals)
   liquor (whiskey)
litterateur
livable
livelihood
loath (unwilling)
   loathe (hate)
locksmith
lockup (noun)
   lock up (verb)
loneliness
lonely
loose (not fastened)
   lose (verb)
lopsided
loudspeaker
lowbrow
luncheon
luster
luxury

mackerel
madcap
magazine
magnificent
mailman
maintain
maintenance
maitre d'hôtel
major-domo
make-believe (noun)
   make believe (verb)
mandatary (noun)
   mandatory (adjective)
manpower
mantel (shelf)
   mantle (cloak)
manual
many-sided
mardi gras
marriage
marshal
mass-meeting

matériel (supplies)
   material (cloth, data)
matter-of-fact (adjective)
matzoh
meager
meanwhile
medicine
medieval
mediocre
Mediterranean
melee
memento
memorabilia
memorandum
ménage
mere
merry-go-round
metal (steel)
   mettle (courage)
meter
microwave
middle-aged
millennium
millionaire
miniature
minute
mischief
mise-en-scène
misspelled
mix-up
mockingbird
mold (make, fungi)
   molt (birds)
monkey wrench
moral (ethical)
   morale (good cheer)
mortgage
mosquito
mother-in-law
mother-of-pearl
mother tongue
motorboat
multicolored
murmur
muscle

mustache
mysterious

naive
naiveté
naturally
navy blue
nearby
necessary
necessity
neither
nerve-racking
newcomer
newfangled
newsprint
nickel
niece
nightmare
noticeable
noticing
notoriety
nuisance

obbligato
obedience
obey
object lesson
obliged
obstacle
occasionally
occurrence
occurring
offense
officeholder
oily
old-fashioned
omitted
omission
oneself
one-sided
onlooker
onomatopoeia
open-handed
operate
opponent

opportunity
optimism
organization
origin
out-and-out
outpatient
outrageous

paean
paid
pajama
palate (mouth)
    palette (artist)
pallbearer
pamphlet
paneled
panhandle
panic-stricken
pantomime
papier-mâché
parallel
pari-mutuel
parliament
paroled
participate
particularly
part-time
passed (moved)
    past (future)
passerby
passkey
password
pastime
payday
paymaster
peccadillo
peddler
pedestal
pejorative
pendant (noun)
    pendent (adjective)
penthouse
perceive
percent
perform

permanent

permissible

permit

perseverance

persistent

personal (private)
   personnel (hiring)

perspiration

persuade

petit larceny

pharmacopoeia

phase (period)
   faze (overcome)

phenomenon

Philippines

philosophy

physical

physician

piano

pickets

pickle

pickpocket

picnic

picnicking

piece (part)
   peace (quiet)

pièce de résistance

piecemeal

pigeonhole

pince-nez

pipeline

pique

pitter-patter

plaid

plain (simple)
   plane (level)

planned

plaque

plaster of paris

playgoer

playwright

pleasant

pneumatic

pneumonia

point-blank

policyowner

politician

politics

possibility

postgraduate

postmaster

postmortem

post office

postpaid

postscript

potpourri

powerhouse

practicability

practical

practice

precede

preference

preferred

prejudice

premier (leader)
    premiere (opening)

prima facie

procedure

proceed

profession

professor

prominent

pronounce

propaganda

protein

proved

proviso

provost marshal

psychiatrist

psychoanalysis

psychology

psychopathic

psychosomatic

publicly

pumpkin

pursue

pursuit

pussyfoot

putsch

pygmy

quantity

quarantine

quartet

quay

questionnaire

queue

quicksand

quiet (noiseless)
   quite (rather)

quintet

quixotic

quiz

rack (shelf)
   wrack (search)

raconteur

racquetball

railway

raincoat

raison d'être

rapid-fire

rapport

rapprochement

ready-made

really

receipt (paper)
   recipe (cooking)

receive

recipient

reclamation

recognition

recommend

reconcile

reconnaissance

reconnoiter

re-enter

refer

reference

reforestation

regime

reinforce

relative

relegate

relevant

relieve

religion

remember

reminisce

Renaissance

rendezvous

repellent

repertoire

resemblance

reservoir

resin

respectfully

respectively

responsible

restaurant

restaurateur

résumé

reverent

rhetoric

rhinoceros

rhyme

rhythm

ridiculous

riffraff

right-of-way

roadbed

role (part)
   roll (verb, bread)

roll call

roommate

roughshod

roundabout

round trip

roundup (noun)
   round up (verb)

rowboat

ruble

saber

sacrifice

sacrilegious

safe-conduct

safety

sailboat

salable
salary (money)
  celery (vegetable)
salvo
sandwich
sangfroid
savior
saxophone
scandalous
scar
scare
scenario
scene
schedule
schoolhouse
scot-free
scurrilous
seacoast
secretarial
seize
semester
senator
sense (brains)
  scents (odor)
  cents (coins)
sensible
sentence
separate
sergeant
serviceable
set-to
several
severely
severity
sexist
sextet
shear (verb)
  sheer (adjective)
shell shock
shining
shipboard
shopkeeper
shortcut
shorthand
showdown

shutdown (noun)
  shut down (verb)
sibilant
sibling
siege
sieve
sightseeing
signaled
similar
simon pure
simultaneous
sincerely
sincerity
sinning
sitdown (noun)
  sit down (verb)
site (spot)
  cite (point out)
skeptical
ski, skis, skiing
skillful
slim (thin)
  slime (grease)
smoke screen
smolder
snapshot
snowstorm
soccer
so-called
solo
soluble
somber
someone
sophistication
sophomore
source
speak
specifically
specificity
specimen
specter
spiciness
spicy
spelled
spilled

sponsor
staccato
stagehand
staid (sedate)
   stayed (remained)
stanch
standard bearer
standby (noun)
   stand by (verb)
stand-in (noun)
   stand in (verb)
stateroom
stationary (still)
   stationery (paper)
statue
stature
statute
stepchild
stepping-stone
stiletto
stimuli (plural)
stockbroker
stomach ache
stopgap
straight
   strait (geography)
stranglehold
strata (plural)
streamline
strength
stretched
studying
stumbling block
stupify
succeed
success
suit (clothes)
   suite (rooms)
sulfur
summary
superintendent
supersede
suppose
suppress
surprise

susceptible
suing
sycophant
syllable
symbiosis
symbol
sympathy
symptomatic
synchronize
syncretism
syndicate
synonym
synopsis
synthetic
syphilis
syrup

tableau
tabu
tailor-made
talisman
tariff
tattletale
technique
telltale
temperament
tendency
tête-à-tête
textbook
theater
their
   they're (they are)
   there (place)
theory
therefore
thorough
   though (although)
   tough (strong)
   through (pass)
   trough (food)
thrash (hit)
   thresh (grain)
tightrope
titanic

to (preposition)
   too (also)
   two (2)
to-do
together
tongue-tied
topcoat
topsy-turvy
totaled
tournament
tourniquet
tousle
toxin
trademark
traffic
tragedy
traveler
truly
tryout (noun)
   try out (verb)
Tuesday
tying
typical
tyranny

ukulele
under way
undoubted
unforgettable
unnecessary
unprecedented
until
unusual
upgrade
useful
usually
utensil

vaccine
vacillate
vacuous
vacuum
various
vegetable
vengeance

venal (mercenary)
   venial (pardonable)
veranda
vice (evil)
   vise (tool)
vice versa
view
vigilance
vigilantes
vilify
villain
virtuoso
vis-à-vis
vitamin
voilà
volume
voodoo
vying

wage earner
waist (belt line)
   waste (not use)
walkout (noun)
   walk out (verb)
wallpaper
warehouse
warranty
warring
weather
weighty
weird
well-known
wheat
whether
whiskey
whole
wholly (total)
   holy (revered)
who's (who is)
   whose (possessive)
woolen
woolly
workday
workingman
worldwide

worship
worshiper
worthwhile
wrongdoer

X-ray

yacht
yield
you're (you are)
   your (possessive)

SECTION **II**

THE TERM
PAPER

CHAPTER 12

THE PREPARATORY
WORK

Despite the glowing remarks made recently in the national press about the dazzling prowess of today's students—the reading, the writing, the poise in classroom discussions, etc.—many college and high school instructors know better. They see that today's students are not any more endowed with great intellectual curiosity and fine work habits than those of previous generations.

Such teachers come by their opinions honestly and usually through that most revealing document, the term paper (research paper, library paper, reference paper, star paper). Since the heart of learning involves investigatory work, students' efforts in putting their curiosity to work are the key to their true scholarly depths. A student who mindlessly copies every word of his term paper from an encyclopedia, or book, or magazine reveals himself to be a dullard. A student who does too hasty or too slovenly a job on a term paper appears just that way to his teacher. So does a "grind." So does a "brain," and so does a student who can turn out the big words without saying much.

Among the criticisms leveled at students doing term papers are perhaps some that these young writers themselves recognize. Some students turn in the same term paper for three courses. Some have others write much of their term papers for them. Some fail to do more than copy jobs from such sources as the *World Book*. There are those students who pay little attention to the mechanics of term papers and ignore instructions on footnotes, format, and the like. Many students do an excellent piece of work on research but fail to intersperse their findings with their own conclusions. Others seem to have difficulty in organizing the contents of a term paper.

Many colleges and some high schools have been forced by academic dishonesty among students to keep a file on term papers. This is designed to prevent someone from turning in a term paper (and even bibliographies) submitted by another student in past years.

It is easy to see why many rather mediocre term papers earn high grades in some institutions. Even when measured against the sad quality of work turned in by too many of today's students, these term papers have little to recommend them. But they are the best that may be turned in.

Yet there is no reason for you to write a mediocre term paper if you do your research in a thorough manner, if you organize your material and present it clearly and in the proper form. You surely should not set your standards so low as to practice some of the bad habits mentioned.

Picking a Topic

Pick your term paper topic with a view toward interesting the reader. One feature writer on a metropolitan daily said that the key to her success (i.e., having many readers) was that she always asked questions of people that she knew would be of interest to the average person.

In graduate schools, thesis writers know their topics must be approved by an advisory committee, but their committee chairmen will rule on almost every step of preparation, organization, and writing.

The reader must be considered, in short.

This means that you may have to rule out the obscure topics, the too-easy topics, the extreme topics, or topics that will irritate.

You also should consider picking a topic that will benefit your own store of knowledge and one that will not bore you. As long as you're going to all the trouble of doing a paper, you might as well do one that will add to your education and background. Why select a topic you already know a lot about? You're only covering familiar ground. You may find that your research on a totally unknown topic will come in handy for the future. Also, as you labor for weeks on your topic, it helps if the subject does not get to be a complete bore. Boredom often reveals itself in a dull presentation of material.

Term paper topics can be either assigned or the "blue-sky" type.

The assigned topics are given from a list of possibilities set up by the instructor. If this is the method used in your class, pick a topic that you feel will be interesting, as has been said, and a topic that will be challenging to you.

The blue-sky topics are those more generally used in colleges and high schools. The instructor might expect topics to be done on certain specified areas of study. Or he might allow you to make up your own topic, subject to his approval. Because the blue-sky topics involve considerable thinking on the student's part, they are the hardest ones to handle. Your selection will reveal your intellectual ability.

Whichever variety of topics prevails in your class, pick a subject that has a great deal of bearing on what you've been covering in the course. Don't do one on "Scuba Diving" for a political science course, "Hitler's Last Week" for world geography, or "The Kinetic Processes" for literature class. Equally, don't pick a subject that you know has been done repeatedly.

Don't take too broad an approach to your topic. Narrow it to a size that will fit comfortably and somewhat completely in a term paper. If the paper is for a history course, don't take on a huge chunk of a subject as, say, "World War I." It's far better to limit it to some *phase* of this event or to smaller aspects as, for example, "French Mutinies in the Trenches" or "Logistical Problems at Verdun" or "Ludendorff's Use of Infantry on the Eastern Front."

Even in a biographical term paper, you'll be better off if you take but a phase of the person's life. This is especially true since you will probably do a paper on someone famous. It would be more prudent to write a paper on "Napoleon at Marengo" or "Oppenheimer and Security Problems" than cradle-to-grave sketches of these persons.

Narrowing a topic makes it easier for you when it comes to research also. You'll be able to weed out thousands of words and dozens of pages in books, encyclopedias, magazines, and the like. Your paper will have excellent focus and may deal with an aspect of the subject that your instructor has not seen before. And you'll avoid that tempting tendency to copy everything word-for-word out of your sources.

It should be said that if your paper is to be a critical study of something or someone, make it truly critical. This includes both criticism in favor of and against the subject. If your paper is a comparison of one thing with another, it must be filled with both *similarities* and *differences*. If the paper contrasts people or things, ensure that the *differences* are used throughout the work. A paper that deals with the effects of something must include the *effects*. In short, stick with the topic and aspect you've chosen. That's the way an A is born.

Before you formally commit yourself to a topic, it's a good idea to visit the library to see if there's enough material on your subject to suit the requirements of a term paper. You should have a dozen to two dozen good sources for the average research work. Check the card catalogue for books on the subject. Comb the encyclopedias and the *Reader's Guide to Periodical Literature*. If you are doing a paper on such special fields as medicine or home economics, sociology, or drama, these areas often have their own special encyclopedias and periodicals.

If the library's resources are slim for your topic, choose another subject. You can only stretch one or two sources so far and it's rarely long enough for a definitive term paper.

Other students might be working on topics in the general area of your subject. That means that the books, magazines, and the like that you'll need could be checked out continuously. Even if the sources are on reserve, this could happen.

Once you have located materials for your topic, consult your teacher about your choice of subject. Come to an interview with him supported by written ideas on how you intend to develop the subject. The instructor probably will give you some helpful advice on the development of your paper. He may advise you to skip over one aspect of the topic, to shorten that one, or to concentrate on yet another side of the subject. Once the teacher has given you his time and the benefit of his advice, follow his suggestions. No one likes to be solicited for help only to see the assistance discarded. No more than one interview should be necessary with your instructor. You should see to it that it is a productive meeting.

Getting the Information

The best place to get term paper information is nearly always the library. If you're relying on information from government agencies, personal interviews, letters, questionnaires, and the like, you'll have to start gathering such materials weeks in advance. Don't put it off. You must allow for mail deliveries or the tardiness of your sources, the unavailability of materials, and a dozen other mishaps.

Most term papers are based on what is available in school libraries. If your school has only a small library, you're going to have trouble getting materials from obscure sources and will have to resort to that which can be ferreted out from an encyclopedia, the books, or the few magazines available. It is ridiculous to expect a high school or college of 500 students to stock the *Almanach de Gotha* or a *Universal Jewish Encyclopedia*. It is true that you can order material through the inter-library loan system, but here again, it takes time and sometimes what you want is unavailable. Don't expect the impossible from your library.

No matter how small your library, it usually has the three basic reference sources for doing term papers. These are the encyclopedias, the card catalogue file listing the books in the library, and the *Readers' Guide to Periodical Literature*, which gives an index on magazine articles.

Even if your library doesn't have them, there are some other major reference sources for the various fields—political science, music, chemistry, etc.—on which you might be doing your paper. These are specialized sources, however, and it is doubtful if you can find them without going to a large public library. They are listed at the end of the next chapter for your convenience.

Finally, as you decide what reference works to use, don't use the *World Book* or the Collier's encyclopedias. They're fine for the young, but they are not adequate for scholarly work. Most teachers rightly regard them in this light.

Taking Notes

With the advent of the copier, students can amass entire magazine articles, whole book chapters, and complete encyclopedia entries. No more do they have to copy by hand huge sections of material in a notebook or try to boil it down on 3 x 5 cards.

Although the copier has ended writer's cramp, a student still has to comb through sources—to underline or color highlight key passages—to put the paper together. There's no difference between yesterday's and today's student in going through the scholarly pursuit of investigative work that pertains to a chosen topic. Some data may be fascinating, but way off the subject; it has to be discarded. Some data may be boring, but so important that you cheer when you find it because you alone have seen its connection to your term paper topic.

The "card system" is not dead. Neither is your need to dig in and read *all* of the material you've spent money copying. If you can cart home a foot-high stack of copier data, you can read it at your convenience—helpful, considering library hours. The distractions of your room, of course, can keep you from getting to work; this usually has not been the case for students who have camped in a library to go through materials in such a quiet and academic atmosphere. There *is* a trade-off.

The cards *still* are essential standbys for term papers.

They are vital for term papers that require traditional footnotes. They are vital also for bibliographies at the end of the paper (often called *works consulted* or *references*). And they are a godsend for first laying out the organization of the term paper ("these three sources go here, those five sources go there, and I'll end with this source"). When you get to the two paragraphs on, say, Roosevelt, there's your 3 x 5 card with a couple of key words or a sentence—along with the page number—as well as all the bibliographical material; you can comb through your stack of copiered data and instantly work from it.

Smart students use cards primarily for the bibliograpy section; if they're doing footnotes, they have the citation essentials—all in order, to the extent of where a comma or period must be placed—and will have those page numbers with the key quotes. There are at least three systems of bibliographies used today; your teacher may use the traditional one cited in this book, or one called *APA style* or *MLA style*. But no matter what the style, you cannot go wrong if you take that card and list:

> the author(s)'s name (last name first, first name, middle initial, Jr., and academic degree)
> the magazine or chapter title
> the book's title, including subtitle
> the book's publisher and city where published
> the book or magazine's publishing dates
> an encyclopedia's edition number, date, volume, and
> entry heading

Encyclopedias almost always list the initials of the contributors who wrote the entry at its end; the full name is to be found in the set's first volume, where all contributors are listed.

Before you start making out the cards from your copier material, look carefully at your teacher's specified bibliography form. Maybe he or she wants page numbers. Maybe the publisher's name comes *after* the city—or vice versa. Perhaps a magazine citation for *three* authors has to have the first entry with the last name, but the others in reverse order. Some teachers may lower a grade because you forgot to underline a magazine name and put the article's title inside double quotation marks; some are strict about a period coming *after* the name of a book.

Go over the citation style carefully. Circle underlinings, commas, and periods.

When you're ready to make out the cards from that stack of copiered material, write each citation *exactly* the way it will go in the bibliography. Again, for footnoting purposes, you can always put a few words for some specific passages accompanied by the page number(s).

At the end of your labors—when you're getting ready to keyboard the citations—all you have to do is to sort out the cards by authors and put them in alphabetical order. If you should happen upon some sensational additions to your research, the new card just can be slipped into the pile.

The Problem of Sources

The biggest and hardest chore for the paper is reading and understanding the sources.

The sensible way to comprehend your topic is first to read a source that tells you all about the subject in the *briefest* manner possible, a capsule wrap-up. That's why almanacs, encyclopedias, or such works as *Facts on File* are so useful as starting points. In them you will get the overall view that puts the topic in a nutshell. The rest of your readings will flesh out the details.

The detail work will consume most of your energy. There are ways to shortcut through the dozens of leads you might have uncovered in books, magazines, or encyclopedias. To be sure, you're going to have to buckle to the onerous task of following up all your leads. You can hardly turn out a research paper without doing the research. But you can make your reading of more value and save time by first *skimming* the source and catching the salient facts. Then go back for a thorough study of those key points. If you're confronted by entire books, go over the table of contents or the index to see if what you want might not be included in a few pages. Usually, tables of contents and indexes point up this or that focus of the book. If you were doing a term paper on Napoleon at Marengo, for example, the table of contents or the index of any of the hundreds of books on this emperor would single out that battle. You wouldn't have to read entire books to locate what you would need.

Magazine articles don't have tables of contents or indexes, but they do have telling titles and sub-headlines to indicate the various aspects covered. Even if they don't have revealing headlines, you can use that old device of looking for the key sentence in the beginnings of paragraphs. In other words, that first sentence may give the contention, the rest of the paragraph rounding out the contention with examples or quotations to support that key sentence. So check those first sentences. Not *all* magazine article writers might use this style, but enough of them do so that you can be assured of a shortcut to periodicals.

Encyclopedias offer you no table of contents or indexes, but if the entry is a long one, the editors use subheads. Also, encyclopedia entries have the advantage of being much shorter than the usual magazine article and, surely, the average book.

Reliability of Sources

What about the reliability of what you're reading?

Many term paper authorities tell students to be sure to distinguish between fact and opinion as they read through a reference. This sounds like good advice until you realize that no human being can be totally objective. Many authors are quite adept at using a set of facts—statistics, quotations, dates, events, etc.—to support their own views. There are ways and ways of using facts, and, as the saying goes, it's easy to "lie with statistics." Just to be able to distinguish between opinion and fact is not enough as you work through your readings.

What you must be able to do is to judge the *reliability*, or value, of your source to determine what axe the author or the publisher has to grind, what blind spots he might have. Even as you put your term paper together, remember, you too will be subjective. Nobody is immune from this foible, it would appear. You should know that if a magazine is ultraliberal or ultraconservative, the articles it uses will follow these lines. If a publisher prints only books with certain viewpoints, the authors he publishes probably will reflect the publisher's ideas. Newspapers sometimes omit certain stories or aspects of stories or are inhibited by deadlines or space limitations from including the full story that appears. Not even encyclopedias are immune from the subjective view. One highly regarded encyclopedia has only recently begun to back away from its position that England's Richard III was a murderer. None of your sources, in other words, should be regarded as unimpeachable.

You may say "How do I figure out what is really true?" That's easy. You put facts to the test just as scholars and scientists do. You sift through as many *different* sources with as many *different* ideas on your subject as is possible. You'll begin to determine that many authors base their ideas on something another author has written—a "copy job," if you think about it. You'll also have to consider that many authors who deal in half-truths, outright untruths, or in innocent misconceptions do have the gift of being overwhelmingly interesting or convincing writers. By the time you have examined a dozen or more sources, you should be able to find truths emerging.

After you've gone through one source, capsule its information on your card. Use only one card per source, or aspect, if you expect to weather a research paper. Boil down the information so it will fit on one card. If you're planning to use a direct quote, be scrupulous about putting in the exact words. Don't change a thing. And put quotation marks around the passage to indicate that it is a direct quote.

Be sure you get your information right the first time you enter it on your cards. The information and your handwriting must be understandable days later. It's no fun to make trip after trip to the library because you've mangled some vital information on your cards.

It may be that your instructor will ask you to turn in your cards. He may have several reasons for this, but chief among them undoubtedly is to help you to take notes or to see how much work you really did on your paper. Sometimes instructors prescribe exactly how you must take notes on your cards. In this case, you must follow instructions. Even if your instructor doesn't insist on a particular form, your cards should not be so difficult to understand that only a cryptographer could decipher them.

Some Sample Cards

The following examples show how to do cards that are meaningful. Not everyone makes notes in the same way, but these samples should give you an idea of how to enter information.

Even if you have read only six sources, you should be able to begin seeing certain trends or key points that will serve as the foundation of your term paper. In a biographical study, you may spot a half-dozen or a dozen turning points in the person's life. The paper treating with a certain event will use some key occurrences that brought on the final situation. If your paper is an analytical one, you should find in your readings the most important items with which you must deal. If you are writing a how-to-do-something term paper, you should be able to single out all the major steps to be described if you have done a thorough job with your reading of source materials.

What you are doing as you separate items is a form of basic outlining. You'll be able to see also what source materials you won't need to use. Out will go the cards with the irrelevant, though interesting, notes on them. Maybe it has taken you hours to get through the source you're now discarding. But if it digresses from the subject, don't feel that it just must be tucked in somewhere. Stick to the subject.

"IRA's: Costs, Benefits, Problems,"
Consumer Reports, Vol. 45, January
January 1980, pp. 40-46

    Why buy — pros and cons —
front end loading

3 x 5 size card

    Judith S. Wallerstein and Joan B. Kelly, "
"California's Children of Divorce," Vol. 13,
January 1980, pp. 66-76.

        fathers — pp. 71-76
        how they are as adults — pp. 74-75
        money/support — p. 68
        statistical sources — p. 70
        parental adjustment p. 72

4 x 6 size card

Alexy Tolstoy, <u>Peter the First</u>, translated by Tatiana Shebunina, New York, New American Library, 1961, possim.

Azov victory was a Pyrrhic one. Russia not prepared. Had to find allies, improve the army and get money. One of the reasons of Peter's interest in the West.

3 x 5 size card

Marc Slonin, <u>An Outline of Russian Literature</u>, New York, New American Library, 1959, p. 90.

"Nekrassov's social poetry, as well as his poems of self-recrimination, continued the moral trend so typical of Russian literature... Nekrassov questioned man's behavior in man's society and explored the twists of conscience resulting from social environment or practical responsibility."

4 x 6 size card

CHAPTER 13

ORGANIZING AND WRITING THE ROUGH DRAFT

The writing of their findings is a job that seems to many students to be the hardest part of doing a term paper. Actually, it is not. The most difficult part —gathering the information—is behind you. If you are well organized and have all your information, the writing part of the work should be easy.

If you can sort out your note cards into main areas or aspects, you are organized to tackle those portions of your term paper. There are few subjects that do not lend themselves well to categorizing, as you will see when you begin this part of term paper work. Examine the way the following three students categorized their topics:

Some effects of life in a Housing Development

    A. financial angle
    B. social   "   for parents
    C.   "   "   for kids to 18
    D. aesthetic   "   for family
    E. community spirit angle

Topic "Why Dunkirk?"
failure Fr. holding effort
* miscal. by Brit.
* efforts of Ger. high command
(air)
logistical snarls for Allies
communications = failure by "

"Some Comparisons Between Gogol & Dostoyevsky"
— use of trivia — great messages
— " " humor (D- little)
— revelations of Russian life
— use of char. as types
— philos. themes (religion, esp.)
— use of dialogue (& a playwright)
— use of description
— use of settings
— points of view used
— use of history, social structures

Once you have sorted your notes into categories as shown above, you will have to decide which category will be taken up first. Generally, you're better off if you put the most important category first. Follow it up with the second most important aspect and so on. If you have a difficult time deciding which really is the most important category, don't do any sorting until after you've completed a rough draft of the paper. Once things are formalized on paper, many students immediately see just which category should begin the term paper. You can always shift things around by using scissors, glue, and pen.

Informal a method as you might think it is, sorting your cards into categories will provide the simple outline that will carry you through the entire paper. There need be nothing elaborate about the outline unless your instructor directs you to turn one in that is more formal than the basic ones shown here.

The Writing Itself

The next step is the actual writing of the rough draft.

What style of writing should you use? Mainly, it should be formal and scholarly. There should be nothing remotely chatty or chummy about it. Neither should the paper be overloaded with whimsy, sarcasm, or cynicism as you take up opposing viewpoints. You shouldn't reflect the attitude that you think yourself superior in intellect. Nor should you go to the opposite tack of obsequious and syrupy humility ("Although I'm only a novice in . . ." or "I did not understand all that I read, but . . ."). Don't overdo enthusiasm ("What a poet Heine is!!!!!" or "Never have I enjoyed things so much as in reading what the Marquis said of him in his review"). Use a kind of quiet and measured dignity in your writing.

The paper's vocabulary will depend on the kind your instructor prefers in the classroom. A teacher might like to see an elevated vocabulary on term papers. Likewise, another teacher might like to see a kind of basic vocabulary in your paper. Don't forget that great ideas often have been conveyed by simple words, as any reader of Plato or the Bible knows.

Try to keep from mentioning yourself in the paper. If you find you must do so, use the third person as in the formal "this student saw that . . ." or "this researcher determined that . . ."

One important bit of phraseology that would be well to include is what might be called the "scientific hedge" of "it seems," "it appears" or derivations of these two expressions. Mathematics and science are said to be far more exact than, say, history, literature, and other fields where many conclusions are possible on the same thing. Yet even if a scientist has an experiment come out the same way 99 times out of 100, he still qualifies his findings by using the preface of "it would seem" or "it appears that . . ."

When you actually get into the term paper, you'll have to have an introduction to indicate the subject and its scope. This is the place in a page or so to mention all the major aspects you will cover in the paper. If you like, you might also mention what areas will *not* be included.

Some like to leave the introduction and ending until they are finished with the body of the term paper. The advantage is clear. They'll know exactly what's in the paper and can write an appropriate preface and ending. If you are well organized, though, you'll know what you are going to include in the paper and can set it out in either the introduction or summary.

Whether you do introductions first or last, the finished opening paragraph should be diagrammed in the following way with the most important contention or point placed first:

OPENING SENTENCE (reveal topic)

Point No. 1 (most important point)

Point No. 2

Point No. 3

Point No. 4

Point No. 5

Point No. 6

Point No. 7

What such an opening paragraph looks like when it's set to words could be this one:

Nearly 23,000,000[1] Americans are now living in modern housing developments and most are not really happy about it. They have found that buying such a home might have had a good reason originally, but it is far more expensive than they planned. Americans also have found that a development seems to stifle aesthetic values since there are only four or five architectural styles available. Parents object to the rigid social life they must carry on with the neighbors. Children are seemingly affected in that they know children only of the same economic and social levels. Even the community spirit, so high in small towns, undergoes a remarkable transition for the worse in a housing development.

Or if you don't like to waste words, your brisk and short introductory paragraph could look like this:

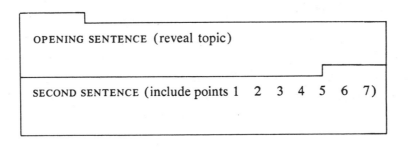

OPENING SENTENCE (reveal topic)

SECOND SENTENCE (include points 1   2   3   4   5   6   7)

Once he got beyond the opening sentence that revealed the term paper's subject, the writer in the example above has used only one long sentence to *combine* each of the points he took up in the body of the term paper. This is how such a condensed introduction looks:

Nearly 23,000,000[1] Americans are now living unhappily in America's housing developments. They find it has more than a dozen important drawbacks in such things as their finances, aesthetic values, social life for the entire family, and does nothing to underpin community life as has always been the case in small communities.

The introduction could be more than one paragraph long, or it could involve three or four paragraphs. Perhaps you feel uncomfortable if your term paper introduction does not fill up the first page of the work and move on into the second for half a page or so. The introduction should *not* run beyond that second-page limit, however.

The introduction finished, you will swing into the body of the term paper.

Your rough outline, setting out the major points (or contentions, steps, etc.), should indicate to you in what order to use them. Put the most important sections first, the second most important section next, and so on down to the least important section. This is not to say you shouldn't change your mind later. All you need do in any shifting of sections is to get busy with scissors and paste. You could also use the "insert" method shown in the chapter on editing, saving yourself much time.

No matter what order you use for sections, the construction of each should be done in the same manner.

How is this done?

You start with a key sentence or sentences (or even a whole paragraph) to lead off the first part of the section. This done, you then follow up those key statements with your specific examples to support what you say in those statements. As you deal with your specifics, you may run into several pages. This is much the same writing pattern that has been shown in the theme-writing portion of this book.

This is what it looks like, diagramed in paragraph-by-paragraph order:

KEY SENTENCE (point No. 1)

Example No. 1

Example No. 2

> Example No. 3

Written out, such a section might be done this way:

It seems that many readers do not feel Salinger's confused teenager, Holden Caufield, is worthy of sympathy. Critic Nancy Roboz said that because Holden has plenty of money and opportunities, he should not be pitied. "It seems to me," she wrote, "that teenagers who are plagued with poverty, perhaps only one parent in the home, acne, poor grades and other attendant difficulties will wonder just what troubles Holden. Worrying about phonies will seem a very small problem to them."[1]

key sentence

example No. 1

This observer has known many poor people, and they have none of the questions that Salinger gives Caufield. One of the boys from the Upward Bound program said he felt Salinger's hero had things pretty nice. What he said is echoed by Prof. Francis Karam in a comparison of Salinger and Charles Maturin. He wrote: "A boy who has been facing life in its cruelest terms knows that life is made up of phonies by the million. But so what?"[2]

example No. 2

example No. 3

You can use more than one paragraph for each example, of course. You need not limit yourself. You might even want two or four paragraphs to do justice to your examples. But as is seen above, you should offer commentary or some observations as you work in the examples.

Using the same structure as shown in the previous diagram, an analytical term paper would look much the same as the next example:

Another important difference between Shaw and Ibsen is humor. Shaw had far more of it and a greater variety than did the Norwegian. When Ibsen used humor, it was with the heavyhanded approach of the North European. There is nothing subtle about it.

key sentence

In *An Enemy of the People,* Ibsen thunders almost without letup on the venality and mendacity of mankind. Near the end of the play, Ibsen sees fit to employ some comic relief of the earthy variety so dear to the Germanic races. Dr. Stockmann enters, trousers damaged, from his street orations about the water pipes and certain individuals of the town. At one point he says: "You should never wear your best trousers when you go out to fight for freedom and truth."[1] This is hardly even Wildean humor.

example No. 1

By contrast, Shaw's many-sided humor turns up constantly. It is as if he cannot help himself. Even his prefaces to his plays are full of it. The preface to *Pygmalian* cannot help making the reader smile. Says Shaw: "The English have no respect for their language, and will not teach their children to speak it. They cannot spell it because they have nothing to spell it with but an old foreign alphabet of which only the consonants—and not all of them—have any agreed speech value."[2]   } example No. 2

Where can Ibsen match such wit as that given Cusins by Shaw in *Major Barbara* when explaining why he [Cusins] will not join her for prayers: "Well, you would have to say before all the servants that we have done things we ought not to have done, and left undone things we ought to have done, and that there is no health in us. I cannot bear to hear you doing yourself such an injustice."[3] Ibsen would never make humor out of the *Book of Common Prayer,* but Shaw dares and tastefully so.   } example No. 3

If one of your contentions has *many* aspects to it, use the key sentence to touch upon the *overall* contention. Then, give substance to each additional paragraph with an aspect of the main point. Follow it up with the illustrative example or fact. The next diagram shows you how to do it:

OVERALL SENTENCE (covering *all* aspects)

KEY SENTENCE (aspect No. 1)

SPECIFIC EXAMPLE

KEY SENTENCE (aspect No. 2)

SPECIFIC EXAMPLE

KEY SENTENCE (aspect No. 3)

SPECIFIC EXAMPLE

```
┌─────────────────────────────────────────┐
│                                          │
│  KEY SENTENCE (aspect No. 4)             │
│                                      ┌───┘
├──────────────────────────────────────┤
│                                      │
│  SPECIFIC EXAMPLE                    │
│                                  ┌───┘
└──────────────────────────────────┘
```

This is how such organization looks as in this example from a descriptive term paper:

The press of this country, in the main, still refuses to meet its responsibilities to the public when it interferes with the publishers' pocketbooks. } overall key sentence

When it became clear that there were a lot of meat processing plants—nearly 9000[1]—that cut meat products under appalling conditions, the posture of many papers was that it was happening some- } key sentence (aspect No. 1)

where else, if it were happening at all. One liberal magazine was moved to say: "Here we have meat processing plants that work amid flies, vermin, rodents and who stoop also to adulterating old meat or meat from diseased livestock. Yet only seven daily newspapers really pursued the matter relentlessly."[2] } example No. 1

Many newspapers also shirked their duty to the public, especially the elderly and sick, in the matter of overpriced drug scandals. } key sentence (aspect No. 2)

Profits on drugs were admitted to be based on what the traffic would bear. This was sometimes a 1000 per cent mark-up, according to the findings of the late Senator Estes Kefauver's famous drug investigation more than two decades ago.[3] } example No. 1

If the nation's publishers covered the drug hearings at all, they put the play in back pages or editorialized to the effect, as did one Midwestern paper, that "when the millions spent for research on just one medicine are considered, the drug industry is only getting its fair return on its investments."[4] } example No. 2

Too many newspapers also fought child labor laws, knowing their carrier boys would come under such legisla-tion. } key sentence (aspect No. 3)

One California daily argued that "there is little wrong in helping train a child to meet adult responsibilities. He has an opportunity to earn his own money and to contribute to the family income. Perhaps he will be too tired at the end of the work day to engage in mischief or crime."[5] } example No. 1

When advertising revenues were jeopardized if newspapers reported too fully the recent housewives' strikes for lower grocery prices, the stories were played down if they were } key sentence (aspect No. 4)

covered at all in most papers. Checking 47 dailies from areas affected by the lady pickets, I found that only four really covered the story at all. Of these four, only one followed the event until the end of the strike. This is a shocking but fairly regular happening where the seemingly public-minded newspaper business is concerned. } example No. 1

If your paper is a biographical study, it would be set up in the same organizational structure as the one in the next example:

aspect No. 1
{
His temperament proved to be irresponsible also in many ordinary things. Take his regard for editor's deadlines. One editor told him over lunch that he'd like two paragraphs changed by the end of the week. Two years later, the changes were still not made. His publisher had at least six editors quit because of his carelessness with deadlines.[1]
}

> key sentence for overall section
>
> example No. 1

Other irresponsibilities had to do with his family life. He was divorced from six wives. All but one declared in court that once he had shown up for the wedding, he considered his marital duties as over.[2] He was an affectionate father to his 15 children, but even his favorite, Sean, admitted to one magazine reporter that his father felt devotion to irresponsibility was a kind of responsibility in itself.[3]

> key sentence aspect No. 2
>
> example No. 1
>
> example No. 2

Financial responsibilities put him in poor shape through most of his life. He seemed to have the perpetual beer pocketbook and champagne tastes as well as a generous heart that could be taken advantage of. When times were good as with that important first novel, he spread around most of the royalties to his friends. His parents received a new house in Shreveport.[4] Two down-on-their-luck poets he met in an uptown bar were startled to learn they were to join him for an opulent midnight supper at the very expensive Four Seasons.[5]

> key sentence aspect No. 3
>
> example No. 1
>
> example No. 2

Each section of your term paper should be done using the same pattern as has been demonstrated in diagrams and examples for a single section.

Endings

Your ending section should not be hard to write once the rest of the paper is finished. Don't make it more than two or three paragraphs long, however. Generally, sum up your views on the main points detailed in the work. Don't gush. Don't ramble. Don't give the impression that the world is now wiser for having had your investigatory talents at work on a topic. One student who wrapped up his term paper without flourishes wrote it this way:

It has been seen that the Empire ruled the Emperor rather than the other way around. Militarily, he was forced to accede to his generals rather than the Senate. Even in the Senate, he was at the mercy of the five chief politicians. The populace even had his services which he was afraid to curtail at all. His family was so insistent in its demands that he was at pains to continually pacify them with his influence and extensive holdings. Nations crushed by his armies made vociferous demands; and he believed it was far less costly to grant such demands rather than to brutally crush any uprisings in the manner of his predecessors. It's no wonder that his contributions to the Empire were so minimal.

Special Reference Works

The most commonly used special reference works are listed below for your convenience. Some are for fields that may overlap and, as has been said, some entries are found only in major libraries.

OVERALL REFERENCES

Bibliographic Index
Guide to Reference Books
How and Where to Look It Up: A Guide to Standard Sources of Information
Index to Indexes
United States Government Publications
U.S. Catalog, with Cumulative Book Index
World Bibliography of Bibliographies

GENERAL ENCYCLOPEDIAS AND ALMANACS

American Year Book
Encyclopedia Americana
Americana Annual
Encyclopedia Britannica
The Britannica Book of the Year
Chambers' Encyclopaedia
Columbia Encyclopedia
Encyclopedia International
New International Encyclopedia
Facts on File
New International Year Book
The Statesman's Yearbook
Information Please Almanac
The World Almanac

PERIODICALS

International Index to Periodicals
The New York Times Index
Nineteenth Century Readers' Guide
Poole's Index to Periodical Literature
Reader's Guide to Periodical Literature
Ulrich's Periodical Directory

AGRICULTURE

Agricultural Index
Cyclopedia of American Agriculture

ART AND ARCHITECTURE

Art Index
Art Through the Ages
Bryan's Dictionary of Painters and Engravers
Harper's Encyclopedia of Art
History of Architecture
Index to Reproductions of American Paintings
Portrait Index

BIOGRAPHIES

Current Biography
Dictionary of American Biography
Dictionary of National Biography
International Who's Who
Webster's Biographical Dictionary
Who Was Who in America
Who's Who in America
World Biography

QUOTATIONS

Bartlett's Familiar Quotations
Oxford Dictionary of Quotations
Stevenson's Home Book of Quotations

BUSINESS

Business Information: How to Find and Use It
Business Periodicals Index
Encyclopedia of Banking and Finance

DRAMA AND SPEECH

Dramatic Index
Index to Plays in Collections
University Debaters' Annual

ECONOMICS

Dictionary of Modern Economics

EDUCATION

Bibliographies and Summaries in Education to July 1935
Cyclopedia of Education
Education Index
Encyclopedia of Educational Research
How to Locate Educational Information and Data
Introduction to Educational Research

ENGINEERING

Engineering Index
Sources of Engineering Information

GEOGRAPHY

Columbia Gazetteer

HISTORY AND POLITICAL SCIENCE

Bibliography in American History
Cambridge Ancient History
Cambridge Medieval History
Cambridge Modern History
Cyclopedia of American Government
Dictionary of American History
Encyclopedia of World History
Guide to Historical Literature
Literature of American History
Guide to Materials in Political Science
Guide to the Study of the United States of America
Public Affairs Information Service
Reference Shelf
Yearbook of the United Nations

INDUSTRIAL ARTS

Industrial Arts Index

LAW

Index to Legal Periodicals

LITERATURE

A.L.A. Index to General Literature
Articles on American Literature
Authors Today and Yesterday
Baker's Guide to Historical Fiction
Baker's Guide to the Best Fiction
Bibliographical Guide to English Studies

Bibliography of Writings on the English Language
Book Review Digest
Cambridge Bibliography of English Literature
Cambridge History of American Literature
Cambridge History of English Literature
Columbia Dictionary of Modern European Literature
Concise Bibliography for Students of English
Contemporary American Authors
Contemporary British Literature
Dictionary of World Literature
Essay and General Literature Index
Firkins' Index of Plays
Firkins' Index to Short Stories
Granger's Index to Poetry and Recitations
Literary History of the United States
Living Authors
Oxford Classical Dictionary
Oxford Companion to American Literature
Oxford Companion to Classical Literature
Oxford Companion to English Literature
Sonnenschein's Best Books
Twentieth Century Authors

MATHEMATICS

Guide to the Literature of Mathematics

MUSIC

Grove's Dictionary of Music and Musicians
International Cyclopedia of Music and Musicians
Song Index

PHILOSOPHY

Dictionary of Philosophy
Dictionary of Philosophy and Psychology
Guide to Readings in Philosophy

PSYCHOLOGY

Dictionary of Philosophy and
    Psychology
Dictionary of Psychology
Encyclopedia of Psychology
List of Books in Psychology
New Dictionary of Psychology

RELIGION

Catholic Encyclopedia
Catholic Periodical Index
Dictionary of the Bible
Encyclopedia of Religion and Ethics
Jewish Encyclopedia
New Schaff-Herzog Encyclopedia of
    Religious Knowledge
Universal Jewish Encyclopedia

THE SCIENCES

Applied Science and Technology Index
Chemical Publications

Dictionary of Scientific Terms
Guide to the History of Science
Guide to the Literature of Chemistry
Harper's Encyclopedia of Science
Hutchinson's Technical and Scientific
    Encyclopedia
Library Guide for the Chemist
Quarterly Cumulative Index Medicus
Thorpe's Dictionary of Applied
    Chemistry
Space Encyclopedia
Van Nostrand's Scientific Encyclopedia

SOCIAL SCIENCE

Encyclopedia of the Social Sciences
Reader's Guide to the Social Sciences
Social Work Yearbook
World List of Social Science
    Periodicals

SPORTS

The Encyclopedia of Sports

CHAPTER 14

THE MECHANICS
OF THE PAPER

When you have finished the rough draft(s) of your term paper and are ready to type it, you will need to consider some of the mechanics—footnotes, bibliography, etc.—of working up the final copy.

Some schools have their own rules on term paper mechanics and issue a pamphlet or mimeographed sheet on the form they want you to follow. Others leave you to your own devices, subject to what you are able to find in composition books and guides. There are still some ground rules on term paper mechanics, however, that you will find in any guide.

The instructions here are for the traditionally *typed* term paper. If you decide to use a computer program that sets your work like a "printed" page, contact your instructor *immediately* about rules for this kind of format; better to be safe than sorry.

For one thing, typewriter ribbons must be blue or black. There must be no typing in reds or other vivid hues even if your purpose is to accentuate something in the paper. Your writing itself should carry the burden of emphasis.

Paper should be the 8½ × 11-inch size unlined typing paper. You can get it at virtually any drug, dime, stationery, or book store. It need not be an expensive stock although some students like it to be heavy enough not to show erasures. If you want to make carbons of your paper, get some thin "second sheets." Be sure to check the carbon paper before you begin typing each page, to see if it is inserted properly. There's nothing quite so irritating as to have to retype an entire page just because the carbon was in backward and everything is reprinted on the reverse side of the master copy.

What should your form look like on the term paper?

Your form depends on which of the half-dozen term paper styles are in use at your school or even in your class. The traditional form is emphasized heavily in this book; if your style uses other forms, you still will have a full backup for your citations. In some universities and a few high schools, students have been chagrined to find that they may have to master a different form in different classes. One student recently found that she had one instructor who wanted a term paper done in the traditional form, one demanded his term papers be done in *MLA style*; and a third insisted she use *APA style*.

Indeed, if traditional form is *not* the requirement, you may be relieved at not having to reserve room at a page's bottom for a footnote (as well as not doing all the switching to single spacing and underlining) and at not having to do a run-through of the Latin terms when repeatedly citing a same reference.

To figure out the form, look at the way you are asked to cite your sources in the term paper itself; second, check the bibliography style (MLA calls it *works consulted* and APA calls it *references*).

In APA style, your content citations will look like this:

> Monroe (1975) explained the situation in his remark about the poor: "Loud noises and violence make life for the fortunate people in the community insecure and dangerous" (p. 106). Many agree (Grim, 1981).

In MLA style, however, a citation looks like this:

> He took meticulous care to underscore his artistic agonies to craft *The Scarlet Letter* (Wade 140). The economy of words is seen in, "The rope did not work." (Voltaire, Aldington, 120).

Note the differences in placement of parentheses and the use of commas and periods. Let's now get into that traditional form for a term paper's mechanics.

The examples on the next five pages will show you how to do a title page, a table of contents, and the first page of your paper. Two examples of title pages are shown, both very popular styles, although your instructor may have a specific form to be followed. If you've received no instructions from him, use one of these shown here. Both carry all the important information commonly required of a student.

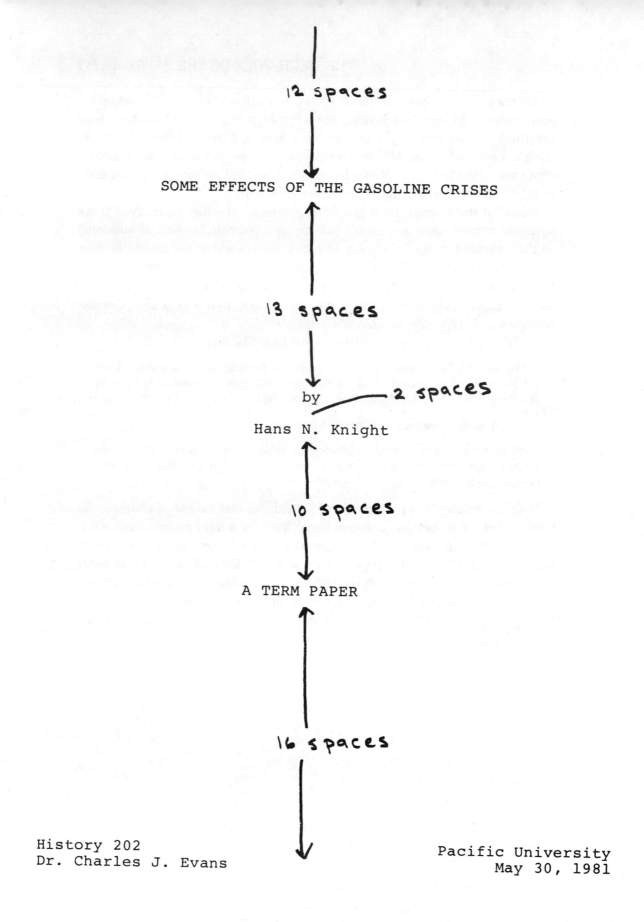

12 spaces

SOME EFFECTS OF THE GASOLINE CRISES

13 spaces

by ⟶ 2 spaces

Hans N. Knight

10 spaces

A TERM PAPER

16 spaces

History 202
Dr. Charles J. Evans

Pacific University
May 30, 1981

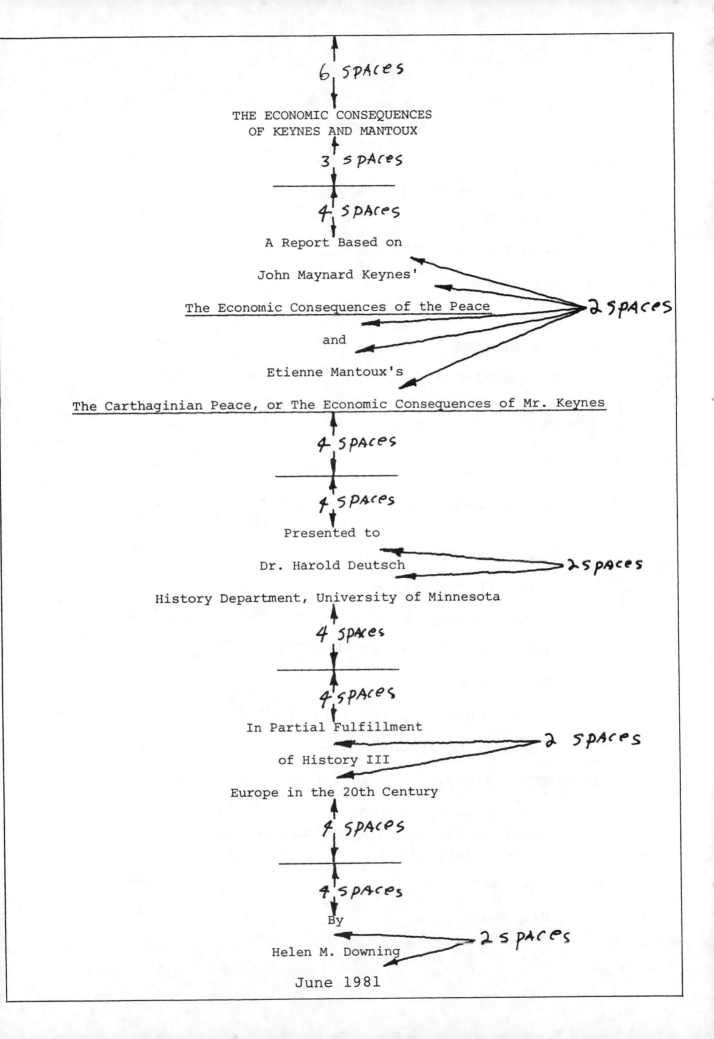

6 spaces

THE ECONOMIC CONSEQUENCES
OF KEYNES AND MANTOUX

3 spaces

4 spaces

A Report Based on

John Maynard Keynes'

The Economic Consequences of the Peace

and

Etienne Mantoux's

The Carthaginian Peace, or The Economic Consequences of Mr. Keynes

2 spaces

4 spaces

4 spaces

Presented to

Dr. Harold Deutsch

2 spaces

History Department, University of Minnesota

4 spaces

4 spaces

In Partial Fulfillment

2 spaces

of History III

Europe in the 20th Century

4 spaces

4 spaces

By

Helen M. Downing

2 spaces

June 1981

TABLE OF CONTENTS

A CRITIQUE OF THE PHILOSOPHY OF LETTING GO

When management consultant Garry Kinder spoke to insurance executives recently, one rule offered was to set mutual guidelines with employees. No fire under the feet. Just trust that a self-starting, resourceful agent needs no checkrein.[1] Add to this rule the comment from economist James Betteridge: "When you take responsibility away from someone, you intrude into his dignity and pride of accomplishment."[2] Or the words of a California banking official: "I do all the footwork in my daily duties, but I leave the results to God."[3]

All were talking about the same thing: the philosophy of letting go.

It's a terrifying, yet profound, idea that enriches work and living, making it efficient, easy, and totally enjoyable. It means to resign as Overseer of the Universe. We become more resourceful, energetic, and creative. We work harder. Michelangelo did the Sistine Chapel frescoes by papal fiat, but the magnificent work itself was left to him.

Letting go runs counter to the prevailing philosophy that "we are the masters of our fates," able to control people and even ice storms.

The rest of Nature lets go all the time. Rivers shift courses

---

[1]Garry Kinder, speech before American Council of Life Insurance, February 12, 1979, Dallas.

[2]James R. Betteridge, Productivity Today, Los Angeles, Argosy Publishers, 1978, p. 404.

[3]Jerald S. Stimson, "Religion in Business, " Business Week, Vol. 107, 1974, p. 66.

Gösta Berling flits like the mystical wraith he is through one adventure to another, each with some religious overtones, unlike Ibsen's famed Peer Gynt. The world of the fanciful seems to exude out of several Scandinavian writers of poetry, prose, and drama in much the same way the reader sees it in reading extensive passages of Lagerlof. She is said to have preferred this manner of prose since it enabled her to use the lore central to a Northland background.[1] Trolls, curses, midnight rides with the Devil---guised as bears, wolves, inebriates, bon vivants, etc.---abound in this work.

The similarities in Ibsen's Peer Gynt are particularly striking as when Solveig declares her love for Peer. She says simply "I will wait for you."[2] Lagerlof has the Countess and the Major's wife weeping and declaring utter devotion in almost simultaneous action midway through the fourth episode.[3]

Such a theme as she sets up is explained possibly by Ole Dragseth in his massive work on Scandinavian themes in literature. He attributed this to a certain ideé fixe in the Nordic character, declaring that the long, dark nights had much to do with the emphasis on the supernatural.[4] Introspection, he wrote, is far more characteristic of the Scandinavian in such a climate than almost any other part of the world. He found that the Germans also were capable of such introspection, but they stopped short of the dependence upon symbolism and myth and concentrated on the here and the now---with the exception of some writers. Thus, such literature from the Far North does have the brooding quality hardly seen in Lampedusa or Baroja to the South.

---

[1] "Lagerlof, Selma," Encyclopaedia Britannica, (Chicago 1964), XIX, p. 713.
[2] Henrik Ibsen, Peer Gynt, translated by Una Ellis-Fermor, The Master Builder and Other Plays, Middlesex, England, Penguin Book, Ltd., 1958, p. 315.
[3] Selma Lagerlof, The Story of Gösta Berling, translated by Robert Bly, New York, The New American Library, 1962, p. 205.
[4] Ole Dragseth, Scandinavian Literature, New York, Jackson and Associates, 1954, p. 113.

The title page examples show you not only what letters must be capitalized, but the actual spacing between lines. On most typewriters there are about six single-spaced lines to an inch. In the second example, the divider rule lines are also counted out for you.

The first page of a term paper, like all other pages, is typed on only *one* side. There is no need to be stingy with paper on a major work. That first page also has no page number in the upper right corner, but it is counted as the first page. The next page does carry the number *2* in the upper right corner. The impression of space and roominess should be given on that first page. That is why the spacings are so generous above and below the capitalized and underlined title.

What about the other margins?

The left side of the page must have a margin that is at least 1½ inches wide. You need room to put the finished paper in a term paper binder or to staple it. The right and bottom sides of the page should carry 1-inch margins. Note that the bottom must have that 1-inch margin *after* the footnotes are all in. If you're afraid you might overrun the bottom margin, put in a faint pencil mark so that you won't exceed that 1-inch point. If you know you're going to have a lot of footnotes on one page, figure the bottom margin and then consider that most footnotes run at least two typewritten lines apiece if the citation is single-spaced.

The second and subsequent pages of a term paper allow a 1-inch margin at the top. The left, bottom and right margins are all the same as for the first page. The pages are numbered with consideration given to that top and right margin allowance of one inch.

If you decide to use a computer's word-processing program, do *not* "justify" the lines as is done on this printed page. (*Justify* means all lines end at the same space.) In typed copy, it means extraordinary readability problems for your instructor because of the wide spacing between words.

Double-space the body text of your paper. There is not so much rigidity of rules where footnotes are concerned. Some instructors like double spacing between citations with the citations themselves single-spaced. Some teachers prefer single spacing throughout footnotes. The examples shown have the single-spaced form.

We have purposely said nothing here about prefaces, forewords, dedications, lists of illustrations, and the like, because the chances are that you'll not be involved with these unless you're doing some kind of advanced work on the graduate level. The average term paper is not long enough to require such treatment. A guide to thesis work should give you help if you do intend to use such materials, however.

Use Arabic numbers (1,2,3, etc.) for page numberings, and don't use any other embellishments such as periods, circles, parentheses, brackets or other decorative motifs. They take time to do.

You don't have to pack a page solid with writing. If you see that you'll have a lot of footnotes for one page, you might have room for only one short paragraph for that page. That's fine. The rest of the page will be devoted to footnotes. Always feel you have plenty of paper and need not crowd the page. This is true only in the case of having many footnotes for one page. Otherwise, work down to the one-inch bottom margin of the page.

Ideally, writers do not split paragraphs in manuscript work from page to page. They would rather end up short on one page than to divide the paragraph with the second half placed on the next page. They reason that things are easier to understand that way. But this is a fine point. If you break a paragraph from page to page, try to have at least two sentences for the page that gets the balance of the paragraph.

Watch the breaks of words from line to line. No word should be broken from page to page. Short words such as *an* or *oh* should never be split. If you see a word is going to be too long for a line, begin the long word on the next line. Don't worry about the line above looking forlornly short. If you must break words, break them by syllables and be sure to put a hyphen where it belongs. If you're not certain about how to syllabicate, consult a dictionary.

The cover binder of your paper may be prescribed by your instructor. If it isn't, there's no reason why you need to buy an expensive thesis binder. You can find covers at little cost in many drug stores, stationery stores, or the student store. It is well not to construct your own binder, incidentally, even though you may be handy with wood or construction paper, and paints. Such cover binders might be welcomed in grade school, but that is not the case in upper-division work. The concentration of efforts should be on the content of the term paper, not on an artfully contrived cover.

Handling Quotations and Excerpts

Direct quotations and excerpts for term papers should never be too long, surely no longer than one short paragraph or it might appear that you don't have much judgment when it comes to selecting the important portion from your sources.

In quoting directly, you must copy the material *exactly* from its source. Don't doctor or twist words and sentences because they don't quite illustrate the point you are making. If the source is learned sounding or ungrammatical, you still must quote with exactness.

Here are some tips for the average use of quotations and excerpts:

Omitting Part of a Quotation

You might want to leave out words or entire passages in a direct quotation. Perhaps the entire portion of your source is unnecessary to convey your point. If this is the case, use ellipsis periods. The word *ellipsis* is Greek for "to fall short" or to leave out something.

If you want to leave out *part of a sentence*, use three spaced periods (. . .). It works this way:

> Four score and seven years ago, our fathers brought forth . . . a new nation, conceived in Liberty, and dedicated to the proposition that all . . . are created equal.

To leave out *whole sentences*, use four ellipses (. . . .) as in the next example:

Now we are engaged in a great civil war. . . . The world will little note, nor long remember what we say here, but it can never forget what they did here.

To omit *entire paragraphs,* use a centered line of three periods between the paragraphs:

He had never once looked at me. He stood with his back to the fire, which set off the herculean breadth of his shoulders. His face was dark and expressive; his underjaw squarely formed, and remarkably heavy. I was struck with his remarkable likeness to a Gorilla.

. . .

I looked up; he had already forgotten my presence, and was engaged in pulling off his boots and coat. This done, he sank down in an arm-chair before the fire, and ran the poker wearily through his hair. I could not help pitying him.

Using Quotation Marks, Long and Short Excerpts

Suppose the excerpt involves only a half-dozen words. If so, put them *in the paragraph you are writing* and include quotation marks around the excerpt. A short quote looks like this:

Who can forget his reminder that "going home is pain"?[3]

If the quotation is longer than a half-dozen words, use a colon before the quote and *still* include it in the paragraph you are writing. This is shown below:

One can see this with Voltaire's famous remark: "I do not agree with what you say, but I will defend to the death your right to say it."[24]

When you are quoting an *entire paragraph* or a *lengthy* sentence, indent the passage on *both* sides to set it off from the text of your term paper. Such a long quote, without quotation marks (since the indentations show that it is an excerpt), is usually handled this way:

Juan worked out all the important actions very skillfully, paying little attention to details. His friends suspected he was an anti-christ. He was too thoughtful, too secretive, too occupied with writing. As for his enemies, they thought him rather stupid and stolid. Only his mother knew what went on inside his soul.[2]

The excerpt above is single spaced. It is indented from the rest of the text.

Using Poetry Excerpts

Special problems often arise when students use poetry in term papers. One thing is essential in the use of such sources: you must quote *exactly.* With many modern poets using typographical devices (e.g., indentations, noncapitalized letters, no punctuation, etc.), this is especially important. Some poets are aiming for visual as well as aural effects.

If the selection you use has only one or two lines and you want to put it in the paragraph that describes it, use quotes and slash mark (/) where the poet breaks the lines, like this:

The poet put it well when he wrote that "I have a rendezvous with Death/ At some . . . barricade."[6]

If you're including more than a couple of lines, set them up with an introductory line, then break to a new paragraph. Break the poet's lines, of course, just where he breaks them. The quotation would look like this:

Donne showed this same spirit of defiance when he wrote these lines in "Death":

Death, be not proud, though some have called thee
Mighty and dreadful, for thou art not so;
For those whom thou think'st thou dost overthrow
Die not, poor Death; nor yet canst thou kill me.[3]

What should you do when the line of poetry is far longer than your typewriter margins for excerpts? Obviously, you will have to break lines. Be careful that you indent perhaps 10 spaces, for poets often use indentations as part of their thought or technique. True, much poetry includes a capital on the first letter of a line, indicating a separate line, but in modern poetry the writer may not use this traditional typographic device. So watch out.

Here's how to break lengthy lines:

Now as I was young and easy under
                           the apple boughs
About the lilting house and happy as
                           the grass was green,

Or

With floods of the yellow gold of the
            gorgeous, indolent, sink-
            ing sun, burning, expand-
            ing the air
With the fresh sweet herbage underfoot,
            and the pale green leaves
            of the trees prolific,

Maybe you'll want to omit some stanzas of the poem you're using. To do this, show the omissions by centering asterisks as is shown here:

Come, fill the Cup, and in the fire of Spring
Your Winter-Garment of Repentance fling;
    The Bird of Time has but a little way
To flutter—and the Bird is on the Wing.

*   *   *   *

Some for the Glories of This World; and some
Sigh for the Prophet's Paradise to come;
    Ah, take the Cash, and let the Credit go,
Nor heed the rumble of a distant Drum![4]

The example above shows how important it is to put capital letters where the poet uses them since some use a word as a personification. Equally, indented lines sometimes indicate suspended thoughts. If the poet uses underlinings, you must follow suit. If he uses strange indentations, you do it too as with this poem:

see
the fiery windmills
            turning,
                    churning,
                            whirling,
                                    swirling,
                                            shriek-
ing,
creak-
ing
                    on
the hill[3]

Using Dialogue from Plays

Quoting dialogue or other material from dramatic literature also requires scrupulous attention to exactness. A short quote would look like this within a paragraph of textual material:

Hamlet shows this attitude with his remark that "there's a special providence in the fall of a sparrow."[3]

A longer quotation would have the introductory line and resemble the next example:

Gertrude is shown to be afraid not for Hamlet's sanity, but for her very life in the scene at the end of the third act:

QUEEN: What wilt thou do? thou wilt not murder me? Help, help, ho!

* * * *

HAMLET: How now! a rat? Dead, for a ducat, dead!

POLONIUS: O, I am slain!

QUEEN: O me, what hast thou done?

HAMLET: Nay, I know not: Is it the king?

QUEEN: O, what a rash and bloody deed is this!

HAMLET: A bloody deed! almost as bad, good mother, as kill a king, and marry with his brother.

QUEEN: As kill a king![1]

If blocking instructions make the point needed, handle your excerpt this way:

The playwright couples important action with dialogue in many places such as this important scene:

JOHNSON: I cannot do it. (*He slams his right fist into the wall in futility. Raina comes toward him, but halts at the table and grips the chair.*)

RAINA: You will have to do it.

JOHNSON: I . . . All right. (*He moves behind her, his hands gripping her neck. She struggles briefly but slumps against him. He lets her fall to the floor. She is quite dead.*)[2]

Using "Sic"

The word *sic* is Latin and means something has been copied exactly from the original with all the mistakes. It is placed in brackets *after* the expression that may be misspelled, ungrammatical, of archaic language, or untrue. Used, it looks like this:

When I am going hoame [sic] tomorrow.[5]

Using Brackets

Many authors themselves use parentheses in the source materials you may be quoting. For you to do it also would only confuse the reader of your term paper. You yourself should use brackets around any comments or clarifying points you want to make with excerpts. This may clear up a misunderstanding that the author might have created as with this example:

They [the Ministry of Agriculture] considered it necessary to issue a warning of the hazard of going into [arsenic] sprayed fields, but the warning was not understood by them [the livestock, wild animals and birds], and reports of poisoned cattle were received with monotonous regularity.[2]

Footnotes

Contrary to what you may have heard, there is nothing hard about doing footnotes correctly. Briefly, they involve *notes* of acknowledgment to your source material and are placed at the *foot* of the page where they are used.

Study the next page carefully and you will see how easy they are to put together. Be sure you check the text also for the identifying number.

Libraries and More Effective Schools

This need already has been reported by Mrs. Stickney and the state committees fairly recently.[1] It was not until Professor Davies investigated and pointed up the discrepancies,[2] however, that action was taken. He indicated there were more reviews and critiques of sources than there were the actual sources in the Teachers' College library and called the whole situation "lamentable" so far as the student body's education was concerned.[3]

That some need other than stack room or work space is essential to the construction of the modern high school library has been singled out also as one of the distinct shortcomings of such a system as that in New York state.[4] There, the necessary 10-books-per-pupil ratio[5] is easily reconciled with the Average Daily Attendance criteria in an administration office. But as Mrs. Stickney has indicated repeatedly in her monograph, there must be other considerations. She suggests that such considerations involve financing, departmental needs, recommendations by national and state groups, new architectural designs, climatic conditions, the community's bonding strength, and greater public knowledge about what is being done.[6]

The work done in encyclopedia references, particularly those akin to one field, has indicated the needs that must be met in the More Effective Schools programming.[7] Even a reference source to cover current events does show the need of some kind of restudy of the program, as Kitchener has repeatedly demanded.[8]

---

[1] Lorraine Stickney, "Planning New Libraries," Saturday Review, Vol. CCV (October 1967), p. 52.

[2] Robert Davies, Liberals and Libraries, London, Oxford University Press, 1970, p. 101.

[3] Ibid., p. 230.

[4] Stickney, loc. cit.

[5] Stickney, op. cit., p. 795.

[6] Stickney, passim.

[7] "Libraries," Encyclopaedia Britannica (Chicago, 1964), IX, p. 201.

[8] "Judgment at the Card Catalog," Time, Vol. 90, December 22, 1969, p. 33.

The example shown includes the three most common types of sources—books, magazines, and encyclopedias—as well as some footnote shortcuts—the *ibid.*, *op. cit.*, *loc. cit.* and *passim*.

When you begin your footnote inclusion, pay attention to this sample page and follow the form exactly, right down to the indentations, commas, underlinings, and periods. Your note cards should be set up like a footnote entry anyway, saving you a lot of time and effort when you get this far in your term paper.

As has been said, sources must be acknowledged on everything but commonplaces or everyday truths ("it is sweet to do nothing and sweeter still to rest afterward"). All you do is to put numbers where your sources are used in your writing and match them at the bottom of the page with the full-dress citation of those sources. The numbers are in consecutive order.

The source's number is slightly *raised* from the rest of the line. It is done this way so that the footnote number will not interfere with the passage too much, and also so that it will not cause confusion. You could see that if a number were put on the exact same line of the text, a reader might think the number was part of the context of the material. So put numbers in the body text *exactly* as you see them on the sample page.

When you get ready to add the footnotes to the bottom of the page, again follow the example shown here. There is a 15-spaced rule line fencing off text from footnotes that must be in your paper. The numbers in the footnotes must be raised slightly also. Indentations must be followed. Commas must be used to separate authors, titles, publishers, dates, cities, and pages. And periods must end each citation. All of this is done for clarity. If you like, consider footnote citations to be sentences which must be punctuated. Although single spacing is easy to understand within the lines of a single citation, the material is easier to read if you double-space between citations.

Don't forget to underline the titles of magazines, books, pamphlets, and encyclopedias or to put quotes around magazine articles and encyclopedia entries.

While some teachers and editors simply use the name of an author and page (e.g., Stickney, p. 42), few universities seem to allow such informality where footnotes are concerned. They prefer students to use the traditional Latin terms for the four expressions of footnote shortcuts. These terms are *ibid.*, *loc. cit.*, *op. cit.*, and *passim*. If it were not for these words, you would find yourself wearily typing the same citation with all its punctuation, underlinings, and indentations many, many times per page.

Ibid.

The expression *ibid.* is an abbreviation for the Latin *ibidem* which means "in the same place." You will use *ibid.* when you are going to include a footnote for the same source, if it is identical, used directly *above* it. Follow the example right down to the capital *I*, the period after the *d*, and the comma after the period, and then add the page number and a period. The *ibid.*

should be underlined since it stands for the title of a magazine, book, or other source material.

Loc. Cit.

Loc. cit. stands for the Latin *loco citato* and means "in the place referred to." It is used when the student finds he has to repeat a citation already on the page, but discovers that he has an intervening citation from another source. Check the sample page again to see how this is done. The Stickney citation, for example, is interrupted by a citation from the Davies book and, then, by an *ibid.* to the Davies work. When you use *loc. cit.*, you won't need a page number with it since it is presumed the material came from the *same* page as the original citation on the page. If you're going to be using *loc. cit.*, set it up exactly as it's done in the sample.

Op. Cit.

The *op. cit.* footnote citation is Latin for *opere citato* and means "in the work cited." This shortcut expression performs much the same function as *loc. cit.* except that it refers to a *different* page from the orginial citation. Again, if you use *op. cit.*, see to it that you have the expression underlined, proper punctuation, and page.

Passim

This Latin expression, meaning "everywhere" or "throughout," is not used too often, but when it is, it means that the student is citing the source as a whole, giving the overall flavor or tenor of the material. If he is trying to say that a novel is gothic but does not want to include every excerpt that proves it, he will use *passim* to indicate that the overall atmosphere of the book has given him his impression.

Some teachers might want an English form of these shortcut Latin words, just as they might have a rule about footnote numbers running consecutively from 1 to 50 or more. Some teachers might even want all footnotes on separate pages at the *end* of the term paper so the text will not be interrupted constantly by footnote references. But if you're given no special footnote rules by your instructor, use these traditional forms. They're in vogue in most high schools and colleges throughout the country.

One special reminder about using the shortcut Latin terms: your instructor might not let you use them unless the *first mention* of the source on which they are based is included on the page where you use them. He may feel that clarity is of first importance, and that to have to go back several pages to hunt out what the *ibid.* or *op. cit.* alludes to does not make for clear comprehension. This makes sense, but it also means some work on your part.

It has been said that the footnote instructions and sample shown here will work for most citations. There are many special situations as with pamphlets, newspapers, poetry, essays, speeches, law cases, and the like that have a particular footnote form. The main ones germane to most high school and college term papers are the following:

BOOKS BY TWO OR MORE AUTHORS

[1] Stokely Carmichael and Charles V. Hamilton, *Black Power: The Politics of Liberation in America,* New York, Random House, 1967, p. 90.

BOOKS WITH TRANSLATORS

[2] Jaroslav Hasek, *The Good Soldier: Schweik,* translated by Paul Selver, New York, The New American Library, 1963, p. 43.

BOOKS IN A MULTI-VOLUMED SET

[3] Winston S. Churchill, *Their Finest Hour,* Vol. II of *The Second World War,* Boston, Houghton Mifflin Company, 1949, p. 337.

[1] James Boswell, *The Life of Samuel Johnson,* Vol. III, New York, The Heritage Press, 1963, p. 213.

BOOKS IN A MULTI-VOLUMED SET WITH TRANSLATOR

[1] Victor Hugo, *Les Miserables,* Vol. I, translated by Sir Lascelles Wraxall, New York, Thomas Nelson and Sons, 1893, p. 232.

A SECTION FROM AN ANTHOLOGY

[6] Fay Gillis Wells, "Mata Hari for a Day," *Eye Witness,* New York, Alliance Book Corporation, 1940, p. 237.

MAGAZINE ARTICLES BY TWO OR MORE AUTHORS

[1] George Hishmeh, Francis Karam, Hikmat Sabah and Alice Williams, "Translating for the Newspapers," *The Overseas Press Club Journal,* Vol. 34 (June 1964), p. 791.

MAGAZINE ARTICLE WITH TRANSLATOR

[3] Marit Lindemark, "The Transition from Askim to Los Angeles," translated by John Braaten, *Elite,* Vol. XXXII (April 2, 1966), p. 952.

PLAYS

[1] Eugene O'Neill, *Strange Interlude, O'Neill's Ten Best,* Boston, Vanity Press, 1960, p. 14.

PLAYS WITH TRANSLATOR

[4] Moliere, *Tartuffe,* translated by Bennett Cerf, *Plays by Moliere,* New York, Modern Library, 1950, p. 120.

PLAYS IN A MULTI-VOLUMED SET

[1] George Bernard Shaw, *The Millionairess, Complete Plays With Prefaces,* Vol. VI, New York, Dodd, Mead & Company, 1963, p. 181.

POEMS

[2] Henry Wadsworth Longfellow, "Chaucer," *The Mentor Book of Major American Poets,* New York, The New American Library, 1962, p. 80.

POEMS IN A MULTI-VOLUMED SET

[5] Rudyard Kipling, "Gunga Din," *Kipling,* Vol. VI, New York, P. F. Collier & Son Corporation, 1923, p. 18.

POEMS WITH TRANSLATOR

[1] Boris Pasternak, "Summer Day," *Poems,* translated by Eugene Kayden, Ann Arbor, Michigan, The University of Michigan Press, 1959, p. 125.

POEMS IN A MULTI-VOLUMED SET WITH TRANSLATOR

[1] Johann Wolfgang von Goethe, "Wanderers Nachtlied," Vol. V of *Goethe's Complete Works,* translated by Toby LaForge, Forest Grove, Pacific University Press, 1967, p. 94.

EPIC POEMS

[4] Henry Wadsworth Longfellow, *Evangeline, Longfellow's Poetry*, New York, Downing Press, 1960, p. 34.

EPIC POEMS WITH TRANSLATOR

[2] Johann Wolfgang von Goethe, *Faust,* translated by Bayard Taylor, New York, The Modern Library, 1950, p. 161.

ESSAYS

[4] Sir Francis Bacon, "Of Studies," *Great Essays,* New York, Washington Square Press, 1960, p. 34.

ESSAYS WITH TRANSLATOR

[1] Arthur Schopenhauer, "Of Women," *Essays of Schopenhauer,* translated by T. Bailey Saunders, New York, Willey Book Company, 1929, p. 75.

SHORT STORIES

[34] O Henry, "The Gift of the Magi," *The Pocket Book of O Henry Stories,* New York, Pocket Books, Inc., 1956, p. 4.

SHORT STORIES WITH TRANSLATOR

[11] Alexander Pushkin, "The Queen of Spades," translated by Ethel O. Bronstein, *Pushkin,* New York, Dell Publishing Co., Inc., 1961, p. 196.

THE BIBLE

[1] *Job* 7:19.

NEWSPAPER STORIES

[9] The New York *Times,* August 21, 1966, Sec. III, p. 12, col. 4.

LETTERS TO THE EDITOR

[1] Hugh Martin, "Letters to the Editor," The Washington *Post,* CVI (August 21, 1967), Sec. A., p. 10.

[2] Eric Bentley, "Future of German," in "Correspondence," *The New Republic,* Vol. 157 (November 25, 1967), p. 38.

PAMPHLETS, GOVERNMENT BULLETINS, BROADSIDES

[3] John Kenneth Galbraith, *How to Get Out of Vietnam,* New York, The New American Library, 1967, p. 20.

[9] *National Parks,* Washington, D.C., U.S. Government Printing Office, August 1966, p. 5.

LAW CASES

[5] Hannegan v. Esquire, 327 U.S. 146,148 (1946).

A PERSONAL LETTER

[1] Letter from Patricia A. Franks, July 14, 1959, p. 2.

AN INTERVIEW

[3] Interview with Sister Pauline Sumonka, Oklahoma City, Oklahoma, November 10, 1967.

A SPEECH

[4] Ronald M. Ross, "Interpreting the News From Vietnam," a speech to the National Press Club, Washington, D.C., September 1967.

The Bibliography

The bibliography for a term paper involves separate pages or a page at the very end of the work. It gives a listing of all the sources you *actually* used to put the project together. It shouldn't include all the false leads you ran down or citations from footnotes found in a source. There is no need to pad the bibliography if you've done an adequate amount of research work.

If your list of readings is long—over one page—sort out your sources according to categories for magazines, books, newspapers, and encyclopedias. If you use only enough sources to fill a full page—14 or less—alphabetize them. Even if you are categorizing sources by magazines, books, and the like, they must be alphabetized.

Check the next two pages carefully on how to do your own bibliography. The first example is for a short bibliography; the second is for a long one that is categorized.

Carmichael, Stokely and Hamilton, Charles V. Black Power: The Politics
of Liberation in America. New York, Random House,1967.

Churchill, Winston S. Their Finest Hour, Vol. II, The Second World War.
Boston, Houghton Mifflin Company, 1949.

Galbraith, John Kenneth. How to Get Out of Vietnam. New York, The New
American Library, 1967.

"Getting the Money," Pen Weekly, LX (July 1960), 45-70.

Hasek, Jaroslav. The Good Soldier: Schweik. Trans. Paul Selver. New
York, The New American Library, 1963.

Long, Stephen. Bold Trip. Boston, Merrymount Publisher, 1946.

                Equal Rights. New York, the Grove Press, 1948.

                The Human Soul in Transfiguration at Scarsdale and White
Plains, Los Angeles, The Humanist Company, 1950.

Minton, Claude R. He Who Dies That Others May Live. London, Oxford
University Press, 1932.

O'Neill, Eugene. Strange Interlude. O'Neill's Ten Best. Boston,
Heritage Press, 1960.

Overton, William S. "How Now is Tulsa Today?" The Tribune Magazine.
Vol. 15 (May 4, 1965), pp. 10-12.

                "Moving Day is Poverty Day." The Ransomer, Vol. 1
(August 21, 1969), pp. 201-11.

                "The Arkansas River Project." The Southwestern
Review, Vol. IX (September 1966), pp. 64-81.

Ross, Ronald M. "Interpreting the News from Vietnam." Speech to the
National Press Club, September 1967.

"Remagen Bridge." Encyclopaedia Britannica. 14th Edition. New York,
Encyclopaedia Britannica, Inc., 1929, XVIII, 14-15.

(General Reference Works)

Casates, Marjorie. "Bridges." Encyclopaedia Britannica, 20th Edition. New York, Encyclopaedia Britannica, Inc., 1947, II, 173.

"Medicine." Encyclopedia Americana, 25th Edition. New York, Encyclopedia Americana Co., 1954, XII, 45.

(Books)

Carmichael, Stokely and Hamilton, Charles V. Black Power: The Politics of Liberation in America. New York, Random House, 1967.

Hugo, Victor. Les Miserables. Trans. Sir Lascelles Wraxall. New York, Thomas Nelson and Sons, 1893.

Long, Stephen. Bold Trip. Boston, Merrymount Publisher, 1946.

The Human Soul in Transfiguration at Scarsdale and White Plains, Los Angeles, The Humanist Company, 1950.

Minton, Claude R. He Who Dies That Others May Live. London, Oxford University Press, 1932.

(Magazine Articles)

Hishmeh, George and Williams, Alice. "Translating for the Newspaper." The Overseas Journal, Vol. 34 (June 1964), pp. 791-3.

Kenworthy, E.W. "Eugene McCarthy at the Hustings." The New Republic, Vol. 157 (November 25, 1967), pp. 5-7.

"Many Thanks, General." The Nation, Vol. 205 (December 18, 1967), pp. 642-3.

Overton, William S. "How Now is Tulsa Today?" The Tribune Magazine. Vol. 15 (May 4, 1965), pp. 10-12.

"The Arkansas River Project." The Southwestern Review, Vol. IX (September 1966), pp. 64-81.

(Newspapers)

The Cincinnati Inquirer, January 20, 1956.

The New York Times. March 15, 1962.

The Wall Street Journal. October 19, 1930.

(Pamphlets)

Animal Industry. U.S. Government Printing Office. Washington, D.C. August 1965.

Galbraith, John Kenneth. How to Get Out of Vietnam. New York, The New American Library, 1967.

Van Eycthe, Nicholas B. The Holy Land. Jerusalem, Franciscan Printing Press, 1960.

The examples shown have *no* page numbers although it is obvious if you go beyond two pages for the bibliography that you will need to begin numbering the pages by small Roman numerals (ii, iii, iv, etc.). Notice the word *bibliography* is in caps and centered.

Each source, as is shown, is listed alphabetically with the author's name listed first. Where the author is unknown as sometimes happens with magazine articles, encyclopedia entries, pamphlets and the like, the alphabetizing is done according to the *first letter of the title*. The articles (*a, an* or *the*) do not count.

Follow the punctuation shown in the examples also. It is not the same as that found in footnote citations since periods instead of commas are used.

The page numbers of the citations are used only on magazine articles and encyclopedia citations. These are not just the pages where material was used but the *complete* page numbers for the *entire* article or entry.

Spacing rules should be evident and so should indentation margins. The indentations are the reverse of those for a footnote. The first line of a citation is flush with the left margin. The second line is indented five spaces. Single-space within each citation, but double-space between citations.

In the case of articles or books by the same author, omit the author's name after the first entry for him. Other material must be included, however.

TABLES, GRAPHS, AND OTHER ILLUSTRATIONS

Illustrations have accompanied written material since recorded history began. As our prehistoric forebears talked about danger or the weather, they either made descriptive gestures or drew pictures with a stick in the dirt. Whole civilizations have been revealed by pictographs on pottery, jewelry, walls, and other artifacts. Symbols like the cross, swastika, and hammer and sickle say volumes.

Some fields such as technology, the sciences, education, the government, and advertising rely heavily on illustrations to tell their stories. Stockholders may not read every word of an expensive, glossy annual report, but they pore over all the tables, graphs, pie charts, or diagrams to see how a company is doing.

Illustrations also give vital information in seconds for certain research papers in high schools and universities.

Computer software has eliminated a lot of the hard work in doing tables and graphs and other illustrations. Instead of the painstaking care required to draw by hand a bar graph with crosshatched and solid lines, students simply have to to dump their numerical data into a personal computer and out comes the illustration—professional looking and in a dazzling number of designs: a pie chart, bar graph, or polygraph of extraordinary creative skill. It may even be in color!

That's wonderful, but computerized illustrations generally are done only by students who can afford computers and expensive software programs or those who are attending well-off school systems that can furnish such expensive equipment. Too, even at major universities where computer laboratories are free and open 24 hours a day—and where software and hardware is state of the art— many students have found that the systems "crash" all too frequently; or worse, that to print out a graph (particularly in color) means that it holds up the printouts of other students—who may react with various degrees of hostility.

Too, there still are millions of students who either don't have access to a computer that can churn out such stunning illustrations, or don't know how to use a computer. If you're in this situation, know that your instructor certainly won't think less of your laborious pen and ink work than the work of the class "hacker" with the cyan and magenta trimmings.

In other words, the precepts for good illustrations contained throughout this chapter are just as apt for computer work as they are for freehand line drawings.

A thesis usually includes more illustrations than the ordinary research report. But if your paper has complicated sections, perhaps it would be clearer with an accompanying table, diagram, cutaway, or graph. There are also photographs, drawings, isometrics, maps, and so on. Be sure that illustrations are essential, however, and not a way of concealing a lack of content. A report needs "more matter, less art."

The following pages show you samples of everything from an appendix title page and lists of both tables and figures, to formats for illustrations when they occupy separate pages.

30 spaces

APPENDIX

7 spaces

LIST OF FIGURES

4 spaces

2 spaces

1¼"

7 spaces

LIST OF TABLES

4 spaces

2 spaces

1¼"

7 spaces

3 spaces

TABLE XX. SALES BY AGENCY, INDIVIDUAL
LIFE INSURANCE*
(000s OMITTED)

Agency (1)	Month		Last 12 Months	
	MDRT amount (2)	% to last year (3)	MDRT amount (4)	% to last year (5)
Park	$3,330	138%	$32,321	125%
Hopkins	2,935	172	21,289	109
Robbinsdale	3,149	139	20,274	76
Wayzata	2,784	83	16,976	105
Bloomingdale	1,490	313	14,840	98
St. George	2,010	96	12,624	110
Centerville	300	29	10,416	112
Martinsdale	928	75	9,844	113
Farmington	991	89	9,836	110
Northfield	901	103	8,384	100
Hamlin	1,299	118	8,363	100
Haupe	385	58	8,291	89
Fergus Falls	1,148	100	6,862	87
Lakeville	521	68	6,117	77
Albany	550	149	5,481	69
Vinsanto	538	171	5,469	120
Excelsior	303	21	5,264	114
Morton	580	82	5,046	127
Benton	186	28	4,900	86
Folger	415	169	4,021	123
Marysville	418	334	3,372	88
Hannibal	2,341	315	23,105	110
Vale	457	55	5,890	113
Company Totals	$28,207	108%	$250,478	108%

*Michael Pertschuk, Cost Disclosure Studies, Washington,
D.C., Federal Trade Commission, 1979, p. 543.

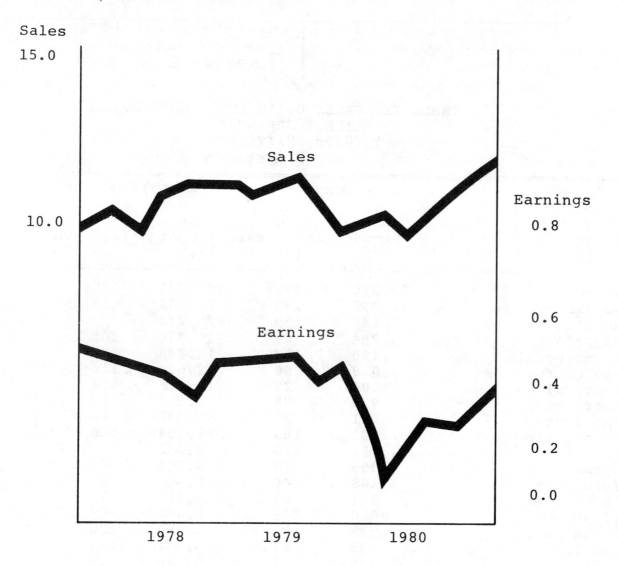

Figure 14.   Quarterly Sales and Earnings (Millions of Dollars)*

*Iberian Totaling Company, <u>1980 Annual Report</u>
Philadelphia, Iberian International Enterprises, 1980,p.8.
Used with permission.

In using illustrations, follow the rules used by all annual-report designers: 1) one large illustration makes a stronger point than several small ones, and 2) the right illustration must be chosen for the right point. If you're showing trends, for example, bar graphs traditionally convey the point best. Pie charts show how something is divided. Tabulations are suitable in tables. Flow charts depict cycles. Perhaps you'll need a diagram, map, or photograph.

Before you pick up pen or ruler, however, ask your instructor for directions. Fields such as mathematics have specific guidelines for graphic presentations of ordinates and abscissas, for example.

Materials

The paper will depend upon the illustration. Tables can be done on the same paper stock as the rest of the report. Graphs can be drawn on stock set up to various centimeter measurements, purchased in any stationery store. But be sure it can be photocopied; some blue graphing stock won't reproduce in black and white.

Fold-out illustrations generally are 8½ inches from top to bottom and are any width. Such illustrations are folded into the rest of the paper. Thesis writers should be aware that trimmer knives may sheer illustrations at the right-hand side of the manuscript if they're not tucked well inside the margin. You may need to buy large paper stock and cut it to the required measurements.

Black India ink and a set of mapping pens will give you different line widths, particularly good for bar graphs. Black felt pens are excellent if width is not a consideration in line drawings. Also, they don't smear. Circular illustrations such as flow charts will require a compass for consistency in diameters. Metal rulers are essential for straight-edge work. Pencil in preliminary sketches and erase with art gum after the ink work has been done.

Placement

Put each illustration as close as possible to its mention in the text. The text reference is:

> The usual cycle of turnover (Figure 19) is begun when the employee decides the job has no future.

If the illustration is small, put it on the same page where it's cited. If it's large, give it full-page treatment on the next page. Reference it this way:

> The usual cycle of turnover (Figure 10, page 18) is begun when the employee decides the job has no future.

If you mention the illustration elsewhere, use the same form of citation. Help the reader find the material with ease.

At a few schools, students are allowed to place illustrations directly across from the page where they are mentioned. Because reports are written on only one side of a page and this treatment means a reader will be confronted by a blank page (with the illustration on the back), indicate what's afoot by placing a centered message in the middle of the blank page:

Figure 20

Comparison of Annual Returns for
S & P 500 Stocks and Real Estate Properties

(Facing Page)

Numbering

Number illustrations consecutively. Tables require Roman numerals, but *all other* illustrations are marked "Figure 1," and so on. Capitalize the *F* in figure. If you have more than six illustrations, set up a page for a "List of Tables" or a "List of Illustrations" to follow the title page or table of contents. (See pp. 173-174.)

Page numbering itself follows a common-sense rule: Put it where you've numbered the rest of the pages in the report.

Now, if you've grouped the illustrations in an appendix, the pages should be numbered with small Roman numerals, centered, at the bottom.

Titles

An illustration's title explains clearly and briefly, like a newspaper headline, what the material covers. It's placed *above* a table, but *below* any other illustration. Titles for photographs are put on the mounting paper—not the photograph— *before* you mount the picture.

Titles for tables generally are centered and in all capital letters. If you are using both capital and small letters, however, capitalize the first letter of each word except articles (*a, an, the*) and short prepositions and conjunctions. Titles for all other kinds of illustrations also are centered and capitals and small letters are used, again with no capitalization for the types of words listed above. Neither tables nor figures use periods at the ends of titles, by the way, but they do follow punctuation usage elsewhere. A period follows the figure or table number.

Figure 10. Performance of "Seminar Fund," 1934–76,
Initial Investment $250, Adding $100 per Month

TABLE XII. PERCENTAGE YIELD NEEDED TO
MAINTAIN PURCHASING POWER

As shown, all titles are single-spaced and centered. If you are using fold-out illustrations, titles still must be centered with regard to the ultimate width of the page.

Avoid long titles because they detract from illustrations. If headline writers can boil down long stories into a few pithy words, so can you. Don't repeat material word for word from the text of the report. And don't use obvious expressions such as "This table shows . . ." or "This is a drawing of . . . ." Readers recognize that fact.

Spacing and Margins

Spacing is shown in the specimen pages (176-180). Margins depend always on leaving room for binding on the left-hand side of any report. If you plan to use a vertical illustration, leave room at the top for the binding area in the report. Don't run the risk of obscuring a title. In tabulations, space once between every five or ten figures. The result is easier to follow and looks inviting.

Footnotes

It's scholastically honest to credit sources if the illustrated material has been based on other people's work. If you've taken a poll, however, or originated the work, you'll not need footnotes.

Basically, the regulations for footnotes in reports apply. Put the original citation at the end of the title, the matching footnote at the bottom of the page. If the illustration itself is full of numbers and numbered footnotes prove confusing, use asterisks or daggers (doubling or tripling them, as needed):

TABLE III.   THE EFFECT OF A 5.2% INFLATION
RATE ON YOUR PURCHASING POWER**

Number of years (1)	Annual dividend (2)	Loss of purchasing power (3)	Adjusted purchasing power of dividend (4)	Effective yield (5)
5	$900	16%	$756	7.5%
10	900	40	540	5.4
15	900	53	423	4.2
20	900	64	324	3.2
25	900	72	252	2.5

**Venita Van Caspel, The New Money Dynamics, Reston, Va., Reston Publishing Company, Inc., 1978, p.59.

Figures

A sample page for a list of figures is shown on page 177.

As has been mentioned, titles go below the illustrations. They're centered and single-spaced. If you have a draftsman's or cartographer's neat penmanship, hand-letter words on your illustration. Most students prefer to type data, however, which means that you should do a practice set to ensure that there's room in the artwork to insert words. Keep in mind also that typing may mean errors. Allow for corrections.

Line/Curve Graphs

Line or curve graphs show patterns or compare two to five elements. One line can be solid; another can be dots. A line may be wider than its mate:

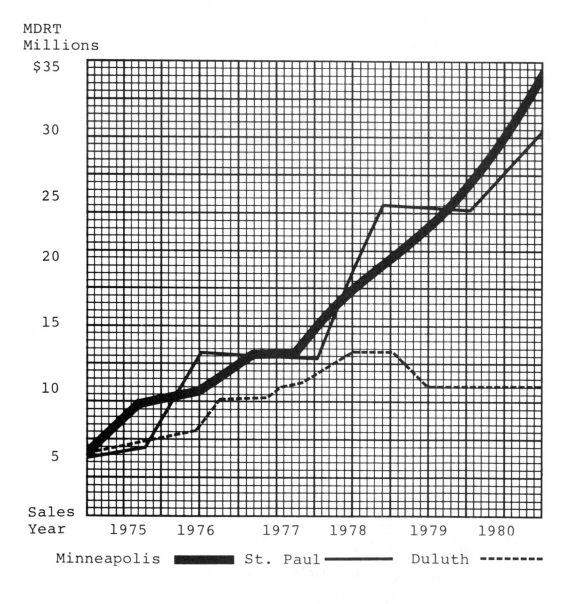

Figure 18.   Whole Life Production

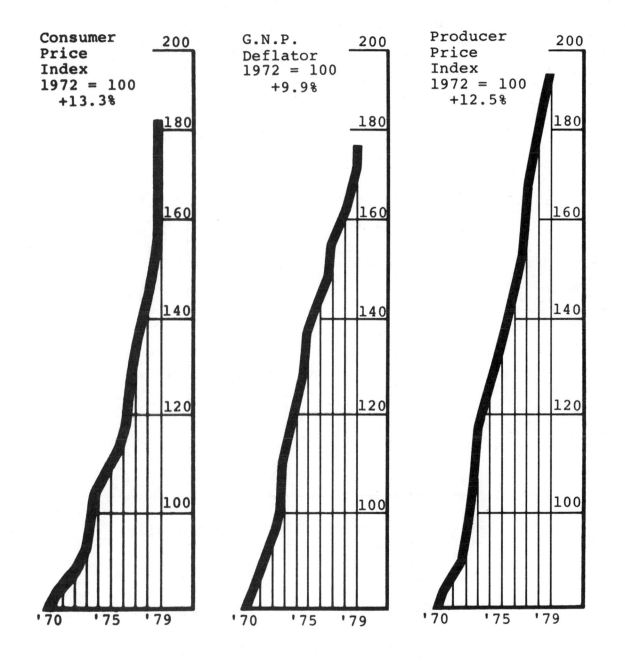

Figure 5. Measuring Inflation: Three Different Yardsticks*

*Idea for graph from Financial Federation Inc., used with permission

Bar Graphs

Bar graphs use horizontal or vertical lines for comparisons. Bars often are distinguished by making one wider than the other. Or one bar can be shaded; another made solid. Cross-hatching can be used. Sophisticated graphs have used more than one dimension:

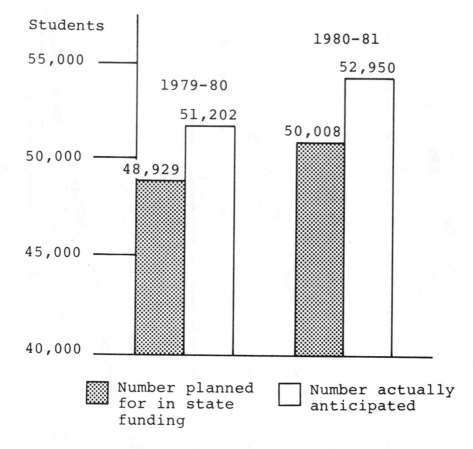

Figure 15. Oregon Community College Enrollment Increases

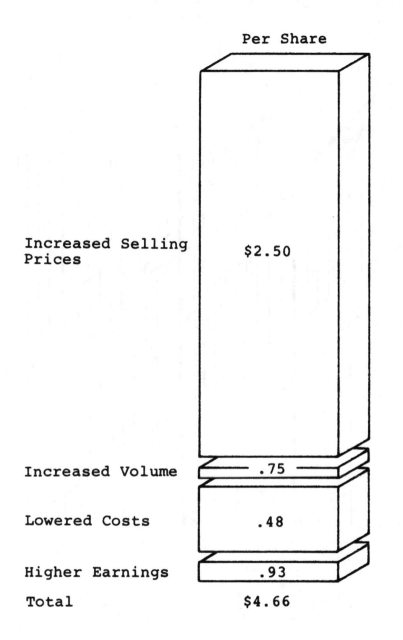

Figure 2. Major Factors That Increased 1974 Earnings from 1973*

*Form of graph from Scott Paper Company, <u>1974 Annual Report</u>, used by permission.

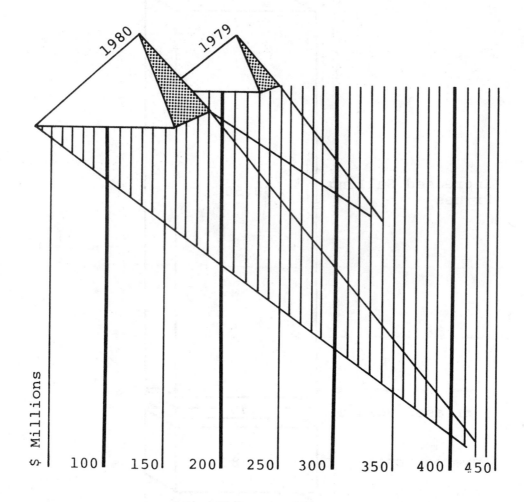

Figure 12.   Notes and Contracts Receivable*

*From United California Bank, <u>1975 Annual Report</u>, used by permission.

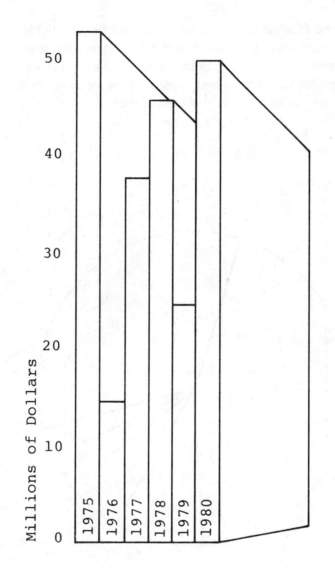

Table 14. Federal Home Loan Bank Borrowings at Year End*

*From Financial Federation, <u>1975 Annual Report</u>, used by permission.

Pie Charts

Pie charts are familiar to anyone who's learned how to divide. One caution: Don't use too many slices (no more than eight), lest you confuse the reader. Also, you'll need room to include words inside slices. Pies can be done in "color" (shadings, crosshatches, solids, and whites). Annual-report artists have offered new wrinkles on this old type of illustration, too:

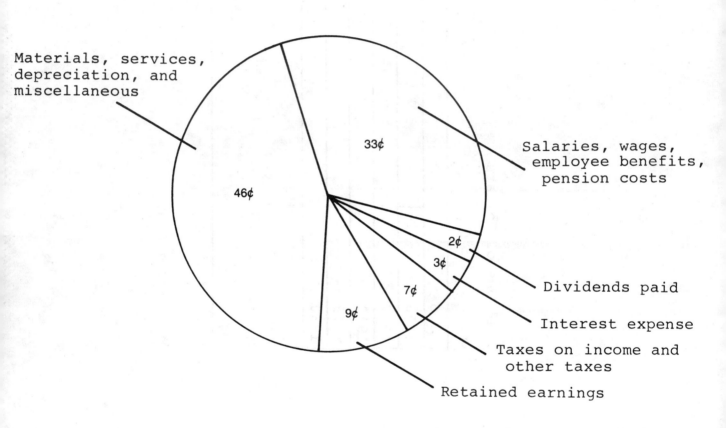

Figure 9. Where the Sales Dollar Went

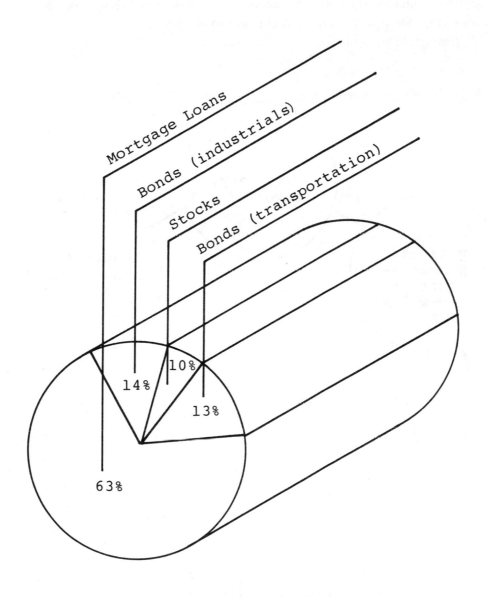

Figure 4.   Sources of Investment

Flow Charts

Flow charts are excellent to show sequences or cycles. Circles need to be large enough to contain information, yet small enough to fit the entire flow on one page. Arrows move the reader's eye from one area to another.

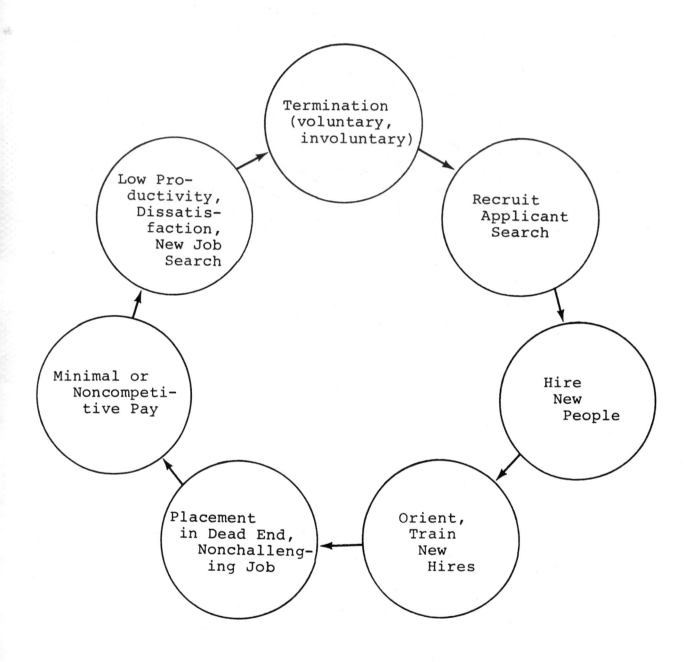

Figure 1.   The Warm-Body Syndrome

A variation on a flow chart is what's known in the business world as a chain-of-command chart. It looks like a family tree. Set in a pyramidal design, it has the key factor at the top, subordinate items at various levels below it:

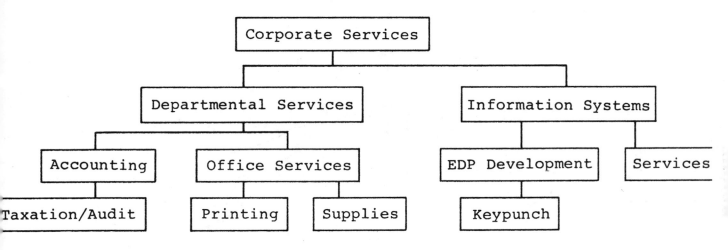

Figure 6. Chain of Command for the Corporate Services Division*

*From Standard Insurance Company of Oregon, 1980 Annual Report, used by permission.

Maps

Maps should be confined to the essentials. Don't add any places not mentioned in the report; you'll only confuse the reader. Again, solid or dotted lines can convey the message. So can arrows.

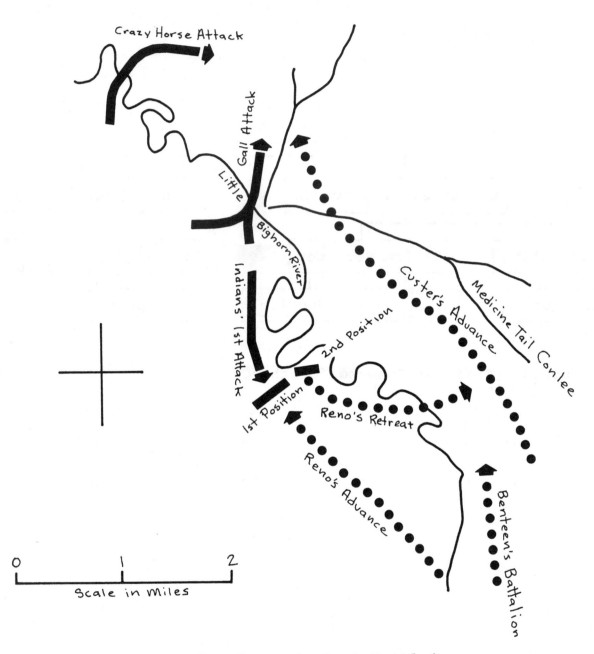

Figure 8. Custer's Last Battle*

*Courtesy of the National Park Service, 1969.

Other Illustrations

For all other illustrations, the principles are the same. Keep them simple, clear, and consistent with the format of the report. Check with your instructor on the requirements before you begin the work.

Tables

A sample page for a list of tables is shown on page 178.

A table should present only one fact or a series of *related* facts so that it is easy to understand.

The title is in capital letters and appears *above* the table, as has been mentioned. The number is in Roman numerals.

Once you move into tabulated material, however, you will use capital and small letters for columnar titles. Such titles should include only one word (two if they're small) to a line. They are single-spaced, and each line may be centered or all lines may be aligned at the left-hand side of the column. Capitalize the first letter of the first word, but don't use any other capitalization. If you are numbering the columns, center the numbers and enclose them in parentheses:

```
     Number                Number
       of                    of
    positive              negative
    responses             responses
      (3)                   (4)
```

What about tabulated numbers? Align them at the right, and put decimal points or commas directly under each other so readers can keep track of the statistics. If you're using a dollar sign, put it only before the first figure at the top of the column and then before the last figure when you do the totals. Temperature-degree and percentage marks are used only after the first figure:

MDRT amount	% to last year	Temperature for July 9
$3,330.00	138%	103
2,935.00	172	98
300.00	29	88
928.00	75	110
1,148.00	100	49
$8,641.00		

Suppose that a figure is missing in one of the tabulated columns? Use either a blank space or dots, *never zeros;* these confuse. If there are many omissions, you may use horizontal lines to prevent misunderstanding. Generally, horizontal

TABLE V. OFFICE SALARIES IN PACIFIC NORTHWEST

Monthly average	Seattle			Portland			Boise			Spokane		
	1979	1978	1977	1979	1978	1977	1979	1978	1977	1979	1978	1977
File clerk	$620	$542	$559	$623	$524		$637		$481	$589		$559
Accounting clerk	841	702	698	750	737		676	628	568	724		758
PBX	888	706	659	767	741		698	633	680			654
Typist/clerk	862	676	633	745	633		689	654	568	620		641
Secretary	901	828		845	776		810	789		758		
Keypunch oper.	771	715	646	715	732		676	602	555			
CRT operator	780	750		728	715		698			659		589

TABLE V. OFFICE SALARIES IN PACIFIC NORTHWEST

Monthly average	Seattle			Portland			Boise			Spokane		
	1979	1978	1977	1979	1978	1977	1979	1978	1977	1979	1978	1977
File clerk	$620	$542	$559	$623	$524		$637		$481	$589		$559
Accounting clerk	841	702	698	750	737		676	628	568	724		758
PBX operator	888	706	659	767	741		698	633	680			654
Typist/clerk	862	676	633	745	633		689	654	568	620		641
Secretary	901	828		845	776		810	789		758		
Keypunch oper.	771	715	646	715	732		676	602	555			
CRT operator	780	750		728	715		698			659		589

TABLE V. OFFICE SALARIES IN PACIFIC NORTHWEST

Monthly average	Seattle			Portland			Boise			Spokane		
	1979	1978	1977	1979	1978	1977	1979	1978	1977	1979	1978	1977
File clerk	$620	$542	$559	$623	$524	---	$637	---	$481	$589	---	$559
Accounting clerk	841	702	698	750	737	---	676	628	568	724	---	758
PBX operator	888	706	659	767	741	---	698	633	680	---	---	654
Typist/clerk	862	676	633	745	633	---	689	654	568	620	---	641
Secretary	901	828	---	845	776	---	810	789	---	758	---	---
Keypunch oper.	771	715	646	715	732	---	676	602	555	---	---	589
CRT oper.	780	750	---	728	715	---	698	---	---	659	---	---

lines are limited to the top of a column for headings and the bottom for conclusions or totals. Horizontal or vertical lines within columns make the already formidable appearance of tables even more forbidding. "Air" makes a table look inviting.

Double horizontal lines are a graphic technique for fencing off data. Single lines distinguish headings and statistics. See the table on page 196, which illustrates the various possibilities mentioned above.

If you're working with thousands or millions and the figures can be rounded off, you can save time and wear on the 0 key on the typewriter by indicating under the table's title that the zeros have been omitted:

TABLE V. SALES BY AGENCY
INDIVIDUAL LIFE INSURANCE TOTALS
(000s Omitted)

Should you need more than one page to complete a table, use the "continued" format. On subsequent pages, repeat column titles on top of the table, using the same form for single and double horizontal lines. If material requires a repetition of subtitles from a left-hand column, they will have to be repeated too. This avoids the inconvenience of having to turn back to the first page of the table to find the subtitles. See the table on page 198.

You may use either the short or the long form for continuing a title on subsequent pages:

TABLE III. SOME EFFECTS OF THE TELETYPSETTER
ON THE NEWSPAPER (Continued)

TABLE III. (Continued)

Last, for both figures and tables, make sure your information is accurate. Use a calculator to check mathematical totals. Proofread statistics to make sure there are no omissions or transpositions as you move data from notes to finished report page. Sometimes students have worked with information for so long that they cannot see their errors. Check and double-check. Your instructor might find your report flawless—except for a careless mistake in the illustrations.

TABLE V.   LIFETIME INCOME (Continued)

Age of payee, nearest birthday	Life annuity (1)	Refund annuity (2)	60 (3)	100 (4)	120 (5)	240 (6)
40	$ 6.55	$ 6.52	$ 6.54	$ 6.53	$ 6.53	$ 6.49
41	6.58	6.55	6.58	6.56	6.56	6.51
42	6.61	6.58	6.61	6.59	6.59	6.54
43	6.65	6.61	6.64	6.63	6.62	6.57
44	6.69	6.68	6.66	6.66	6.66	6.60
45	6.73	6.68	6.72	6.70	6.70	6.63
46	6.77	6.72	6.76	6.74	6.74	6.66
47	6.81	6.76	6.80	6.79	6.78	6.69
48	6.86	6.80	6.85	6.83	6.82	6.73
49	6.91	6.85	6.90	6.88	6.87	6.76
50	6.97	6.90	6.95	6.93	6.92	6.80
51	7.02	6.95	7.01	6.98	6.97	6.84
52	7.08	7.00	7.07	7.04	7.02	6.88
53	7.15	7.05	7.13	7.10	7.08	6.92
54	7.22	7.11	7.20	7.16	7.14	6.96
55	7.29	7.18	7.27	7.23	7.21	7.01
56	7.37	7.24	7.35	7.30	7.27	7.06
57	7.46	7.31	7.43	7.37	7.34	7.10
58	7.54	7.39	7.51	7.45	7.42	7.15
59	7.64	7.47	7:60	7.53	7.50	7.21
60	7.73	7.55	7.69	7.62	7.58	7.26

WRITING ABOUT COMPLEX SUBJECTS

CHAPTER 16

WRITING ABOUT COMPLEX SUBJECTS

What do you do if you want to write a theme on a complex topic—science and technology, statistics, business, or public affairs?

This chapter will help you translate all your research—reading and interviewing—into a paper that is easy to understand, well organized, and accurate. You will not have to resort to a "copy job" (plagiarism) as is the case with some students—writing material word for word or changing only a word or two from an encyclopedia, a book, or magazine. Indeed, your theme or report may be easier to understand than some of the efforts of professional authors. Best of all, you will feel you understand the material thoroughly and that you have done a first-class job on the presentation.

Consider how many papers your instructor has to correct. If there are 30 students in your class, that means correcting papers that might be half finished, poorly organized or researched, or that either barely scratch the subject or have such a broad focus that the material is overwhelming. If you follow the instructions from the previous chapters and from this one, you will turn in a paper that is on target, says something, and is clear and perhaps even easier to read and understand than the original material of research.

What makes a paper or theme on a complex subject stand out?

The secret is as close as your newspaper or television screen. Reaching a wide audience is the goal for any newspaper publisher or television producer. The more people in the audience, the more advertising potential they have. That has been the bottom line in the media since the first newspaper was published or the first broadcast was made. Most of the people in that audience do *not* have college degrees. In the state of Oregon—as well as other parts of the nation— nearly 25 percent of the adults have not attained a high school diploma. We have been reading and hearing a lot lately about the growing rate of functional illiteracy. The media has recognized that to explain complex things like space shots or black days on Wall Street, they must keep things *simple*. Simple words. Simple sentences. Examples that are simple. And the whole thing must be organized because there is only so much space in a newspaper column or time in the broadcast world to deal with such complex subjects. Most of all, writers must be teaching with those simple words, sentences, examples, and that organization.

What they are doing in print and broadcast mediums, you can do with themes or special reports, too. Borrow their working principles.

Some of those principles have been mentioned. Let's take examples or analogies (taking an example of something we *know* to teach us something we *don't* know). That's when you use the short "breather" paragraphs to be sure the reader does not get overwhelmed in the presentation of some subject. It's a typographic break for the eyes as well as the mind.

The specialist writer who does science, business, government, or statistical stories for the general public knows how to use those skills to explain things for the average person. People read *Consumer Reports* magazine, for instance, without realizing that the content is based on highly complex research procedures that have been put into statistical data. Some writer had to translate that complex material into words that ordinary readers could understand. When there is a space disaster, the television industry immediately gathers all the complex factors known; and in the evening news, the viewer gets both words and pictures that have translated the vast amounts of research done earlier in the day into something they can understand.

There is a great sense of satisfaction for this kind of writer.

Never dreaming of plagiarizing from encyclopedias or newspaper articles, this writer gains the pure pleasure of taking the complicated and changing it into words the average reader or viewer *can* understand. It's not too different from the thrill a teacher receives when almost an entire class understands one aspect of geometry or the use of nominative-case pronouns. That is *real* communication.

And you can do it, too, in what you write.

Students in one university class who were not particularly good at science once translated a complex article from *Scientific American* about research on cancer cell metastasis to something a 10-year-old reader—or a 10-year-old reading level person—could understand. The writers first acted out in class what happens when an original tumor breaks apart to form new tumors. The analogies might get frowns from some science teachers, but readers would understand such things as a cops-and-robber race through the blood and lymphatic systems, a greedy subdivision builder, or trendy teenagers trying to get everyone to wear a pair of "jeans" with the H-2D label (it is the oncogene *H-2D* that appears to spread cancer).

If you decide to do a theme about, say, the Josephson switch, the U.S. Navy's sonar buoys, Wall Street's program trading, this chapter and those you've read previously should help you to deal with such complex subjects in terms that are clear to anyone—your instructors or friends. You will have mastered a difficult topic. Best of all, you will not have had to resort to the ''copy job'' that can get you into trouble.

Use Simple Words

One thing you must keep in mind is that the average person in this country is said to have that 10-year-old reading level. Readership studies taken year after year have reported this fact. There is a computer program, in fact, that charts writing by such reading levels. The *National Geographic* magazine is said to be aimed at the 13-year-old reading level. *Scientific American* magazine is aimed at university levels. That computer program placed some of the writings of William Faulkner at the doctoral level.

This is important for you to know. For example, your instructors have a college education. Yet when it comes to understanding *all* of today's complexities, they probably would prefer such subjects in these areas to be written clearly. That means a return to simple words by which to teach *them* something new.

In an earlier chapter, it was pointed out that Aristotle perhaps was the last man on earth to understand *everything*; after that, science, politics, literature and all the rest of our knowledge became complex. No one can know *everything* today—not even with computers and hundreds of data bases. To learn about something new, someone will do best with a simple presentation about the subject.

Think about the genius of the television writing teams who by the six o'clock news program, explained the Chernobyl nuclear disaster so that most viewers could understand it. In that instance, most people were able to master enormously complex engineering and physics concepts because of the mastery of the simple by writers and artists. Such a team was not out to impress intellectuals or the scientific community. Their aim was to get the facts to as many Americans as possible, including those of the six-year-old reading level and the millions of functionally illiterate adults.

Both Plato and Jesus did the same thing. They explained highly complicated philosophical and theological ideas to those around them. No matter what the translation of their words has been, the concepts almost always have been easily grasped by ordinary people. In fact, when you are about to explain something complex, you might first try it out—using words alone (no pictures)—on a bored or antsy six-year-old child. That sounds strange, but if a six-year-old can understand your explanation, almost every other reader will do the same. And if you can make that child sit still while you're doing it, you might have a future in writing. Writers wrestle daily with each stroke of a key to hold onto audiences with short attention spans.

In talking to that child—or the 10-year-old reading level person—you can't use big words that might be found in encyclopedias or presentations in scholarly journals. You can't lay down concepts that only your trigonometry instructor could follow. Instead, you are forced to keep things simple and to go slowly. You also pay careful attention to organization and keep things that are similar tied together.

To seize a reader's attention, you will have to use most of the techniques taught in this book. To keep that attention, you must have substance. You will have to know your subject or any reader will see that it is lightweight and heavily padded. Keeping things simple does tend to reveal froth and lack of content. Complex words can conceal a lack of content.

One of the great principles of teaching is to lead the student from the known (familiar) to the unknown. Most people do not like to be pioneers. They balk when a new word or a new concept is thrown down at their feet. Minds close. After all, when a mass of unknown material comes our way without a user-friendly warm-up of relating it to something we already know, we become overwhelmed. Fear enters the picture. And fear keeps us from learning. But if Sally or Darren know what a pie is, she or he can be moved quickly along the path to understanding fractions. For example, chocolate pudding that has been left too long in the refrigerator is *known*. To explain what solid fuel looked like, one student likened it to that chocolate pudding. Another student told his readers to think about a room full of mousetraps, each rigged with ping pong balls. When one trap was sprung, it flung a ping pong ball to another trap—which then triggered it to fling its ping pong ball to another trap, and so on. He followed that up by saying this is the principle of nuclear fission.

That is leading from the *known* to the *unknown*.

Let's return to Plato. Now, Plato was not worried about other teachers' sneers (and there are such things!) that he was "popularizing" or "dumbing down" Socratic ideas. That is elitist talk, for in knowledge there is power to be exclusive or a snob. Plato was concerned only about making complex ideas understandable to his readers. Lucky for him that Socrates was using simple examples, simple words, and simple techniques. He recorded that Socrates once asked students why they blew on their hands in winter. They replied that this was the way to keep hands warm. But then he asked them why they blew on hot soup. They— and readers for thousands of years—suddenly understood life's paradoxes and have applied it to philosophical concepts. Our hands and soup are examples that are homespun, familiar. One of the reasons that Shakespeare's poetry is still understandable to many is that he used nature constantly as a source from which to draw his examples and analogies. And Jesus had his lilies of the field and the Good Samaritan to make his points.

Thoroughly Understand Your Explanation

To begin writing about complex topics, you first must understand—*thoroughly*—what you are trying to explain. If you don't, your bluff will be recognized by any instructor. Further, if you are asked to give an oral explanation of what you wrote, you will be exposed as a fraud. It's far, far better to take the time and to make the effort to master *all* aspects of a subject. Don't sit down to do a theme or a paper the night before it's due for any subject; but particularly don't do it on complex subjects. You'll never make it.

Narrow Your Focus

To write about such topics, you must take a narrow focus on one thing rather than try to tackle a wide range of a subject. Instead of writing about, say, the Vietnam war—a scope that would boggle even professional writers—take just a *slice* of it: a skirmish, a single mission, a small part of its logistical challenges. If you decide to do a theme on electricity, four or five pages never will do; take one *small* part of electricity. If you are going to do a paper on Emily Dickinson or John Keats, zero in on just *one* aspect of either their lives or their poetry. That will keep you from checking out every book in the library on such authors or historical subjects—or *any* topic.

Once you've narrowed the subject, you can deal with learning about it far more comfortably. You will not feel so overwhelmed with the scope of it that you will put off doing the paper.

Speak with Experts

Even if you're only dealing with a narrow wedge of a topic, you probably won't know much about it when you start. The key to real mastery of a subject—instead of a lick and a promise—is to *admit* you know little about it. Go back to what was said about Aristotle. Nobody expects you to be a Junior Aristotle, even in your field. One physician in the specialty of family practice once admitted that although he was chief of surgery at a major Washington, D.C. hospital, it was a challenge to stay current in that specialty. It required going to continuing education short courses and seminars and reading the many journals dealing with that specialty. If he could admit he was ignorant of some areas in his own specialty, you have the right to admit you are not state of the art in the subject you have chosen, too.

Moreover, think of the courage it takes to raise a hand in class to ask a question—particularly if the instructor *has* explained the material once. It takes heroics to do that. Before you start off on researching your topic, why not stop in and see an instructor who specializes in that subject. If you're doing a history paper, talk to a history instructor. If you're going to take up a business topic, talk to the faculty member in that field. These experts can give you leads and/ or advice that will save you going down blind alleys. Librarians also are helpful. So are experts in the field—"outsiders."

Check Out and Study Sources

The upshot may mean that you have to check out 10 books on the same subject just to see how the authors have presented the material. You may then make the fascinating discovery that many of the authors either have copied other authors' broad concepts or information or write in a fashion so that no ordinary readers can follow what is being said. You doubt that? Well, for example, one encyclopedia mirrored —edition after edition—what the major history textbooks said about England's King Richard III: that he was a hunchback who killed two boy princes as well as a host of others. But such "facts" were based on those given out by the enemies of Richard III, facts mandated by his successor (Henry VII) who needed a one-sided story to keep the throne in Tudor hands. Such facts were picked up by Shakespeare, of course, when he wrote his play *Richard III* and perpetuated for more than 400 years. Today, historians know better. But this single instance demonstrates that you need to have more than one or two sources about a subject. And if authors are copying each other, you will *not* get an unbiased piece of information.

Another advantage of checking out materials and studying several sources or in talking to many people (if you are doing a poll or a study that requires interviews) is that if a subject is unclear, the fifth or sixth version of it may bring the light. Take the experience of one university student who, in her practice-teaching unit, found she was supposed to teach high schoolers about the correct pronoun to use with gerunds when the situation was possessional. She had never mastered this section on possessive pronouns. She was not about to ask other would-be English teachers because, as she explained it, English teachers usually do not want to look dumb. She later learned that most of them didn't know how to teach it anyway, in her experience.

So this is what she did:

She checked out 13 books on grammar, making sure from the index that each covered gerunds. She was determined to do the first explanation of pronouns with gerunds that was clear to both readers and listeners. She knew about the short attention spans of her assigned sophomore English class students. She knew it was dangerous to bore the audience. Most of all, she also wanted to master this aspect of gerunds even though she knew they might not come up except once per year.

The first two textbooks were like reading Greek, she said. But the thoughtful writers had picked examples from ordinary conversation. By the fourth book, she began to pick up patterns just by reading the examples; the explanations were poorly written for basic comprehension. Soon, she was no stranger to the sentence structure that contained a possessive pronoun used with a gerund. By the eighth book, she was able to follow the explanations easily even though the language was hardly the kind she used with her friends—and certainly not with students. By the tenth textbook, she not only understood that aspect of gerunds, but had figured out a fresh and clear way to explain it to those easily distracted high school sophomores. This took a Saturday. All day. It might take you a *week* of study. For mastery of the complex on a narrowed-down basis, the time elements do differ. But you will have to spend some time. Once you do, however, the fun is in thinking up a way either to do an oral or written presentation that will instantly be understandable to a resistive or even hostile audience. That is what students have done on cancer, DNA, booster rockets, or a billion-dollar business takeover.

Now, let's apply all this to you.

To explain something complex, you will need to get out those books or journals—or talk to those experts. You can choose to use the same old examples or analogies (which the teacher undoubtedly will recognize because they *are* so familiar) and wording. But why not come up with material that is all yours and clear to any audience. One student began her explanation of DNA by talking about the ''Nitrogen Air Force Base'' and used couples who were going steady (Sweet Adenine and Thyamine) for the hydrogen elements. No textbook has that kind of jazzed-up explanation, yet it perhaps was clearer than any DNA explanation now in the science textbooks—and a fresh, memorable approach as well. Another student, explaining photosynthesis, used "little green kitchens" as an analogy to explain the vital process.

Use Unorthodox Techniques

Another way to master complex materials takes methods that may strike you first as strange. But that's just because you haven't done them in years and your friends might think of them as goofy. But your friends don't have the writing assignment. You do. Many who have "cracked the codes" of the complex have done some highly unorthodox things.

Like drawing pictures. Or reading source materials aloud. Or trying to explain things to fidgety youngsters, as mentioned previously. Or acting them out with a drama or skit.

Perhaps you haven't drawn any pictures since first grade. Maybe someone laughed at your art efforts. Maybe someone corrected your pronunciation of words. Or perhaps you're so shy, getting up in front of even your closest friends is enough to paralyze you with fear. But forget those years! Those things happened long ago. You have matured emotionally far more than you think.

Be Dramatic

Nobody is going to laugh at you if you privately use those methods to explain lasers to yourself or the latest in wave research or what can cause the corporate bond market to disintegrate. One pair of students explained a new and complex educational philosophy (metacognitions) in a class of delighted graduate students via a scavenger hunt that involved eating chocolate cream pies, rushing around under blankets, and tying strings to a ceiling, all followed by the rewards of big bags of chocolate kisses; the philosophy they were teaching was highly complex, yet almost all students grasped it far more easily than if they had had to read a textbook or journal on the subject. And it was fun!

Another group of "science boneheads" easily understood lasers when they did a skit that cast up the entire class into the various elements of a laser, including a chorus line that kept in "step" at the end. One biology professor teaches mitosis by borrowing dance students from the physical education department. An English teacher teaches the nominative-case pronouns by getting the school cheerleaders to do the "Nominative-Case Locomotive" ("I, you, he, rah, rah. I, you, he, rah, rah! We, you, they, hey. We, you, they, hey" etc).

If you don't feel like being dramatic, try either drawing or reading aloud—or both.

Draw Pictures

Now, the kind of drawing recommended here is not too different from what is done in television when cartoonists or writers have to translate something complex for viewers. They are not worrying about their old art teachers. They are worrying about understanding something that will be presented to millions on the evening news or a special. They get out big pieces of butcher paper or other large-sized paper—big because it forces *overemphasis* of something mysterious and lets them truly see the small elements in a large form. They use wide-nibbed felt-tip pens or crayons.

Such people go through a process—whether it's explaining fiber optics or program trading—of mastering the essentials. They may come up with several sketches. If they are involved in a space disaster, the puffs of smoke may be enormous, the rocket seams may be equally exaggerated; but they can see at a glance the fundamentals of what they will be presenting. The trick then is to recast them into an analogy. Wind shear that wrecks airplanes may look, in the drawing, like a garden hose with its spray directed at a driveway. A volcanic lahar looked to one student like an avalanche and he used that extended analogy all the way through a theme on the eruption of Mount St. Helens.

Perhaps you are the type who blenches at just drawing. If so, why not try reading *and* drawing? Here you will read and stop instantly when the author says something confusing. Then reread it (perhaps that may take several rereadings.) When you've mastered a section, draw a sketch of what it means to you alone. Do things *slowly.* Are you trying to explain how a bill gets through Congress? Draw boxes that stand for each stopping point of a bill. One student who explained the latest videoing process read aloud from his source and sketched out—as the text described—everything from heads to tracking; it took more than one piece of paper. As he said, the source (a magazine) was aiming for an audience that understood the material; it was written over the heads of ordinary readers. Once he figured out the process, he merely found an analogy or two that most readers would understand and wrote a paper far more interesting and far clearer than his original source. He was willing to ''look dumb,'' something so many dread; he both read and drew until he understood the subject. Part of the work involved having to call up two local electronics dealers to clarify some points. But he was more interested in being accurate, complete, and clear than he was in worrying about what has been called a ''look-good.''

In any event, when you're reading aloud, drawing, or acting out a subject, let yourself go. Double-check yourself when you finish a phase to make sure you are accurate. Page 210 shows what a student did to teach herself how the video cassette industry now records things on a single tape. Her source was a high-technology magazine that used jargon that many ''high-tekkies'' employ everyday. But she drew crude pictures as she read the text. These pictures will mean nothing to you, but they certainly did to her. Your drawings, equally, will make no sense to anyone else, but you are drawing only for your own understanding of a topic.

Read Aloud

Let's talk now about reading things aloud.

You did this as kindergarteners and perhaps as first graders, but probably have not read aloud since then. As has been mentioned, perhaps you mispronounced words; today, you'll never put yourself in a situation where you have to go through that again. Or perhaps you feel reading aloud is only for babies; grown people don't do that unless they're part of a Greek chorus in some arena theatre production from antiquity.

But reading the complex material aloud is helpful in trying to understand it. And nobody will be around to correct your pronunciation or to riducule you for being "too old to do that sort of thing."

First of all, consider that in many encyclopedias, books, or magazines that there is limited space. Authors know they must be economical with words. Often, they pack one sentence with so many ideas that the reader is unable to sort them out. Just for fun, take a passage from a textbook you have that you have had trouble understanding. Circle the sentences. Chances are you will find they are long. You also may find that if you circle the commas, the sentence carries two or more thoughts; commas fence off clauses and phrases. Such sentences are "packed." Such a sentence is difficult to understand for sound psychological reasons. Nobel laureate Herbert Simon has shown that most people cannot concentrate on a lot of things; he says six things are our limit if we are of ordinary intelligence. The point is, then, that an overloaded sentence results in an overload of subject mastery for you. If you read aloud, however, you will spot such a heavily laden sentence and can break it apart. The read-aloud system means you can halt in mid-sentence to absorb the data. That also gives you time to look up words in the dictionary. When you write in the future, then, perhaps you will give your reader a break and find a simple word that says the same thing, one that will be understood.

Another surprising discovery in reading aloud is that some material is poorly organized in terms of how ordinary readers think. You may find that authors forget to lead the reader from the known to the unknown. Perhaps you may feel that the topic would be easier to understand if authors did not start off in a certain way. Or instead of starting with details and working up to major concepts, the presentation should have been handled the other way around.

In your theme or report, you can fix the organization so that it matches your view on what should come first, second, third, and the like. You are not being arrogant here. Nor are you out-experting an expert. Instead, you are organizing material so that a wider audience can understand it. Right now, your audience is your teacher, an excellent source for trying out a change in presentation.

Use Analogies and Examples

Analogies and examples have been laced throughout this chapter so far so you will be familiar with them up to this point. They are crucial in a translation process, as indicated. When you use either an example or an analogy, you need to think about your reader: what's the person's age, sex, interests, experiences, to name just a few elements. You cannot do well in teaching mathematics if all the word problems are geared to males. Those who design IQ tests found out a few years ago that oranges were not common to the tables of poor people, and that using oranges in problems would be a "stopper" for some children.

A professional writer cautions that good analogies and examples never are dated or drawn from fads. Anyone using the Lindy Hop to explain a complex maneuver will perplex readers unfamiliar with this 1940s dance step. When a teacher talked about one politician as being a "little left of Himmler," he perplexed the class because no one in it was that familiar with this notorious Nazi.

Moreover, an analogy or example must fit. One student has found that almost everyone understands his food analogies. Everyone has to eat, so he has no difficulty with dated analogies that "stop" readers. Be careful not to use brand names, however, for companies come and go or are merged into conglomerates.

Now, let's apply all the foregoing to the fields that are highly complex, yet ones that are used by many students in themes, reports, or term papers.

Science and Technology

If ever there is a temptation to do a "copy job," it is when you decide to do a composition on a science or technology subject. You may copy for several reasons: you have a tight deadline and no time to do a decent job; you just know a professional writer can do a better job on the subject; you don't understand the material and figure that the teacher would fare better with the original source material.

Unfortunately for "copy-jobbers," instructors usually can detect such plagiarism because of the organization, scientific jargon, and packed sentences. Other giveaways are the scientific hedge ("it appears," "it seems,") or writing that is geared to the author's colleagues. Too, your instructor has been reading student themes and reports for months or years and knows that most students turn in first drafts with minimal skills at sentence construction, mechanics, and spelling. A polished piece often is a giveaway; so is the dry-as-dust scientific abstract. Moreover, plagiarism is considered such a serious offense in college that you could be expelled. The word certainly spreads about plagiarists in both university and high school faculty rooms; don't risk your reputation by copying. In other words, don't do a copy job.

After all, you *can* do a good job on writing about science. Your worst enemy is fear. Obviously, you can't if you leave a project until the last minute. Most of all, you have to begin to believe that you *can* explain something complex just as well—sometimes better—than an original source. Much of this chapter is filled with examples of the creative way students explained complex subjects. If they can explain the complex without plagiarism, so can you. You need to start trusting in your own writing ability.

One of the most refreshing stories about *Discover* magazine is that its earliest chief copyeditor—the person who must approve every word in the publication—said she absolutely would *not* pass any writing that was not clear to the ordinary reader. Even though scientific types generally frighten the layman, here was one person who refused to be intimidated even by the nastiest of the world's scientists. She argued that *Discover's* circulation is built on sales to the general public. *Discover* still does not have a super-scholarly readership. Its stories also are so varied that a reader drawn to one probably will read others; there must be a unity of treatment in writing style. Obviously, such a stand might not go down well with scientific writers who fear they are "popularizing" research data; but the data for *Discover* had *better* be popularized if the publishers are going to obtain and retain millions of readers. If readership slips, they will not be able to get advertising; and if advertising slips, a magazine folds.

It's also refreshing to note that the writing in the science sections of the daily

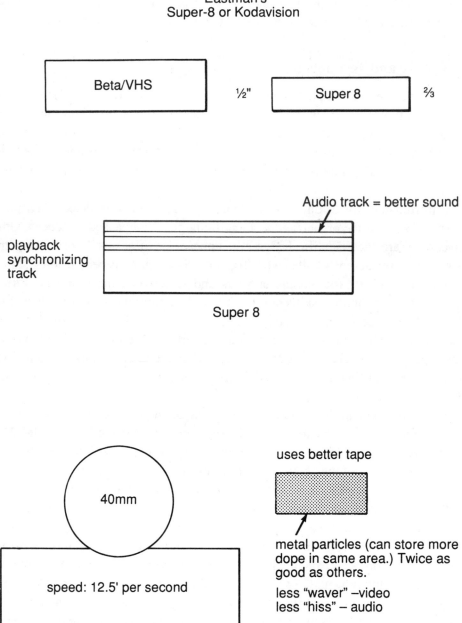

newspapers is geared to the ordinary reader. In the mid-1980s, 22 daily newspapers had started science sections because they knew ordinary readers were interested in this subject; their editors took the same tack as that *Discover* copyeditor and her editors. Today, there are nearly 70 daily newspapers with science sections—all following the rule of keeping things simple. *Popular Science* magazine has existed since 1872 because it does translate the complex to the simple for its millions of readers.

Writers on such publications do exactly what you will learn here. Their work tends to fall into such categories as *people, processes,* and *phenomenon.*

When writers take on a Gallileo, an Eve Curie, Thomas Edison or Steve Jobs, they begin by doing research in encyclopedias, books, or magazines. The student who does the same will understand how quickly a writer can be overwhelmed by data. Generally, that student winds up with a kind of ''obituary'' of dry facts: birth, childhood, school days, work days, things invented or discovered, and death.

Avoid the Chronological Approach

The problem is that there's no life in such a chronological approach. The scientist does not come to life as one who had head colds, and family problems, or was curt with lab assistants. There's no emotional pain, no exasperation on the seventy-eighth run of an experiment. Nor do most students spend one drop of ink on the day-to-day single-minded drive that possesses scientists. Not *everyone* wins a Nobel prize. There's no smell of the laboratory in the writing, the discouragement of being unable to get research funds, the petty jealousies— all possible if a writer tackles a *segment* of a scientist's life instead of a birth-to-death rendition. But why not?

Writing involving inventors or scientists can be exciting. One of the discoverers of DNA certainly had no difficulty making it interesting to the ordinary reader as he recounted what went on in the lab in the best-selling book *The Double Helix*.

Focus on One Achievement

If you are going to write a theme or paper about people—a scientist or someone in technology, put some meat on the bare bones as you recreate the constant trial-and-error/trial-and-error that led to some achievement. Something must be in your paper about the repeated experiments that went nowhere— despite the cost, time, and energy. Thomas Edison's struggle with perfecting the light bulb is an excellent example of such inspiration and exasperation. If you have read one or two sources about a key figure—you certainly can find some instances of the difficulties surrounding one of his or her major efforts. Ideas *do* consume such people, often making home life difficult or impossible for their families.

Put yourself into an imaginary lab jacket and your composition suddenly will have the smell of reality and real people. One help might be to turn to the section on how to write profiles (page 42). Once again, it must be said that key quotations usually are excellent ways to reveal someone's real personality.

Once in that lab jacket, you must understand the discovery you are detailing, whether it's radiation or jet propulsion. The source book might explain it, but if it offers little information, look up the work in an encyclopedia or science book. To understand a scientist's work, you also may have to do those unorthodox things suggested previously in this chapter (draw, read aloud, dramatize).

Organizing the Personality Piece

After this, organize your paper. It can be done exactly as explained in the chapter on organization. A ''quick-and-dirty'' outline is an excellent way to go for you (page 6). But you certainly could use a more formal outline system.

Open your paper with an inviting lead, one that will want to make a reader go on. An anecdote or an event usually seizes such interest.

The next paragraph can be devoted to briefly summarizing the person's achievements, but get into only the *major* ones; most people in technology or science have a long list of awards. Did the achievement start a host of spinoffs? Did it trigger a trend? Or, is it a ''one-shot?''

The rest of the paper can be handled chronologically, especially if you have decided to focus on just one or two achievements. Bear in mind that the organization should move the reader from one major attainment to another. You also should give generous credit to the work done by others that led to such a benchmark. Most scientists are quick to insist on this, in fact. They know that one discovery is built upon the yeoman's work that has gone on before by others, much of it unsung. For example, Jonas Salk may have been given credit for polio vaccine, but his work was built on the untiring labors of others. Apple computers evolved from the unheralded work by others in the past.

When you begin mentioning a singular achievement, take a historical approach that not only includes previous work, but what got the scientist or technologist interested. For instance, the laser beam began on a park bench in Washington, D.C. while its inventor sat gazing at the nearby flowers. The Post-its of 3M got started because an employee complained his place markers kept falling out of his choir hymnal. These are fascinating starting points of interest to ordinary readers.

As you write about the week-to-week work, try to give the flavor of lab life whether it's bringing in sandwiches or worrying about paying the bill for the burning of midnight oil.

Include a paragraph or so on the significance of the work and its scientific or commercial impact. Has the work set off a whole new industry as has been the case with space shots? Radar certainly did. So did the discovery that selenium was useful in television's infancy. The close of the composition could involve such results or perhaps a significant quote that sums up the person's chief work. Pick quotes with extreme care; they should sum up a personality or a work.

The structure of a personality piece is set out in the quick and dirty outline structure that follows.

When you are writing about *processes* in technology or science, you will see that they tend almost to organize themselves. This leads to this. Then, this leads to this, and so on.

Link the Reader with the Process

Whether you write about installing an artificial heart or grafting genes, try to seize the reader's interest from the start. Why not begin with an action-filled little story—an anecdote—that is tied to that process? "As he sat eating his lunch, he began to watch a group of bugs as they ate into the tree trunk. Moving closer, he noticed that their jaws moved a certain way. Out of this observation came the chain saw." That was how one student explained the process that radically changed how loggers work today. This anecdote also is loaded with the human factor.

Such a "little story" as an opener also should tell the reader what the process is. What will it do? When inventors excitedly tell you about their widget, the thrust is always what it will *do*. Tell readers how it fits into their lives. Will it keep death at bay? Will it create jobs? Will it open new vistas? If you're writing about stars, you'll need to work at relating them to those who seldom look at the heavens except to see whether they need snow shovel or raincoat.

In short, try to link the reader with the process.

Organizing the Process Piece

Once you establish that tie, remember that what grabbed your attention about a process probably will work with your reader. There's nothing wrong with writing a paragraph early in the composition that explains how *you* got interested in a subject.

Move next to a paragraph or so on the historical development of the process. Include some sentences on pioneer efforts. After all, computers did not just spring up from nowhere one afternoon. The use of historical material also has the advantage of getting reader interest because it begins at the process; it does not overwhelm the reader with current advancements until one has been led through the generational steps. Once again, it is the known to the unknown. History also is full of people lending the human touch to something scientific or technological. Many might be interested to know, for instance, that the invention began in someone's garage as did Tektronix's famed oscilloscope.

That should bring you to explaining the process.

You will find that processes almost always move in that one-two-three step order mentioned earlier. Think of the amoeba's cycle of birth to death. It goes through several stages. So does a star. A helicopter of the fourth generation will take to the air in stages. An offshore oil rig is built in stages as well.

So organize the rest of the paper by those stages. One stage may be so extensive that it requires several paragraphs. If you want to be truly understood, you will break down a complex stage by giving each element its own paragraph. Breathers between major stages are a godsend to readers. So are those two most beloved expressions "for instance" or "for example." And you will need analogies throughout. Try to pick an analogy that fits *every* stage, something called an "extended analogy"; that makes it easy for a reader to follow as was the case in a student's surgical explanation involving a bypass of the heart; he likened it to a freeway's exits and entrances.

This kind of writing demands simple words, simple sentences, simple exam-

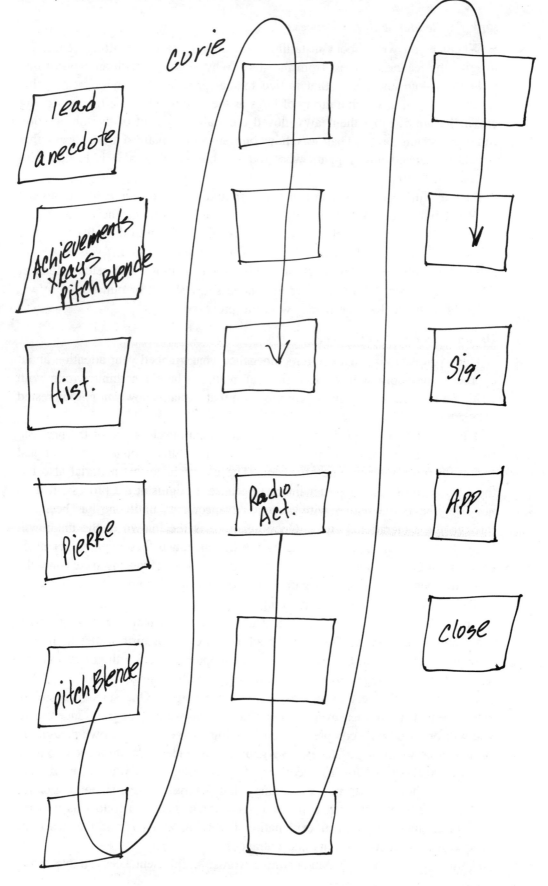

ples. Avoid packing a sentence with too much information. Readers will follow each of your stages if you remember their difficulties with jargon and assume that they don't know all the fundamentals. Be careful not to skip a stage that you think is self-evident; it often isn't. Assumptions lead to omissions that frustrate readers.

Move then into the significance of the entire process.

What are the ultimate results? The eventual applications? Again, tie them to our daily life. Think about why the reader should care about this process. The significance also might provide you with your ending. ''The teletypesetter was the keystone that changed the newspaper backshop forever,'' is one student's economical blend of significance and close.

A quick and dirty outline for a process might look like this one:

Apply a Human Interest Touch

Suppose you decide to write a paper about a *phenomenon*—the Northern Lights or El Nino. Again, you must check several sources so that you *thoroughly* understand such a phenomenon. Again, you must seize the reader from the first paragraph. It can be done if you apply a human-interest touch to your subject. For example, a paper on the greenhouse effect might be started by a graphic description of what the earth will be like 100 or 1000 years from now if the earth continues to warm. Readers want human life to continue. They want the earth to stay the same. If you begin by pointing out that the greenhouse effect will make things difficult for our descendents, they will read with enormous interest.

In *The Silent Spring,* Rachel Carson riveted readers' attention with an opening that had a world where no birds existed because the insecticide DDT had killed them off. Her book was not written in scientific terms for an elite and small audience; it was intended to carry the message about what chemicals do to the food chain and life itself. She put her views in terms ordinary readers could understand. The book was a bombshell! President John F. Kennedy instantly became concerned enough to push for an end to using DDT on crops. The chemical industry was hard-pressed to stop the simple message Carson sent— all put in simple words crafted around the dire results that any human could understand.

You can do the same thing.

Organizing the Phenomenon Piece

Once you have aroused reader interest, you then move into the paragraphs that describe what causes the phenomenon. There may be many interworkings that bring about the phenomenon. For example, the Northern Lights involve light reflection, metal particles, gravity, among other things. Each element you take up should get a paragraph or more. There is nothing wrong with including two examples if you feel the first one might not register with the reader. ''Put another way'' is another welcome expression if you decide to go for super clarity and more than one example to explain a phenomenon's element.

Analogies are essential throughout compositions on phenomenon. Readers

who have coped with physics topics will be delighted if you use analogies that are in everyday life rather than straight from a textbook or journal. Make them apt, however, and familiar to ordinary people.

Some writers like to present the phenomenon itself and then follow it with several paragraphs about the history of its observation and scientific explanations. There are writers who intersperse history with the phenomenon because they seemingly feel that a Ben Franklin flying a kite does spark up what could be a dull presentation. The human element absorbs readers.

The close should contain a paragraph or so—on how a phenomenon is significant to our lives. Again, why should we care? An El Nino assuredly can change our lives. So can the shifting of tectonic plates off California's coast. A Mount St. Helens has impacted people's lungs, the wood-products industry, tourism, and botanical life.

A quick and dirty outline of a phenomenon might look like thison page 218.

One spin-off of learning to write about technological or scientific subjects is that you could decide to make a career of it. The salaries are considerable in both fields for this kind of writing. Companies that want the general public to buy their wares have found they need to put instructions and sales materials into "plain English." Foreign manufacturers may have technical writers who understand English, but who cannot master our idiomatic expressions; they need someone who can.

The growth of science and high technology sections in the newspaper and the spawning of high-tech magazines is another avenue open to you if you master the art of translating complicated jargon to simple writing. Best of all, you will be writing about subjects that fascinate you; your writing truly will be a labor of love.

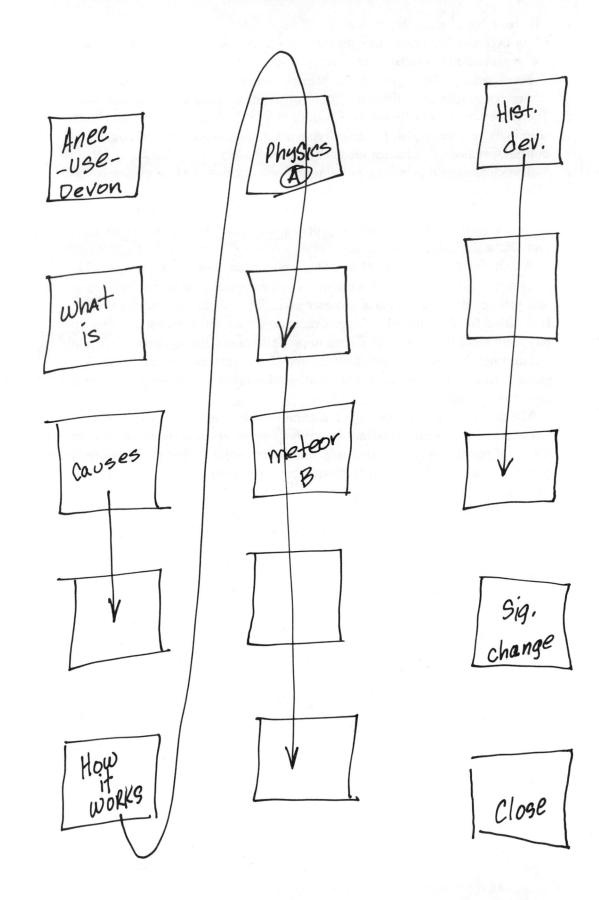

Statistics

The magazine *Consumer Reports* and almost any political poll both show how you can translate dry research data into something lively and interesting. Even something so seemingly boring as life insurance statistics can become fascinating in the hands of, say, a Metropolitan Life writer who reports that the men who live the longest seem to be symphony conductors ("they love what they're doing; all creature comforts are taken care of by agents, students, families; and they live a life of limousines, great restaurants, and attention").

Consumer Reports is built on product testing and toting up the number of times a car's engine conks out, the durability of exterior paint, the safest lawn mowers, and the sharpest kitchen knives. Its entire thrust is testing products that ordinary people buy, something that has kept its circulation in the millions for decades. It has charts that indicate advantages and disadvantages and other factors. These illustrations help readers enormously. But the prose that wraps up the subject has zip, bounce—and meat. The lead paragraph on electronic keyboards lured its readers in with such everday language as:

> Today's hills are alive with the sound of computerized music. More than 25 million people now play electronic keyboards. You can find little under-$50 keyboards with miniature keys in toy stores; you can find more elaborate keyboards, costing up to $500, next to the stereo rigs in department stores; and you can pay anywhere from $500 to $10,000 or more for "professional" keyboards and synthesizers at music stores.

The words that held all the research together for a dishwasher article included such terms as *snazzy, boosted, wrapped, swaddled,* and *thrifty.* The sentences concerning 35mm cameras were equally simple ones like: "Sales of compact cameras have boomed," "Some are trim enough to slip into a shirt pocket," "You can squeeze more people into a group shot without having to back up too far, for example."

Doing a Poll

You may decide to do a theme or term paper that involves doing a poll, the usual introduction to statistical writing. Statistics, after all, basically involves counting things, people, or events. Then there are special formulas by which you check the numbers to see if they really prove something. For now, if you take on a poll, no readers will expect you to apply a test like chi-square or an f statistic, however. But they *will* expect you to be able to report numbers and to draw conclusions from them. Too, they will want to be able to understand you when you write up your conclusions. This includes whoever reads your composition, especially your instructor.

When you draw your conclusions, always use the scientific hedge of "it would seem," or "it appears." Scientists use such terms because they know that even if tests show 100% of something happens 100% of the time, there is always the possibility that they could be wrong. Even though the link between smoking and lung cancer seems to be a beautiful example of cause and effect—bolstered by years of research—there still may be doubt by scientists as to the connection. After all, 9 out of 10 explorers in 1492 seemed to think the world was flat. So don't say that your results "*showed* that this attitude is prevalent." Say that "*it seems* that this attitude is prevalent."

First, of course, you have to design your poll.

Any question you ask should not be loaded. "Do you still beat your wife?" is the classic example of a loaded question, for no matter how someone answers, the implication is that beating has occurred. The professionals call such a question "biased." They can provide you with methods to do a full-dress poll if you want to take the time to look up their ideas in the library.

Questions must be clear. This is one of the reasons that most statistical researchers try out their questions on a few people before they go to the expense and effort of a poll of hundreds. They get out the bugs of misunderstood words, grammatical errors, and bias. "Would you—or wouldn't you—drive without a seat belt?" is a question without bias. Some researchers suggest that a pollster also soak out the question for any kind of emotional flavor. They also point out that you'll get better results—and unbiased ones—if you don't have a long question. Never write a preface for a question or you *will* get a biased answer, meaning your poll is worthless.

You need to ask the same question in the *same* way of *all* your respondents, of course. Professionals try to ask the question in the same tone of voice, with the same area of emphasis. If you write out your question, you will not have to worry about tone or emphasis.

You will have to pay attention to note many things about the people who respond to your poll. Males and females do not always respond the same way. Age makes a difference. So do experience and background. Ethnic heritage may be a factor. A detail-oriented person will answer a poll quite differently than a creative type. There also are the factors of the time of day you ask the question. The day of the week. The month or seasons of the year. Don't forget that many want to please you—if they can figure out what your *real* view is on a poll question.

The circumstances under which you asked the question also have a bearing on the results. Was it during the excitement of an athletic event or during study hall? Did you leap out at the person being polled or did they see you coming from a long way off? One group of sociology majors once set up a clipboard poll at a major intersection in downtown Portland—at rush hour! They tied up traffic for miles and infuriated anyone they approached for poll responses.

Once you have your results—and you will have at least a representative number of the population you are testing in that sample group—you will tally the numbers. Most experts feel you must have at least 30 people in a sample.

The categories about your sample group will provide the meat for this kind of theme. There is a category for the overall head count. There is a category for males and one for females. There is a category perhaps for freshmen, sophomores, juniors, and seniors. There might be a category on athletes that is split out by the sports specialties. Maybe there's one for those who hold jobs and those who don't, or particular kinds of jobs. You might have a category that involves people in a chemistry class as compared to those in math.

The possibilities are endless. So are the ones involving such things as the circumstances or the time periods, all mentioned above.

Consumer Reports often sort products into effectiveness, cost, ease, and safety as well as elements peculiar to the good or service. You will need to figure out your categories and then figure out which one you want to emphasize the most or what elements are the most important to readers. That will help you organize your composition. Once you decide which category will get the biggest play, then determine where you want to put the others.

A quick and dirty outline on a poll about setting up a smoking area looked like this the one on the next page.

Organizing the Statistical Piece

The wording has been dealt with, but you will need to know how to work the numbers into your prose. This is the sticking point of any statistical story because readers will not long endure unadorned numbers or those just strung out in never-ending patterns. You need to give meaning to your results as well as statistical depth to this kind of writing.

One unobtrusive way to include a statistic that does give it fact and impact is this kind of handling:

> Most men (41%) had dropped out of the 11th grade while most women (42%) had dropped out of the 10th grade.
>
> Nine out of 10 Standard employees appeared to crave praise when asked if they got enough. When 56% of the home office's personnel (897) thought about praise, they seemed to echo one employee's lament: "If they can't give a raise, how about praise?"

Quotes should be anonymous, but can spark up the written results as is shown above. Bear in mind that readers always love to see if what *they* think is echoed by others. Do not pick dull quotes or those that don't reflect the tenor of the response in a poll. Nor should you pad out a composition with mostly quotes. Most teachers will spot that kind of padding.

Because professional pollsters always recognize that readers need to know *all* the particulars about a survey, such researchers always include information about how many people were questioned and the percentage of respondents. That is

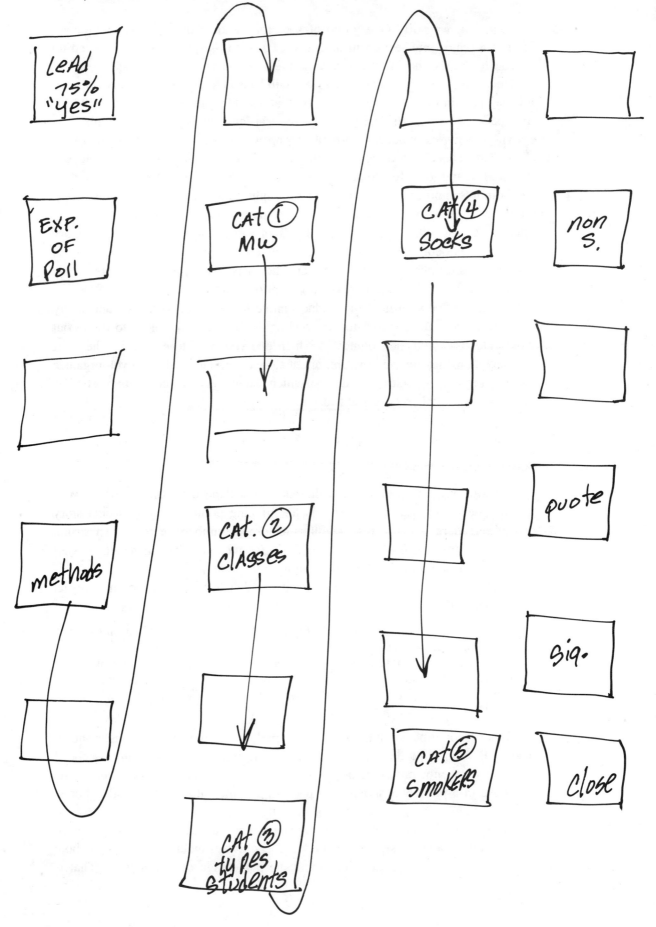

only fair. When the first statistics came in on fetal alcohol syndrome nearly two decades ago, the sample group involved less than a handful of cases. Yet major conclusions were drawn from such a tiny number of instances. This kind of situation shows the dangers of drawing conclusions based on few numbers. But it also illustrates—as you will learn—that there are many, many factors that can make statistical research worthless or highly dangerous if all the methods and circumstances are *not* explained.

In sum, somewhere near the beginning of your composition, you need a paragraph explaining whom you polled and how many responded. Be honest. Professional pollsters usually are, particularly in revealing the percentage of errors. You can add to it the location and what question you asked; you may want to include other particulars surrounding your survey as well.

Business

Are you looking for an exciting topic for a composition—one that will interest both you *and* your instructor?

Why not do one on a business topic? After all, nothing involving money (and what else powers business?) ever has been dull. Business is about "getting and spending." It keeps roofs over heads, food on the table, and provides enormous outlets for translating ideas into goods or services. Even if you feel that love of money is the root of all evil, you'll have to admit that it could be an excellent subject for a composition where you can say just that. Research material is as close as the morning newspaper or last week's business magazine; that can't be said about a topic in history or literature.

Business topics are exciting because they involve people's gargantuan efforts to survive. True, survival often triggers motives like greed and overambition, and it may take tax deductions to force some to be charitable. But as you look around your town, can you honestly say that this or that merchant is not interested in doing the right thing for customers or employees? The unscrupulous generally do not last long.

The business world teems with possible theme topics.

What is dull about the rags-to-riches rise of a Mary Kay Ash who started a cosmetics business with only an idea, energy, and a shoestring budget who today has more than 30,000 people selling her products? What's boring about a shoe company (Nike) that started with using a waffle iron on soles and first sold its product from a truck parked on a Los Angeles street corner? Isn't there high drama about the 1988 Christmas Eve cliff-hanger when the government decided to hold off foreclosure deadlines against 80,000 farmers?

All of these items come from the business and front-page sections of the daily newspapers. Reader interest in business stories equals that spent on sports. You may shudder at four pages of fine print spent on stockmarket results, but if you own even *one* share in Avon or Josten's, you may find yourself turning to those pages before the comics to see if you made or lost money. There's a theme topic in each of the stories below that appeared within a two-day period not long ago.

An introduction of a new hand-held calculator   A mill closure   The rise of wholesale prices   A wheat sale to the Russians   The effort to get a pier for car imports   A bank merger   Employees getting a refund   Dividing the assets of a bankrupt tulip bulb firm   Suspension of three bank executives after a $15-million shortage   A rise in housing starts   Employees rescuing a failing company

Each story could be a "peg" on which to hang a fascinating and solid theme. For instance, the item on wholesale price increases could be spun into what that means in your home because the national price index is based generally on household essentials like food, gasoline, and home heating costs. Housing starts can be the basis for several themes: How many housing starts are there in your town (go to city hall and ask to see the list of building permits)? How are *you* going to finance a house one day? Or what's going to happen emotionally if most Americans wind up in apartments (historically, we demand space)?

As for that bankrupt tulip bulb firm, why not use that as a peg to write about small business failures this year? The *Reader's Guide to Periodical Literature* will reveal many magazine stories on such trends. So will a library's computer data base programs devoted to business topics. There's also a theme topic written from the creditors' side—an aspect few newspapers bother to explore. What's the effect on those who held stock in such a firm or those vendors who expected the company to pay for the goods or services it sold to them?

The story about the pier for car imports also should trigger your imagination if you think about the great effort that many towns and cities put out to attract businesses. New businesses mean jobs as well as a tax source to help pay for police, street and sewer repairs, and community resources like a library or shelter for the homeless. Visit your chamber of commerce office and ask them about what it took to bring a new firm to town. You'll go away with more material then you can possibly put in a theme.

You get the idea.

You'll find that the media uses words in business stories as lively as in any sports story. Those items about wheeling and dealing are sprinkled with color and bluntness that you're welcome to use. There are words like "hammered out," "cutting off arms and legs," "plush," or "skyrocketed." You're likely to see such vigorous and vivid sentences as:

> In spite of all the assertions that personalities don't matter, Milken means more to Drexel than Michael Jordan does to the Chicago Bulls.*

> Businesses have become slaves to finance—and to the billions of dollars of freshly minted IOUs held to their heads like loaded guns.**

> The most valuable asset on Wall Street—it's not platinum, it's not drugs, it's not women, and it's not cash—it's information.***

We seem to be living in a world of Sir Francis Drakes and Bluebeards today in reading about the buccaneer tactics in takeovers. The words are lively and apt as these samples show:

> bear hug   bootstrap acquisition   churning   crown-jewel defense   golden parachute greenmail   junk bond   Pac-man defense   poison pill   radar alert   shark repellants tidal-wave purchase   vulture funds   white knight

---

*From *The Oregonian*, December 23, 1988.
**From *The Oregonian*, June 2, 1986.
***From *The Oregonian*, November 1, 1988.

You can use the same kind of words and sentences in a composition on business. When a farm is saved, when a new product is introduced, or when white-collar crime—or any subject, for that matter—is your theme topic, brighten and lighten the vocabulary you use. Business is *never* dull to those involved. So put some sparkle and dash as well as lively analogies into it. One ingenious reporter tackled the highly complex doings of a major brokerage caught in the toils of the law by likening their fix to "kiting" checks; any reader who has written a check on a Monday, hoping that the Friday paycheck deposit will cover it knows exactly what that brokerage did.

One reason students overlook business topics is that such a field looks overwhelming or complex. But that's not true. Sylvia Porter, the famous business writer, has been translating the most complicated tax laws and business practices for over 30 years. Her best-selling books—mostly bought by ordinary readers—show you how to boil down the complex into words your 10-year-old sister or brother could understand. Her secret is using simple words, simple sentences, and easy-to-understand analogies and examples. That's what is emphasized repeatedly in this book. Porter reduces the vast to its basics. For instance, she knows that even a mega-conglomerate dealing all over the world is basically run like a neighborhood lemonade stand.

The Lemonade Stand—Business Simplified

The lemonade stand is a good key to understanding businesses. Let's look at how it can be applied to a business topic.

Go back 10,000 years to our civilization's beginnings—to that famous valley of the Tigris and Euphrates rivers and its cities of Babylon and Ur. Most civilizations tend to start along riverbanks or other places where people gather. And where there are people, there's an opportunity to buy or sell something. Take the fellow(s) who learned there was a good living in ferrying people across the Tigris and Euphrates rivers—and there was bound to be someone who saw such a financial opportunity. His business was built on lemonade-stand principles: there's money to be made if you provide a product or service that people need. On a hot day, it's lemonade or an air conditioner. But if you needed to get across the Tigris, it was a ferryboat.

Move now to link that lemonade stand to business subjects.

A lemonade stand may have one owner, two, or many. So do businesses. One person owning a business is in a *sole proprietorship*. Two people make a *partnership*. A group is a *corporation*. A corporation is usually formed in the business world so that if it gets sued or winds up owing back taxes, each person's personal property can't be touched. A corporation could have a couple of variations from the traditional grouping; if your lemonade stand is run by family members, it could be what the business world calls a *closely held* corporation; if it's a group of friends, it could be a *Subchapter S* operation, a combination of both sole proprietors and corporation that has all of the advantages and few of the disadvantages of both kinds of business entities. Such groupings shift almost every time the tax codes change.

Lemonade stand owners have to buy supplies. In the business world, the lemons, sugar, and cups are called an *inventory*. An inventory ties up money, especially if the stand folds and the owners get stuck with a lot of lemons, sugar, and paper cups. But to begin, the owners either pool their money or talk parents or friends into giving the start-up funds (capital). In both situations, the owners generally promise either to pay back that initial investment or, as an added sweetener, to give them part of the profits *after* the costs and their own salaries are paid off. The owners might even issue stock, a kind of IOU that promises to do all of that.

To sweeten up such a transaction, the owners might tell their lenders that they will get "preferred" stock, *preferential* stock that means they'll *always* get paid part of the profits; if the lemonade stand fails, they'll be first in line—way before other creditors—when the cash and other assets are divided up.

Once a lemonade stand begins to thrive and needs more *capital* to buy either a longer table or more supplies, its owners might decide to raise more cash by issuing "common" stock. They could peg it at 50¢ a share of stock or $5 if business is really good. The higher the price of a share, the better the stand is doing. The same situation is present in the business world.

When the owners of the stand do buy a longer table or more chairs or additional pitchers and spoons, they are involved in adding to what is called "property, plant, and equipment" in an annual report's balance sheet. That two-page balance sheet is the most important section in an annual report (that thick booklet that scares many people because of all its charts and lists of figures). But a balance sheet is not that complex now that you have begun to understand what has been said about that lemonade stand. You know that the *assets* include whatever *cash* the owners have in the till. You know what an *inventory* is, too. And you know what is involved when an annual report's list of *assets* includes *property, plant, and equipment*.

An annual report's balance sheet—generally found in its center section—devotes a left-hand page to all those assets. It divides the assets into categories that essentially indicate what can give owners instant cash if they had to close the doors ("current assets") and long-term assets. Cash certainly is one of those *current assets*. So are the IOUs from their debtors; these are called *accounts receivable*.

Another current asset might be an income tax refund, due as soon as the stand pays its taxes. *Inventory* also is considered part of the current assets because owners hope that if things don't go well, they can sell off the inventory.

If you can convert all these things to instant cash, it's like ice melting at the lemonade stand—and done as quickly when things get hot. Things are said to be "liquid" (a company is said to have a lot of "liquidity"). An investor in the business world may be interested in nothing more than checking that annual report to see how "liquid" the firm is, especially if the rumors are rife about it either doing extremely well or, by contrast, ready for bankruptcy court.

What about the lemonade stand's items that can't be cashed in quickly?

These items certainly are part of the assets, but are listed after the "current" ones. Here, you'll find the list of "property, plant, and equipment." You also will find "investments" if the owners have put part of the profits into something that can earn additional money ("capital"). In the business world such investments may provide enough capital to expand operations or it may make a company able to enrich stockholders and trickle profits down to senior management or into profit-sharing plans that reach ordinary employees.

The right-hand page of the annual report lists the debts or "liabilities." Sometimes such a page is called "liabilities and shareholders' equity" or "capitalization and liabilities." Nevertheless, "liabilities" are what a lemonade stand (or any business) owes. The term "equity" means the money shareholders (stockholders) have invested in the company.

On such a page, the terms may be fancy, but they all stand for debt whether it's immediate (bank loans, back taxes, bonds), or is equity owed to stockholders (preferred or common).

If you understand the foregoing, you have just mastered the key portions of an annual report, all done via that lemonade stand. If you had trouble, reread it aloud—perhaps draw those sketches.

Such mastery means you can do a theme, as one student did, that looks at four utility companies as investments. She compared them to those classic five factors that any well-informed investor looks at before getting out the checkbook: solvency, liquidity, the amount of inventory accumulated, the property/buildings and equipment, and the price-earnings ratio.

In determining *solvency* she wanted to find out how debt ridden each firm was. All she did was divide the total current assets by the total *current* liabilities. If the firm owed twice or more than that it had in assets, she knew it wasn't able to pay its *immediate* debts (solvent).

To check the liquidity, she divided the cash *plus* the accounts receivable (all highly liquid) by the total current liabilities. If the ratio was *equal* (1•1), the firm could quickly convert its assets to pay off the debts; if there was *less* liquidity on the asset side, however, the investment risk was high.

As for inventory, she went back to the lemonade stand. If the owners have tied up too much in lemons, sugar, and cups—and fall's cool weather approaches—chances are they are going to be stuck with inventory they can't convert quickly to cash. In the business world, a wise investor will look to see if a firm has *less* inventory of products in its warehouse in the current year than the previous one. A firm that has an enormous pileup of products generally is not a good risk, especially in a competitive business where a constant line of new products or services are musts. Generally, a firm with a warehouse full of inventory will try to sell much of it before embarking on something new; this precarious situation forces a company to be fearful, an environment that stifles creativity and thus, long-term survival.

Many investors check the plant/buildings/equipment of a firm to see whether sizable investment has been made in this category. If the entry for the current year is much larger than the previous one, it tells the investor that he or she will not have to worry for a long time about investment dollars tied up in such large expenses. If the current year is a *fraction* of previous years, however, the signs are strong that so much repair to buildings or equipment is coming (or that new facilities and equipment will have to be financed to replace the outdated items), that stockholders will suffer lower profits; the debts for such new expenses will be larger.

Do you now see that almost every complex story about business can be likened to that lemonade stand? Labor troubles are easy to understand. So is a bankruptcy when creditors are fighting stockholders to get their money first.

Even the way the owners originally financed the lemonade stand mirrors what's done in the business world. Often it's done with someone who has a tremendous idea and energy to match—but almost no money. The nation's huge publishing empire, Time Incorporated (*Sports Illustrated, Time, People, Fortune, Discovery, Life,* etc.) was started by two Yale seniors who had only the idea and the work energy; they talked investors into a $90,000 grubstake.

Sometimes a business starts with an idea and almost *no* work involvement. That's how the famed corporate raider T. Boone Pickens got started. He was living in his car and shaving in service stations when he got the idea of playing matchmaker between a landowner who was open to letting someone drill for oil on his property and an independent driller looking for a spot. He introduced them and when two small gas wells resulted, he made $2500 on the "marriage." After many such brokered deals, Pickens attracted financiers who wanted to ride on his coattails. Eventually, he had enough money to take over the huge Gulf Oil corporation. His later attempt to take over Boeing Aircraft resulted in an emergency meeting of the Washington legislature, which passed a law that essentially was what traders today call a "poison pill"; its rules about an out-of-state takeover were not to Pickens's taste. All of his actions show what someone can do with no money, not much elbow grease, but with a colossal idea.

This brings us to the dizzying world of mergers and takeovers (*acquisitions*), something you've heard a lot about in the last few years. There's nothing complex about a merger, for generally it's like two lemonade stands uniting ownership. United, they can pool capital, inventory, promotional efforts, and a place with high traffic. Divided, each makes less, and one may even drive the other out of business.

In the business world, one company may be long on ideas, have a best-selling product line, and a growing territory; the other may have a lot of cash and a well-established, far-flung territory. There is a kind of equality in a *merger* in what the two firms bring to the whole.

A *takeover*, however, is *not* equal. Sometimes, Goliath may swallow David. Or if David is like T. Boone Pickens and can talk enough investors into backing him, he may swallow Goliath. In so doing, he may siphon off all the cash, sell off all the inventory and property/equipment, and close the firm; that means he can add more to his bank account and walk away from a situation that leaves thousands jobless, as has been done in many past takeovers.

Now, a takeover requires a "raider" and a target. You might want to explore such famous raiders as T. Boone Pickens or Irv the Liquidator as a composition topic. The business pages, business data bases, and the *Reader's Guide to Periodical Literature* are full of their deeds and the implications of what they have been doing. To understand their actions, you need to go back to the lemonade stand.

A *raider* may be an outsider who spots certain things about that lemonade stand that makes it a primary target. The raider may want to take over a thriving stand to get in on the profits without putting in too much energy or ideas, or by gutting it. In the business world, there are even raider types who merely threaten to take over a company just so they can drive up the value of the stock; because they usually have bought its stock, they can walk away from such an effort after selling it when they think it's at its highest level and, thus, make a sizable profit. Such a threat is called "greenmail."

Certain factors, such as sizable profits, attract a raider to a target. Buried assets, greedy/lazy management, and refusal to push for a firm's fullest potential are the blood that lures such sharks.

A T. Boone Pickens, for example, has pointed out that he is on the side of stockholders cheated by all these things. It must be remembered that most stockholders essentially are *not* loyal to the firms in which they have bought shares; they buy to make a profit. Fundamental investing advice always has been "never fall in love with your stock." And so when a raider's threats drive up stock prices, investors *do* benefit; when a raider offers to take over a firm and make changes that *will* increase stockholder profits (*dividends*), most stockholders will back that raider; or when a raider raises enough money to buy a controlling interest in a stockholder election (and it might be a *small* percentage of all shares), it's been shown that stockholders will support the raider.

Let's say our lemonade stand owners have been lazy and greedy and unwilling to expand; that now a T. Boone Pickens spots them as a takeover target. Whether it's our lemonade stand or Boeing Aircraft, targets rarely go down without a spirited and expensive fight—another good topic for a composition. To write about such bitter "wars," however, you need to understand some of the tactics; many of the words cited as lively in this section of the chapter are common terms in takeover battles.

Seeing that it doesn't have a chance, a target may rush around looking for a friendly company, i.e., one that will allow it to continue operating just as it has, to take it over. The friendly company is called a *white knight*. Or management may decide to sell off its most profitable product line or subsidiary so that the raider will wind up with a gutted target; this strategy is called the *crown-jewel defense*.

It could be that a lemonade stand's owners may attach so many strings to the deal via employee contracts (large pension arrangements, big severance-salary and deferred-salary payments, big blocks of stocks as gifts) that a takeover may bankrupt the raider who starts running that stand; this is the *poison pill*.

Or the lemonade stand owners might decide to buy out the stockholders and "go private," something that is so costly to a company that it may be the last resort. A raider who cannot buy the stock will be stopped from making any moves on the lemonade stand. In the business world, *going private* means that the owners will have to raise enough money to buy up all the stock issued. Usually, only major banks can gather enough money to lend owners for such a maneuver; they stand to make millions in interest from such loans. Once the loan has been made, such banks tend to keep such a close watch on operations that the owners find the firm cannot grow; the owners also generally spend more time and effort trying to pay off that enormous debt that they look backward more than they do toward future progress. They certainly become timid about developing new products or services. There are many possible theme topics about what has happened to companies that have taken this route. Again, the library is your primary source.

As for the raiders, there are composition topics galore here, too.

Raiders without a lot of capital generally borrow money from banks whose mergers and acquisitions departments have staffs of attorneys and other financial experts to provide superb help in bringing off a takeover without a hitch. Such a bank may get from 5 to 10 percent of the eventual sale price of the target company; imagine the 10 percent commission on the $20 billion sale for RJR Nabisco or the $13.1 billion price tag for Kraft Foods. (Wall Streeters call such a commission *feemail*.)

If you're uncertain how to tackle a theme on such a topic, you may find an idea in the comments of at least one business columnist who was begging for government action against this fast-paced kind of modern piracy:

> These (takeover-protection tactics) are complicated, taking squads of lawyers and investment bankers just to put them together. (The law firm representing Kraft reportedly submitted a bill for $20 million). But they are not all that hard to understand. What happens is this: A publicly owned corporation is taken private. The stock is bought with borrowed money. Then the new owners of the firm [the lenders] sell off various pieces of it to pay for the buyout and trim the costs of what's left. What's created is debt—not new products or new jobs. Stockholders make a killing, but the real killing is made by those who put the deal together. . .Corporate debt is [thus] subsidized by the taxpayer: Interest payments are deductible—a cost of doing business.****

There are one or two more things you need to know about takeovers.

A raider without much cash may borrow a small grubstake to show major investors that there is credit worthiness. The raider may borrow on his or her life insurance or from someone or a firm willing to withstand such a risk. That is called *leveraging*. Another way of raising capital is not to issue stock, but short-term *bonds;* bonds usually are *long-term* IOUs, but even short-term bonds give the impression that the raider is not a quick-buck artist, but a solid source for investment. Fortunately, bond purchasers are protected by the bond industry's credit rating system. Instead of getting an A credit rating, for instance, it may be a BB—a rank low enough to show it's a high-risk situation. Those looking for a quick buck often seek out raiders who have pulled off a takeover and paid off such *junk bonds* handsomely and quickly.

Let's move to the mysteries of stocks and bonds.

Assume that our lemonade stand initially was financed with stocks sold to both preferred and common stockholders. Junk bonds introduce you to the world of the long-term bond. (It's sometimes 10 to 50 years before such bonds mature.)

If the lemonade stand owners want to raise additional capital, they will issue new stock at a certain price. It's usually priced higher than the first stock they issued, just to attract buyers. The initial stockholders love this sort of thing because the value of *their* stock goes up. Sometimes a company will issue new

****From *The Oregonian*, November 6, 1988.

stock only to present stockholders, but at a lower price. Even so, the stockholder may find that a $10-per-share stock has now been changed to two (or more) shares; that even a drop in value to $7 still means a nice profit, particularly if future trading sends each share far *beyond* $7. This is called a *stock split*.

Stock purchases are not complex. If you buy a $1 share of that lemonade stand and the owners do so well that each share rises to $1.01, you've made a profit; if it rises to $2 or $200, you'll understand why real stockholders hang onto their stocks when values are rising.

If you buy at $1 per share and it goes up to $6, you've made $5 if you then decide to unload (sell) the stock. Equally, if you buy at $1 per share and it drops to 10¢, you've lost most of your investment. *Playing the stock market* means that you are gambling; seasoned traders urge you *never* to play the market with rent or grocery money.

You may decide to do a theme on something called *program trading* whereby people who have invested huge amounts of money use a computer program to buy and sell large blocks of stocks. In the famous Black Monday October 19, 1987, part of the fall of the stock market was blamed on such investors deciding to sell those blocks of stock when computers told them to "get out." As such a plug was pulled, smaller investors got frightened and also tried to sell. But the drop was so vast and so quick that most small investors found they couldn't even get a call in to a brokerage. Such major transactions locked up the stock market so that small investors were cut out. Panic drove down the worth of stock.

You now can see how it's possible to manipulate stock prices with such big purchases even if they are *not* bought via program trading methods. When a raider buys enormous chunks of stock to drive up its price, other investors often decide to join such a buying spree. There's a theme topic in what the Securities and Exchange Commission and Congress have been trying to do to stop both program trading and such raider manipulation.

What is *insider trading*?—something that has put a few people in prison. Suppose someone "inside" the lemonade stand finds out that expansion is planned; or that business is going from bad to worse and everyone smart should bail out. If an "insider" either buys/sells stock because of that information or tips outsiders about what is happening "inside" the stand, that is "insider" action. It also is a federal crime.

You need to know also that there even are traders who gamble on whether stocks are going to rise or fall by a certain date. This is called *options buying*. A deal to sell by a certain date is called a *put*, to buy by a certain date is termed a *call*. "Inside" information could help the options trader to make a lot of money as well as help the ordinary stockholder.

Investors who are supercautious about their money or who like a variety of stocks in their *portfolios*, might decide to get involved in a *mutual fund* that includes the lemonade stand as well as many other investments. Often, people who are not rich decide to pool their money and invest it in a mutual fund; or they contact a stockbroker who picks out a mutual fund for them; such modest investors earn more on these collective buys than they could as individuals.

What about bonds?

If you have ever received a savings bond as a present, you know already the principle of bond buying. A bond is like a long-term IOU with interest. Or think of it as passbook savings with such costly penalties for gutting your account that you leave your money in the bank for 10 to 30 years.

Most bonds cost much more than your $25 savings bond. They usually start at about $1000 each and are bought in blocks. They are not for the small investor.

But if they're so costly and don't pay off for years, why do people buy them?

First, even 50 years later, investors will get back every penny they once spent on them. Second, because bonds are so expensive, the interest is equally high. It's paid at regular intervals (quarterly, semiannually, annually, etc.) when you clip the interest coupon and present it to the bond issuer's representative. Many people live well just on the interest alone.

The only risk about bonds is that inflation or deflation can change what you'll get when the bond "matures" down the road. Also, if the issuer sets a stipulation in the original purchase that he or she can "call" in the bond at any time, the owner might not get years of living off the interest and face current inflation or deflation rates as well. The only major risk—one that does happen occasionally—is that the bond issuer goes broke at the time of the bond's maturity and cannot come up with money to pay it off.

One most attractive kind of bond is the *municipal bond*. This instrument is issued by towns, counties, states, and the federal government to get money so that major projects or programs can be funded immediately. A city may need money to repair hundreds of potholes in its streets. A county may need to replace a bridge. A state may need to finance a university building or a highway. The federal government may need to float bonds to pay for anything from weapons to rescuing farmers.

The "muni" generally is a highly attractive investment vehicle because, unlike bonds that private company's float, interest is tax free. Stockholders must pay income tax on their dividends (although they also can get tax relief if they lose money on stocks). But "muni" owners enjoy the best of all investment worlds—provided they investigate the background and credit rating of bond issuers. For instance, if a city can scarcely meet its payroll and is begging a county to take over its fire department, its credit rating will not be high. If a state is losing a lot of industry and a lot of residents, that means that it is losing major tax resources; and because taxes meet payroll and other major expenses, it is not likely that a governmental bond can pay much on a bond's interest or even pay back the initial investment.

An act of God or a major error in the issuer's judgment also can cause a loss to bondholders. The largest default in the history of "munis" happened in the 1980s when the state of Washington's Public Power Supply System voted not to go ahead on two nuclear-power plants they had floated bonds to build. The 25,000 bondholders who had invested the $2.25 billion for the plants had to resort to years of trials and lawyers' fees to divide up the only $700 million awarded by the courts.

If you decide to do a theme on stocks or bonds, you either can resort to some aspect of this kind of investing with material found in business data bases, the *Readers' Guide to Periodical Literature* or the daily newspaper. Or you can pay a visit to a brokerage; almost every town has such an office, and its staff generally has both literature and help available on stock and bond investments. One student wrote a theme based on a week's experience in which he invested $25 in a motel chain and spent his lunch hours and after-school time checking with his broker on this stock.

Explaining the Complex

Some overall precepts in doing themes on business topics are obvious from the foregoing.

The language must be simple—words and sentences—and analogies like that lemonade stand or other homespun situations are the elements that put clarity into what you write. Don't "copy" a source, as been strongly advised; usually you can do a better job than that original source of explaining something to ordinary readers. Give yourself some private applause when you figure out an analogy that clarifies the complex or when you turn a simple phrase that improves on one that is complicated. The complexity of your sentences probably will be directly tied to how many commas you have to use, as has been noted.

Don't forget the *breather* between sizable sections or paragraphs in your composition. And paragraph between sections of something complex.

Another method mentioned for explaining the complex—particularly needed in business topics—is to *humanize* the situation. Readers get and stay interested in a subject if you use examples of people going through a situation. The lemonade stand is especially helpful because every reader can envision youngsters doling out this familiar drink.

Be scrupulously accurate when you cite figures, operations, or the names of those involved. Use the same careful techniques you employ on a term paper where citations of sources are required. Give the name of your sources(s), if any, in the same fashion. Your instructors know you couldn't possibly master all that you include unless you have read about it or have talked to a source; all they want to know is where you got the information. The more sources you cite, the more thorough and academically sound your paper is.

Organizing the Business Piece

What about the structure of the business theme?

The first paragraph must lure the reader into the composition. If you thought business subjects were dull, your instructor also may think so. But these stories can be as lively as anything in the sports page. The rest of the theme must hang onto that reader. A fine composition on a huge southwestern bank failure began with a bystander noticing nearly two dozen Cadillacs tooling into the parking lot of a bank. To most readers, it sounded like a gathering of the Mafia; subsequent paragraphs revealed the cars were full of bank examiners. Another theme put a reader in a Portland store where its Vietnamese owner was repeatedly shaken down by a group of teenaged Asian thugs. Such a humanized anecdote led the reader into the lives of store owners who were too terrified and yet had too much personal pride to call the police about such victimization.

What comes after that opener depends on the subject.

A profile of a business personality should be handled like the structure explained in the chapter on descriptive themes (page 30).

Use a lead that shows a new product being used. Follow it with information about its manufacturer and its significance to the marketplace. Then get into its history. How did the product come into being? Include the trials—particularly the early failures—because a reader is often fascinated and inspired to know what kind of tribulations other humans endure to create something. After this, describe the product, starting with its overall look; then, spell out all its functions. You might then add information about who is likely to buy it, what kind of competition it faces, its price, and where it's going to be sold.

A quick and dirty outline used by one student on an assignment about a new hand-held calculator from Hewlett-Packard looked like the one opposite.

That student who compared four companies as investment possibilities set up her composition with an opening that had them turning on an electric light; that is easier for readers to relate to than coping with a huge tangle of nuclear reactors, kilowattage, and ratios on prices to earnings. Her quick and dirty outline looked like this one on page 236.

A student who used the wave of takeovers as a peg for a theme on ways to stop raiders, did start with Bluebeard and his forays on the high seas. His outline moved in this fashion appears on page 237.

Public Finance

When a city tries to tax a dozen elderly people right out of their homes, public finance is not dull or dry. When the corrupt regime of Boss Tweed and his gang stole $100 million from the New York City treasury in the 1870s and were exposed by *Harper's* magazine, its readers found it shocking. And when school systems have to close down—as has been the case in this decade— because they run out of money, public finance again is full of all kinds of emotions on the part of parents and taxpayers.

Public finance perhaps is the most exciting part of government, for money always has dictated policy. Here are many potential theme topics for you. Your friends who do well in history class may believe wars are fought over honor, high principles, or freedom. But most conflicts are linked to governmental finance or business dealings. Money calls the shots. Our nation fought for independence partly because the founding fathers objected to taxation without representation, but chiefly because British businessmen relied upon the colonies to furnish cheap raw materials and to buy finished goods. Haven't our past city governments refused to punish polluters because they were afraid to lose the payrolls and tax revenues that came from businesses ruining environments? Don't areas become

Lead | "Atlanta"

Sun. | HP 285

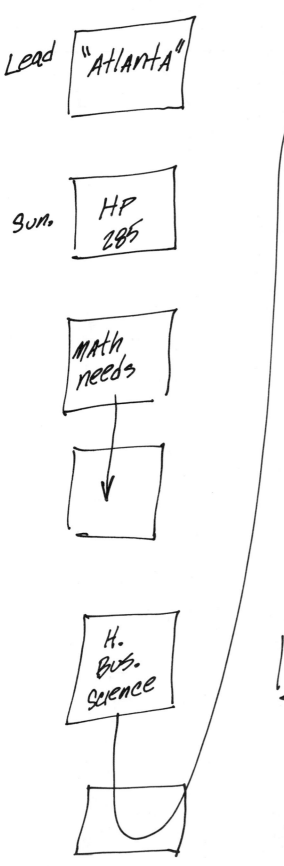

Math needs

H. Bus. Science

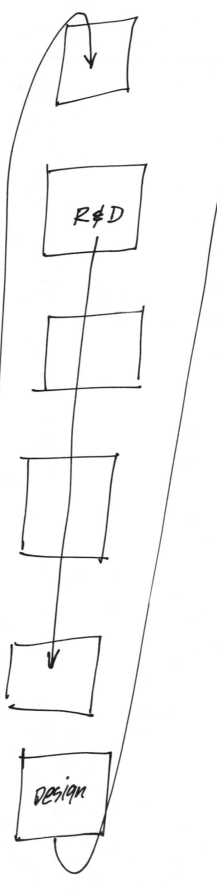

R&D

Design

test

marketing

Comp.

Close

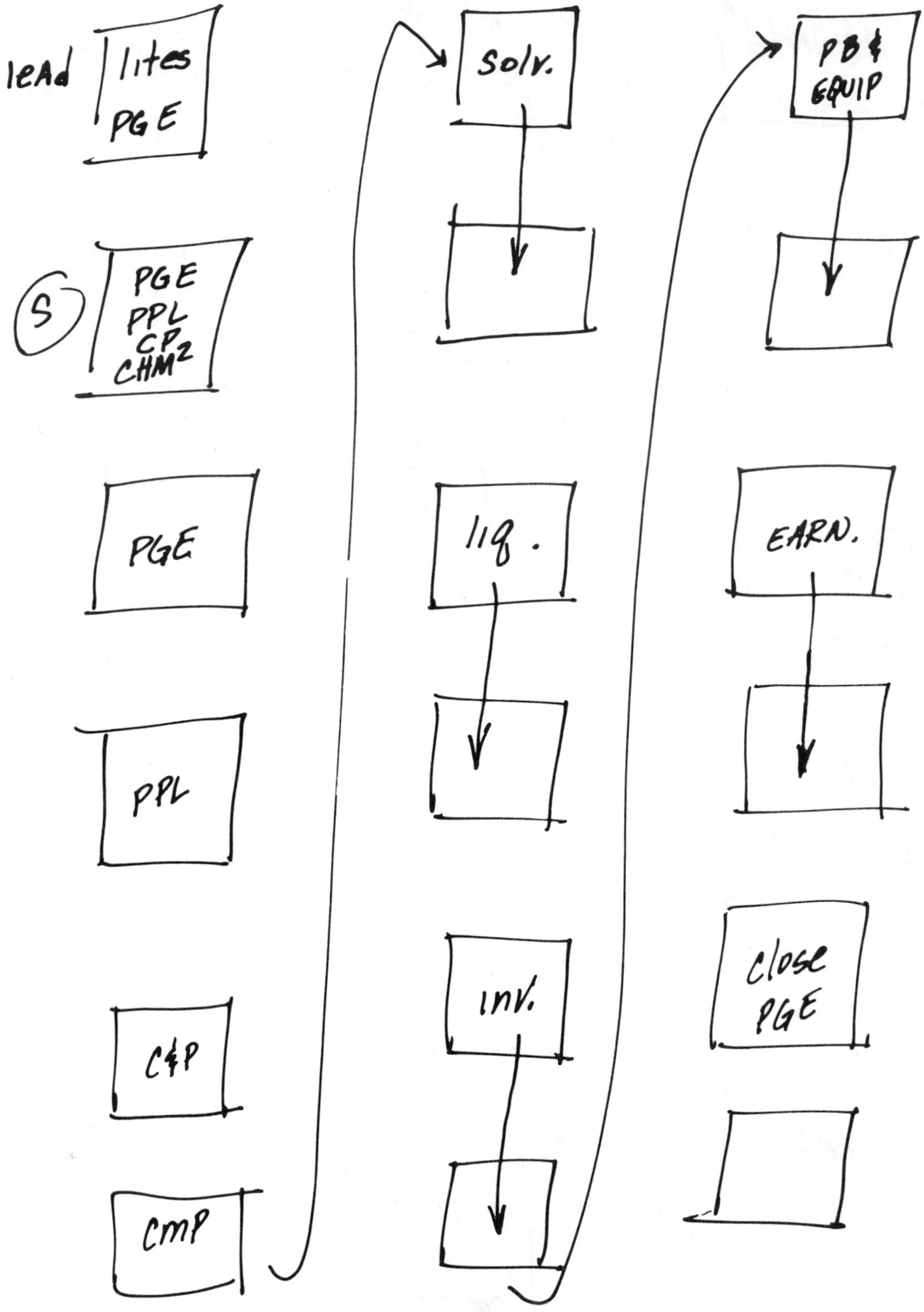
lead
lites
PGE
S
PGE
PPL
CP
CHM2
PGE
PPL
C&P
CMP
Solv.
liq.
inv.
PB&
EQUIP
EARN.
close
PGE

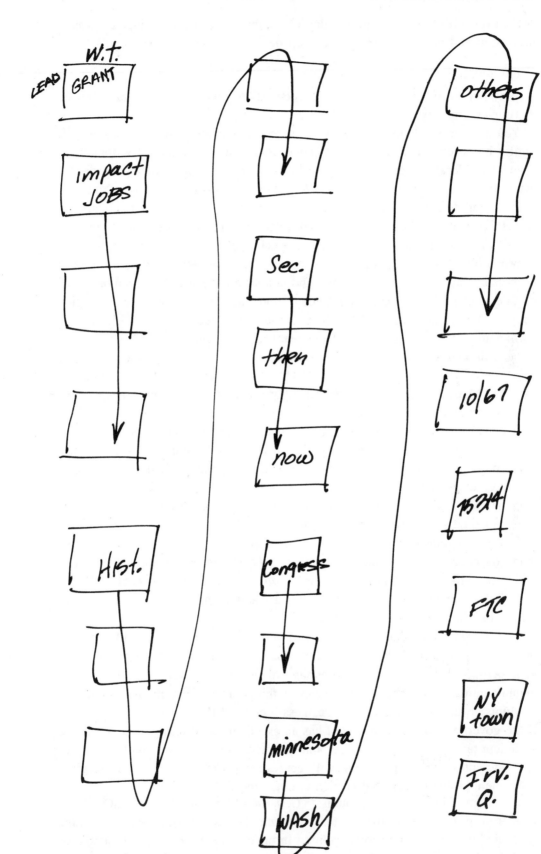

crime ridden because communities don't have the tax resources to increase police protection and public services or to keep public housing in good repair?

Focus on Your Community

Why not write a composition that is focused on some aspect of public finance in your community?

You could do a theme on the usual subject of tracking a federal or state bill until it becomes law. But the investigative work to do a fine job takes contacting state and federal sources as well as a lot of time spent in following up distant leads and interviewing key people a long way from where you live. You also may be tempted to plagiarize articles from national or regional publications, something that could damage your grades and reputation with teachers and your school. But a decision to write about local public finance is far easier, its information at your fingertips. The taxation and budgetary information is only a few steps away, for most city hall and county courthouse staff members will go to considerable lengths to help students understand what looks like a complex subject. The same thing is true about schools, another fascinating element of public finance. You certainly will impress your instructor.

Schools and all other governmental offices by law must open their books at any time to the public. You can get a copy of their budgets just by stopping in for one. Many budgets have been carefully prepared so that the taxpayer will come to understand how money is being spent, and why.

Just like your personal budget, the budget of a governmental body or school has both revenues and expenditures. If you have a job, you have income; and if you buy items you regard as essentials, you have expenditures. If you overspend and have to get an advance on next week's salary or allowance, you're doing what is called *deficit spending*. When you've saved a sizable sum, you have what is called a *reserve* or *sinking fund*.

But if you want to buy something really expensive, something that will cost many paychecks or allowances—a used car, a computer, a trip to Disneyland— what you will be doing is investing in a *capital expenditure*. In public affairs, a capital expenditure could be a bridge, a stadium, a highway, an additional school building.

To fund your own capital expenditure, you might float a loan, with interest, from family or friends. You'll promise to pay it back at some distant date when your savings account has amassed enough money to retire such a debt. Governmental entities and schools do the same thing. They float municipal bonds. ("Munis" were introduced in the business section of this chapter on page 232). If the governmental body or school has an excellent credit rating—that is, it has sufficient taxes coming in to make bond payments—bond buyers will snap them up. The attraction is that they will get every penny back of their original investment—plus the interest (which is not taxable).

There are four types of "munis:" *General obligation* bonds ("GOs") are paid from property and business taxes; *revenue* bonds are paid for from income generated by usage (an airport, stadium, turnpike); *special assessment* bonds are paid for by a single tax against property owners who will benefit from an improvement to their neighborhood (a sidewalk, sewer hookup, road); finally, there are *special general* bonds that are paid off by revenue from a single assessment on *all* property and business owners.

There is a rich theme topic for the student who wants to explore the kind of "munis" a community has seemed to finance over five years or a decade. Such a theme can reveal whether a community believes in putting money aside for capital improvements or whether it lives from hand to mouth and then stuns taxpayers with the news that millions will have come out of their pockets because some long-neglected major project is falling apart.

The main portion of county or town or school revenues comes from taxes, however—which need not be a scary topic. Throughout history, governmental entities have been taxing people. You either pay or lose your property; you could be assessed fines and/or charged high interest rates on overdue taxes; some people have been imprisoned for failure to pay federal taxes. There is high drama connected with taxes, something you can capitalize on if you choose this as a theme subject.

Taxes are figured by an assessor who looks over a piece of property and/or its equipment, and improvements and does an estimate of how much taxes the owner must pay. Let's say you own a house and yard worth $50,000, according to the county assessor. Taxes are figured by a certain sum per assessed valuation. Let's also say that last year you paid a rate of $20 per $1000; your property taxes were $1000. Let's now say that the county has economized as much as is possible, has put off needed capital improvements, closed some agencies, and even laid off workers; yet it still can't meet its expenses despite such wise cost-cutting. The only way it can pay its bills for essential services (fire, police, water, sewer) is to increase your property taxes at a rate of $30 per $1000. Your taxes would jump from $1000 per year to $1500.

You will begin to understand why some property owners around the nation have passed referendums that limit taxes from going beyond a certain level. You also will understand the rage some people feel whose children have grown up and yet their tax bill for the $1500 has $1000 earmarked for the local schools. Last, you may begin to understand the impact that such tax-limitation laws have had on communities where residents demand the best in services. And you'll know why communities send out expeditions to major industries to try to lure them into the city or county with promises of deferred taxes, the attractions of laying in sewer and water lines, and pledges of cutting through a lot of paperwork and ordinances. You'll also see the dilemma of that Oregon city council that had to back down in assessing elderly homeowners on fixed income for improvements done on the street running past their homes; one man living on $8000 per year was billed $49,000. Raising revenues has agonizing human consequences that can be captured in a theme.

Let's move from property taxes to that major source of most of a government's revenues: business taxes.

In the business section of this chapter, the analogy of the lemonade stand was used as a way of helping you to understand basic business situations. Let's resurrect that lemonade stand to explain business taxation.

Obviously, the owners of a *real* lemonade stand won't pay taxes, for they usually stay open for a day or two in summer. The federal government would never ask them to register for a tax identification number, and the state wouldn't ask the owners to go through the chartering formalities. But let's pretend that the stand prospers and there's money enough to open a daily business near the local high school. The minute the stand opens at that location, the owners will be subject to taxes—city, county, state, and federal. And if they don't pay those taxes, their private bank accounts can be seized, their personal property can wind up with tax liens on it, and the padlock can be put on the front door.

Businesses always are confronted with public finance. They must pay taxes on profits. They also must pay taxes on the business property. Owners must send in withholding deductions on their employees. They must do the same with employees' social security payments. And they must contribute to the government's unemployment fund. Additionally, there are payments to the state workmen's compensation fund to cover any employee on-the-job accidents. Finally, they must send in regular reports on their operations, including forecasts of what their profits might be. All such reports, payments, and filings must be done regularly: on paydays, or once a month, once a quarter, or once each year. The paperwork is backbreaking for small business owners.

Remember the Human Element

The complexity ends when you remember the human element.

These are real people fretting over taxes. That's where you could seize your reader's interest. For instance, you might write about a business owner short on cash one month, who failed to send in regularly the withholding sums to the state and federal governments. Then she let the social security payments slide. These two elements are common reasons why many entrepreneurs wind up as bankrupts.

Equally, there's a theme subject in the flower shop owner whose business fails because taxes were raised to the breaking point. Considering that businesses situated in malls not only have to meet all of the above rules, but pay mall owners a percentage of their profits, it's no wonder so many are in physical, emotional, and financial distress. Here, you can find many good and interesting topics. Talk to the owner of a business. It may be where you work. Ask what he or she has to do for the various governmental bodies. Point out you're not asking for their "numbers" (profit figures), but that you are interested in knowing what their tax headaches are, right down to the number and variety of forms they must fill out or to how the government should streamline the tax system. Their quotes should be meaty and colorful, lending a lot of interest to your theme.

What you will have done is to humanize public finance.

There's also a theme topic in the viewpoint of the governmental entity.

Decreasing tax revenues from property owners and businesses mean that services will have to be cut. The result might be temporary school closures or severe cuts among faculty and programs. Some cities may make across-the-board cuts or just amputate the services that will cause the least outcry. There may be fewer police. The fire department might be farmed out to a county unit. Cuts in maintenance crews mean that repairs and replacements will be delayed or cancelled and, in future, cause gigantic capital-improvement expenditures. A library can't pay for itself on fines. And a park and recreation program that has been sliced to the bone cannot offer youth activities or grounds upkeep. Maybe streetlighting will have to be sacrificed with accompanying increase in crime.

You might monitor police department expenses in the last three or four years, for example. You could do a theme on jail expenses over the last decade. Or write about which kind of county employee gets most of the payroll. In case you think line items in the payroll category of a budget are boring, one of the factors that broke open the Tweed scandal ring was that a plasterer was officially on the books for a $50,000-per-day salary, a colossal sum even today.

You could do a composition on the rising costs of the public dump (a landfill), an indicator that residents either must be more willing to approve higher salaries and/or to pay for obtaining additional landfill space or to one day cart away their own refuse. There's always a hot topic in transportation. When fares are raised (to cover salaries, maintenance, new buses, and increasing liability insurance rates), ridership usually drops. Those who suffer most are the poor who may be reduced to walking or giving up a job.

All such topics are right in your backyard. Budgets and governmental staff are readily available and, usually, responsive. They generally are astounded that young people are interested in public finance. You also can go to your local newspaper and talk to the reporter who covers city and county news for leads on the aspect of public finance that has intrigued you; he or she may have tips that will provide shortcuts in your researching efforts.

What goes on locally is magnified at the state and federal levels, of course.

Organizing the Public Finance Piece

Once you have done your research, the next task is to break it all down so that you understand it thoroughly. That may mean drawing a system, or reading aloud until everything falls into place, or talking to more than one source.

Then, you'll need to set up your structure via a quick and dirty outline. That outline will get you started, for it offers a direct effort to write a theme; you will know exactly where you are going and what to leave out and what to leave in.

Once again, the opener must seize a reader's attention. An anecdotal opening paragraph—preferably one involving ordinary people—will do that. One student held readers' attention in her first paragraph by describing what a new city councilman found when he climbed under a heavily used bridge to check for metal fatigue in the girders. Another student, writing a theme with "what-if" overtones, started off with an imaginary house fire that took several lives because a fire station had been closed.

The second paragraph should deal with the point you're making along with the significance of implications spelled out in that opening paragraph. Is the city going to have to cut its court system? Does the failure of a levy mean that a women's shelter will have to be closed? Will the community college be able to pay a $600,000 repair bill on a chiller and meet other major upcoming maintenance costs?

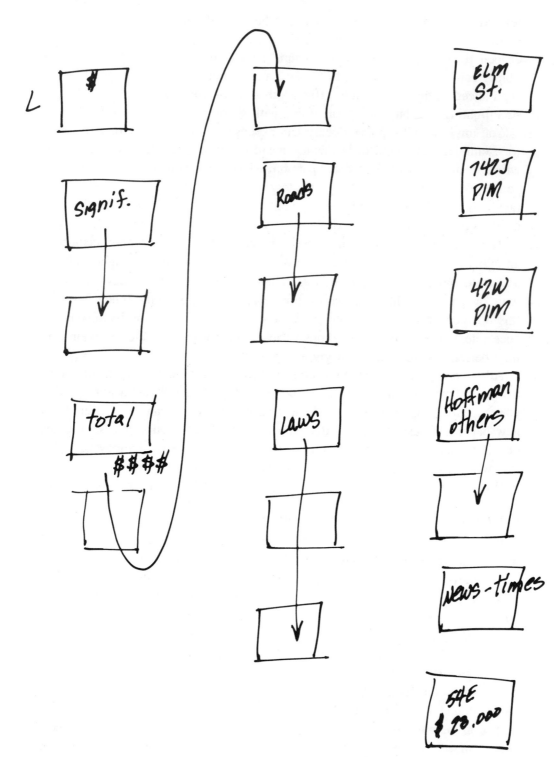

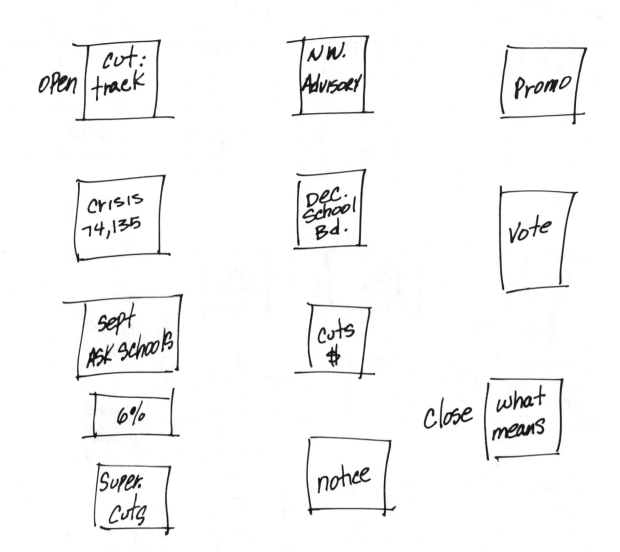

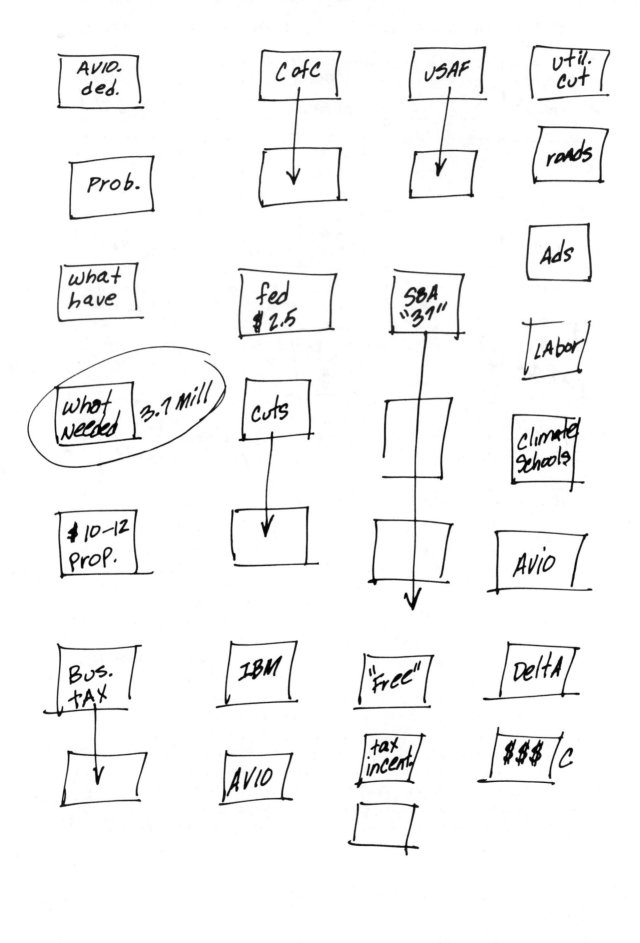

Subsequent paragraphs might fill in the reader about the topic's financial history, including past implications.

After presenting the past situations, move to the future. What's ahead if things continue as they have? Sprinkle in good quotes from your sources, where they pertain to the point you are emphasizing. Quote the source accurately. If you're using items from the newspaper or budget, ensure that those sources are credited. The instructor knows there's no way *you* could be the source for all that information.

A quick and dirty outline for a student who decided to track the awarding of county road contracts in the past five years looked like this the one on page 242.

A student describing the route a school superintendent had to take to get the district's annual budget passed, set up this kind of outline the one on page 243.

Then there was the student who traced the various methods used by a town to increase its tax base over a 10-year period. His outline looked like this:

As you move from outline to writing the theme, remember to use simple words and uncluttered sentences. Stories on public finance need to reduce dollar figures to meaningful terms. For example, when you're writing about how much is being spent on the police department, deal with how much it takes to keep one squad car on the road per day or the kind of daily duties an officer performs—along with the risks—for a certain salary figure. If you're trying to explain costs in the water department, tell the readers how much it costs to fix just one pipe, or include the amount of water the average family goes through in one day.

Use breathers for major breaks in the theme. Start a new paragraph each time you bring up something new or complex. Analogies and examples are vital, in converting financial matters to levels an average reader can comprehend.

Steps in Clarifying a Complex Topic

On writing about complex topics, the first step is getting up the courage to decide to deal with something difficult. The second step requires you to focus on one key aspect of such a subject. Then, you must concentrate on understanding *everything* about that aspect. You may have to draw pictures. Or read aloud. Or go over several articles that deal with the same aspect. The next step is to boil down the subject to its basics and to find analogies or examples that will lead the ordinary reader from the known to the unknown.

Once you complete that kind of groundwork on science and technology, statistics, business, or public finance, you then must take the time to lay down a quick and dirty outline. That way, you'll know exactly what you'll be including— essential to avoid procrastination—and where you're going in each paragraph.

From that point on, take a breath and in your simplest words and sentences, write. Remember what has been suggested about attracting and holding onto the reader throughout the theme. When you finish the first draft, edit ruthlessly for sentences so packed with ideas or facts that they overwhelm. Forget, too, the deathless prose and well-turned line or you'll forget the purpose of the theme. Instead, concentrate on teaching the reader something complicated through basic English.

Last, read your work aloud to spot the clinkers and unclear information. And when all of that is completed, pat yourself on the back. There can be no greater thrill than to take a complex topic and make it clear and absorbing to those who initially would either shun it or flee from it. After all, that is what was accomplished by Plato and all others who found great joy in opening the doors of knowledge to ordinary people.

THE COLLEGE
APPLICATION
AUTOBIOGRAPHY

CHAPTER 17

THE COLLEGE APPLICATION AUTOBIOGRAPHY

It is not very comforting to hear that the trend today is for colleges not to ask applicants to write an autobiography. Many—such as the prestigious Ivy League and Seven Sisters' colleges—still ask for one. So, probably, does yours or you would not be reading this chapter.

Many college officials feel that most autobiographies give insights into an applicant's values, his self-appraisal, and his ability to organize and use English. The admissions dean of Wesleyan University once said he feels that such autobiographies tell more about applicants, their strengths and weaknesses, their aspirations and disappointments, their response to society, and their troubles with it than "we can gather from all the scores, recommendations, and references put forward in their behalf."

Other admissions directors may not agree as they wearily pour over the hundreds of autobiographies that come in each year. They may feel that these brief sketches are untrustworthy, superficial, misleading, and time-consuming. Further, they may indicate that the unsure student may be so afraid that this sketch will be the key cause of acceptance or rejection that he will have someone else write it for him. Some admissions people declare that an autobiography inhibits applicants from revealing their true selves—that it's a "put-on." A shy applicant churns out a busy and glowing portrait of an extrovert. The scholarly type gets a fit of modesty and plays down his intelligence. The fun-loving individual describes himself to be more retiring than a Trappist monk. The pressures to get into a good college today do many things to applicants.

But no matter what the views are on the worth of autobiographies, most people concerned with them readily admit that just thinking about writing them leads to more procrastination by an applicant than does any other single document required for college admission. Students dread writing about themselves, especially for something so important as getting admitted to the colleges of their choice. They are afraid they will seem boastful or too shy. They are fearful of seeming disorganized. They are unable to write well or appear to have too limited a vocabulary. They might even feel that the admissions directors won't give their sketches much attention anyway. And so applicants put off writing the autobiography until the very last moment. Then, coupled with their other real shortcomings, this hasty effort does not make the best impression.

Yet this need not happen.

There is nothing so difficult about writing an autobiography if you know how to go about it. And if you know what you're doing, you'll not procrastinate about this important document. You'll get to it when the college application papers arrive at your house. A careful reading of this chapter will make you feel sure of yourself on writing the autobiography.

To do a good job, you'll need to follow these cardinal rules:

1   Write the autobiography all by yourself.
2   Be truly honest in describing your real goals and values.
3   Be organized in what you write.
4   Include substantial information on yourself.
5   Try to write in an interesting way.

Let's examine each of these requisites.

There should be nobody involved in writing your autobiography but you yourself. True, a lot may depend on that profile, but you're hurting yourself if you cajole someone else to write it for you. It's as bad as hiring someone to sit in on a class for you or to take a test for you. Nor should you try to pick the brains of your guidance counselor or your English teacher on organization, criticism of your writing, or proofreading. Because of the time element, among other things, your teachers probably will refuse aid and wonder if you can cope with the self-reliance demanded of students in university life. Also, you won't be able to take Mom or a friend along with you through four years of college. In addition, many admissions officials can detect an autobiography written by someone other than the applicant. What they will think of the maturity and honesty of someone who leans on others for such important matters needs no comment. So stand on your own feet. If you have to lean on anything, lean on what you read in this section of the book.

Next, be totally honest in describing yourself, your values, and your goals. You shouldn't be applying to a college that does not fit your philosophy of life or your capabilities anyway. You should have done enough investigatory work on the college to which you're applying to know what kinds of students it seeks. You should know if it is aiming for the "late bloomer," the affluent, the religiously oriented, the genius with the work habits to match, the socially or economically disadvantaged, the scientifically inclined, or the person who is well-rounded. Even if you slant your autobiography to the manner you think the college wants certain points answered, you're letting yourself in for a great deal of unhappiness for four years if you don't mean what you say.

More than this, writing an untruthful autobiography is much more difficult to do than a genuine one. It's easier to be truthful. If you're shy, why not admit you're not a hearty extrovert? Colleges understand introspective individuals. If you've spread yourself too thin through many activities so that grades have slumped, say so. Many universities realize that applicants often benefit from earlier mistakes in life. If you really don't plan to work with retarded children or to join the Peace Corps for work with the backward in Yucatan, don't give the impression you are an Albert Schweitzer. It is recognized that everyone is not altruistic. Nor do you have to be ashamed that you were not a leader in high school. It is pretty well understood that the world is not made up of billions of chiefs and only a few Indians.

So be honest in your autobiography. You'll only cross yourself up anyway if you aren't truthful since your application file will include appraisals from teachers and friends as well as your school records. Such appraisals, incidentally, often ask for detailed accounts on such things as the applicant's aptitude and performance, the breadth and depth of his reading, his intellectual curiosity, his facility to express ideas in speech and writing, his participation in discussions, his powers of organization and concentration, his cooperative attitudes, his moral character, his leadership abilities, his relations with others, his citizenship, his work habits, the real depth of his participation in extracurricular activities. Thus, if your own profile is quite a departure from what is said of you by other sources, the admissions officials will draw some interesting conclusions about you and your autobiography.

Let us come now to the rules that have to do with composition of the autobiography: organizing material properly, including substantial information about yourself, and writing in an interesting way.

You still will have to be organized whether the college has set the length of the autobiography at a maximum of 300 words or has prescribed no set limit. Leaping around from aspect to aspect of your life with no connection whatever can give college personnel the impression that you run your life in much the same way. Even those who don't feel life can be lived in a kind of Germanic lockstep orderliness will allow that a certain amount of information must be set down in an easily discernible manner in an applicant's autobiography.

The college either indicates on its forms what points it wants covered in a profile, or it just gives you free rein and tells you to write about yourself. The first will be called here the specific biography; the second, the "blue-sky" biography.

The specific biography, many have thought, came about as the result of colleges setting no word limits to autobiographies or guidelines on points to be covered. Years of receiving rambling profiles that revealed very little of the applicants perhaps drove them to set some limitations on content and length. In the past few years, the admissions people have thought up aspects that are intended to be very revealing. You may be asked to include in your autobiography any of such things as: 1) your immediate and long-range goals in life, 2) your values in life, 3) who or what influenced you to apply to this particular college, 4) what person or book has had the most influence on your life, 5) what you expect to get from the college, 6) your strengths and weaknesses, 7) your greatest disappointment and your greatest happiness, 8) what contribution you intend to make to the college or to life, 9) your work experience, 10) your leadership or "followership" capabilities, 11) how you react to adult responsibilities, 12) your creative talents, 13) your feelings on religion or morals, 14) the activity in school that gave you the greatest (or least) amount of success and satisfaction, 15) how you get along with most people, 16) your evaluation of your education so far, 17) what makes you different from others. There may be many other points asked that are not included here, but these represent most of those asked in one way or another of applicants.

Whether you are to do a blue-sky or specific biography, you should first read the short section in this book on how to do profiles in theme work. Many students who have done profiles by following these instructions merely have rewritten their themes for their college autobiographies. That section will show you how to organize your writing in paragraph-by-paragraph fashion as well as provide hints on composition.

The profile section, however, will not show you how to include some of these specific goals-and-values points the colleges want covered in your auto-biography. That is what the following paragraphs will teach you how to do.

If you are writing a blue-sky profile with no guidelines set by the college, you'll see soon enough that there's nothing wrong with borrowing some of the goals-and-values points enumerated above for a specific biography.

What points should you borrow from the goals-and-values information?

Again, it depends on the college to which you're applying for admission and your impression of the school. You may have a hunch that the college is not interested in your immediate and long-range goals. You may have inferred through its information and your visit to the campus that it feels people change their goals as they pass from youth to adulthood. Thus, you'll skip that point. But equally, the college might set a premium on applicants who have very definite goals and values. So you will include those two points in your autobiography. Maybe you sense that your college couldn't care less about your contribution to the campus and to the world. Then you obviously won't go into that. And so it should go as you feel your way through the goals-and-values list.

On the other hand, if you are writing a specific biography, you'll know exactly what goals-and-values points to include in your profile. If you are asked to cover five points, do only the five stipulated. Forget about the rest even if you are eager to deal with other goals-and-values points. The college knows what it wants applicants to write about.

Now, let's look at how to organize both a blue-sky and a specific biography. Both of them are organized in the same way. You can either *add* the goals-and-values points onto the finished profile or you can *weave* them in throughout the fabric of the autobiography. Some may feel that to weave the goals-and-values material into the profile is a smoother way to handle things. Others may find that it makes for rather bulky paragraphs, bulging with too much information. Decide for yourself whether the *weaving* method or the *adding* method is the more satisfactory for your use and then proceed with the organization.

The following diagrams show how both blue-sky and specific autobiographies can be structured. To understand fully what material is to go into each paragraph, what is to go into the first sentence, the second and so on, you must have read by now the profile portion. Don't go any farther if you've not done this, for you'll not understand what you're doing.

The first example below shows how to organize in paragraph form the autobiography where the goals-and-values information has been *woven* into the paragraphs. The applicant, in doing a blue-sky autobiography, has decided to borrow four goals-and-values points from the specific biography forms for his profile: why he chose the college he did, the most influential person in his life, his work experience, and his school activities. Although he has used the cryptic jot outline taught in this book, you should still be able to follow much of this diagramed outline:

Paragraph No. 1	Introduction (why Stanford, Uncle Joe)
Paragraph No. 2	Boyhood (science at home, school, frogs)
Paragraph No. 3	Boyhood (physique-rheumatic fever, chem set, Dad's help on experiments)
Paragraph No. 4	Boyhood (science fair, Stanford film, pres. of Science Club)
Paragraph No. 5	Youth (job at drug store, Dr. Maberly influence, anecdote on RX)
Paragraph No. 6	Youth (A's in sciences, maths, start Test Tube club-treas., project on ergs)
Paragraph No. 7	Youth (anecdote on Stanford visit, summer in paper mill lab)
Paragraph No. 8	Youth (meet Dr. Millikin, books on physics, anecdote on Millie)

The next example shows how one student organized her autobiography by *adding* the goals-and-values information to the end of the regular profile structure. She has been told to write about six things by the college: her goals, her values, her strengths and weaknesses, the most influential person in her life, her reason for selecting the college she did, and what contribution she might be able to make to that school.

Paragraph No. 1	Introduction (farm anecdote, my birth)
Paragraph No. 2	Childhood (tea party, Eileen, death of Mother)
Paragraph No. 3	Childhood (Eileen's death, reading, Scouts, school change)
Paragraph No. 4	Childhood (anecdote on Benny, berry picking)
Paragraph No. 5	Girlhood (movies, music letter, Jobs's, rally squad sec., describe me)
Paragraph No. 6	Girlhood (troubles in French, find Dickens, anecdote on Ben)
Paragraph No. 7	Girlhood (job at Walgren's, Dad's death, 5 honor rolls, 1 high honors, choir, camera club, 2 skits)
Paragraph No. 8	Girlhood (skiing, home ec. and sewing)
Paragraph No. 9	Girlhood (teaching at Grace Church nursery)
Paragraph No. 10	Goals (teaching, writing, homemaking)
Paragraph No. 11	Values (some materialism—house, etc., simple life—Xenwood Ave.)
Paragraph No. 12	Strengths, Weaknesses (loyalty, generosity, curiosity, perfectionism, temper spendthrift)
Paragraph No. 13	Influential (Dad, anecdote on Bergson)
Paragraph No. 14	Reason for Carolina (English dept., library, proximity, finances)
Paragraph No. 15	Contribution (being good teacher, credit as alum, recruit others)

To decide which of the goals-and-values points should go first, put the most important one first.

Proceed to the actual writing of your autobiography once you have a rough structural outline setting out the organization. The next two examples show you how to include the goals-and-values points by the weaving and the addition methods. The first example shows how to weave in these factors:

While working at Haley's garage, I learned how to change oil and install pinion bearings, but I learned other things too. The owner, Richard Haley, got me interested in car design and engineering. "Detroit should have done it this way" and "Detroit boo-booed here" were common expressions of his. He also showed me how a college education can add to practical knowledge on cars. He also stressed that I should take more math and some mechanical drawing. I'm glad now I followed his advice.

You'll see that this applicant wove in information about the most influential person in his life along with his job experience and part of his course work at school.

The next example shows you how to add the goals-and-values points. This boy is writing on one of those points, the strengths and weaknesses:

> This year has been a reflective one for me. I have had a chance to assess my strong and weak ⎱ key sentences
>
> sides as I've never done before. I have done those things which I ought not to have done as when I resigned as a student court juror rather than lose friends over one case being tried. I have left undone those things that I ought to have done even though this involved small chores like running the garbage cans out to the curb or like making some of the clarinet practices with the band. But I know some of my strong points are such things as getting in my homework, free tutoring of six sophomores on geometry, doing all the home errands involving a car, and sticking to a history project that eventually won a national award. ⎰ examples

The example above illustrates how to start a paragraph with a key sentence that indicates what subject will be used—in this case, the applicant's strengths and weaknesses. Then he deals with his weaknesses, supporting them with specific examples. He rounds off the paragraph by pointing up his strengths, again using specific illustrations to show them. Incidentally, it is good psychology to bring in adverse matter first, countering it with a heavy smattering of favorable material. People are usually impressed with the last thing they read.

The fourth cardinal rule in writing college application autobiographies is to include information with some substance to it. This is important whether you have been allowed only 200 words or an unlimited number in which to profile yourself. Some applicants ramble on with platitudes, quotations from the famous and infamous, sweeping and unsupported statements about themselves, all of which tell an admissions official nothing much. Perhaps that is the applicant's intent. Maybe he's really done very little with his life and has not spent much time thinking about his goals and values. But probably not; everyone's life is somewhat eventful. There are avocational interests and hobbies, engrossing or dull school courses, good and bad home lives, strengths and weaknesses. In short, there is little reason why an applicant has to meander through an autobiography, saying nothing.

You have already read the example showing how one applicant gave specific instances of his strengths and weaknesses. He mentioned what he had done on the student court, chores at home, band, tutoring, and a history project. Here are two other examples to show you how to cope with the more difficult-to-answer points sometimes asked in a specific biography:

The first example shows how a girl wrote about disappointments in life:

> Disappointments in life are no stranger to me. I have come to see how they build character and give valuable experience. I thought my life was } key sentences

> over when all my friends were chosen for Pep Club and I wasn't. The prestige of wearing one of the club's jackets and in being in the school's most exclusive organization meant a lot to me then. But after a week went by, I saw that the world had not come to an end. I looked for other things to do without my friends. Soon I found that the School Door Canteen needed a door checker, the choir needed a second alto. I saw that my German could stand a lot of attention too. Through this single small disappointment, I made new friends and gained some valuable new experiences. } examples

The next illustration displays a boy writing on one of the most difficult goals-and-values points, how are you different from others your age? This is what he said:

> You ask what makes me different from others in my generation. To single himself out as special is a brave thing for a person to do in a society that demands that all men are equal. In my } key sentences

> provincial little world, however, I have seen for a long time that I am different from my friends. I was the type who wrote letters to the President and my Congressmen to protest the Vietnam war. One of my friends offered to ship me to North Vietnam for the duration over that. They thought I was strange also when I went to work in a bakery for the summer. But I figured manual labor left the mind free for some deep thinking. It also introduced me to a stratum of society I hitherto had been insulated against—the blue-collar people. I am the one who slogs along through every line of *Crime and Punishment* unlike my friends who are either reading abridged copies of it or one of those outline series on it. Everyone in my generation seems to be out to be a Tom Dooley. But I see that there must still be people who run stores, gas stations, and small or large businesses. Who else but me in my class wants to open a real estate office? Someone has to mind the economy while others are either deserting the world or are out saving it. } examples

As has been shown, then, it is important to say something concrete in your autobiography. It's not enough to write that you've done well in school courses, that you get along with everyone, that you're civic minded. Give specific illustrations to show what you mean.

The last cardinal rule to follow in writing an antobiography is to make it interesting.

You can do this if you remember how many autobiographies come across the desks of admissions officials each year. The larger the institution is, the greater the number of what some officials have called "those tiresome and adolescent autobiographies." Knowing this and realizing how competitive some universities are, you can see that you'll have to write a profile that will stand out favorably.

You need not be a great author to write a profile that will catch the attention and interest of admissions staffs. Often, just a slight touch of humor will set your autobiography apart from the rest of the sketches which are bland, boring, and banal. Just paying attention to some of the hints on writing style shown in the profile section of the theme portion will put you far beyond a boring autobiography. Read it carefully, especially as it concerns anecdotes and humor.

You'll also be helped if you consider some of the "Don'ts" on writing style. They, too, can give your profile quite an edge over others being read at the colleges.

Initially, avoid the opening paragraphs previously described as poor writing. These are quite popular with most students who do not know any better.

Secondly, don't run to the extreme of being either servile or overpretentious. Both styles are most exasperating. Here is an example of an obsequiously modest bit of writing:

> Who am I to try to believe I might be the kind of top student your university strives to enroll? I am cognizant that my study habits, while good enough for Madison High School, are not what they should be to a high achiever at your fine institution. I was fortunate to be on the honor roll several times in my career so far as a student, but I know that the competition on a college level will turn my efforts to molten dust probably. Your magnificent standards are known throughout this great land of ours. My own small intellect can only try very hard to stay the pace.

The pretentious writer is as obnoxious and usually sounds something like this:

> I and Aristotle agree quite often on the growth of the human spirit. Often have I consulted him and my own favorite philosopher, the somewhat lesser known Lucretius, on the true meaning of life. Is it a *sine qua non*? Nowhere have I found my own quest answered in the "Vision of God to His Universal Form" section of the *Bhagavad-Gita*. As Arjuna says at one point: "Universal Form, I see you without limit,/ Infinite of arms, eyes, mouths and bellies—/ See all the sages, and the holy serpents." This signalizes my feelings.

The applicant above is an intellectual show-off. He thinks he must demonstrate that he can drop erudite blockbusters, that he is well-read. Perhaps a small segment of the college applicants do have a great deal of intellectual background, but most do not. Unfortunately, it is known that most teenagers have no more than a superficial grasp of such subject matter that they sprinkle through their autobiographies. Don't be an intellectual show-off.

Don't write in lists. This fault is best demonstrated by the following all-too-familiar example in autobiographies. Avoid list writing like this:

> I have been active in the following school items: Silver Tri my sophomore year; Red Cross, sophomore and junior, vice president my senior year; Pep Club, sophomore, junior and senior; Glee Club, junior; Oriolians, junior; Leadership Club, junior; Blue Tri, junior and senior; student director, junior class play; Masque and Gavel, junior and senior, vice president, junior; Echo staff, senior; Vocational Club, senior; National Honor Society, senior; Graduation Committee, Senior Honor Roll.

The example above reads like an entry in the senior section of a yearbook. Far better to smooth it out so that it looks as little like a list as you can make it. How it might have been handled is shown in the next example:

> Like my mother and sisters, I have a propensity for many varied activities, most of which I participated in these last two years. Because I felt community service was important, I took part in the Blue and Silver Tri organizations and Red Cross. Music and journalism also held interest for me. I was a member of the Glee Club and Oriolian chorus and worked on the school newspaper, *The Echo*. Dramatic work is another of my passions, and I tried to fulfil this by being the student director of our junior class play and participation in the Masque and Gavel organization. The Vocational Club and Pep Club served as outlets for career ideas and fun, respectively. Academically speaking, I was elected to the National Honor Society and earned a place on the Senior Honor Roll. These scholastic achievements led to my being chosen for the Graduation Committee.

It's true that the second version of this activities paragraph runs slightly longer than the first, but it shows far more imagination, skill in organization, and smooth use of the English language than the list type of writing found in the first example.

Don't use clichés, bromides or platitudes in the writing of your autobiography. Check the list of these to see what expressions to avoid.

Don't lean on quotations of the famous and infamous in your profile. This is especially important if you are given a 200- to 500-word limitation by the college. You'll use up precious footage with quotes. To some, it might seem impressive to quote from Dr. Johnson, Plato, Oliver Wendell Holmes, Oscar Wilde, or Voltaire. But as one exasperated admissions assistant once put it: "If I see one more quote from Emerson or Bacon, I'm going to throw up." Don't feel that leaning on the great lends depth or sets an element of high tone to your writing. Anyone can sprinkle quotes around if he has access to Bartlett's *Familiar Quotations*. What's wrong with saying what *you* want to say all by yourself? Put it in your own words. You probably will come out sounding far clearer than if you had leaned on a quotation. It does take work to shape a quotation to fit your needs exactly anyway.

One last "Don't": Don't exceed the word limit if you've been given one by the college. If you do, it will indicate several things that are distinctly not in your favor. One is that you can't follow directions too well. Another is that you are such a poor writer that you can't condense material. Another impression you might leave is that you are looking for special attention or favoritism. Stick to the limitations set by the college. It is doubtful whether you deserve special consideration.

BIBLIOGRAPHY

Allen, Eliot D. and Colbrunn, Ethel B. *A Short Guide to Writing a Research Paper*. Everett Edwards, 1975.

————. *Student Writer's Guide*. Everett Edwards, 1975.

Anderson, Jonathan. *Thesis and Assignment Writing*. Wiley, 1970.

Anderson, Kenneth E. and Haugh, Oscar M. *A Handbook for the Preparation of Research Reports and Theses*. University Press of America, 1978.

Associated Press. *The Associated Press Stylebook*. The Associated Press, 1977.

Astle, Cedric. *English at a Glance*. Arden Library, 1968.

Atteberry, James L. and Atteberry, Ruth D. *Guide to Research and Report Writing*. Tam's Books, 1974.

Avery, Thomas E. *A Student's Guide to Thesis Research*. Burgess, 1978.

Barzun, Jacques and Graff, Henry F. *The Modern Researcher*. Harcourt . Brace Jovanovich, 1977.

Bates, Jefferson D. *Writing With Precision*. Acropolis Books, 1978.

Behlins, John H. *Guidelines for Preparing the Research Proposal*. University Press of America, 1978.

Berry, R. *How to Write a Research Paper*. Pergamon, 1969.

Cash, Phyllis. *How to Write a Research Paper Step by Step*. Monarch Press, 1975.

Cely, Jonathan. *Writing a Research Paper*. Indiana Scholastic Press, 1978.

Chase, Mary Ellen. *Constructive Theme Writing*. Holt, 1957.

Christianson, Pauline. *From Inside Out: Writing From Subjective to Objective*. Winthrop, 1978.

Coggins, Gordon. *A Guide to Writing Essays and Research Papers*. Van Nostrand Reinhold, 1977.

Cooper, Charles W. and Robins, Edmund J. *The Term Paper: A Manual and Model*. Stanford University Press, 1967.

Corbin, Richard and Corbin, Jonathan. *Research Papers: A Guided Writing Experience for Senior High Students*. English Council, 1978.

Cordasco, Francesco and Gatner, Elliot S. *Report and Research Writing*. Littlefield, 1974.

Coyle, William. *Research Papers*. Odyssey Press, 1976.

Cummings, Marsha Z. and Slade, Carole. *Writing the Research Paper*. Houghton Mifflin, 1978.

Deighton, Lee C. *Handbook of American English Spelling*. Harcourt Brace Jovanovich, 1978.

DeVillez, Randy. *Step by Step: College Writing*. Kendall-Hunt, 1977.

Doremus, Robert B. *Writing College Themes*. Oxford University Press, 1960.

Doubleday, Neal F. *Writing the Research Paper*. Heath, 1971.

Draper, Lowell A. *A Curse on Confusion: An Individualized Approach to Clear Writing*. Cambridge Book Co., 1976.

Draper, Samuel. *Simple Guide to Research Papers*. Avery Publishing, 1978.

Ewing, David W. *Writing for Results*. Wiley, 1974.

Fergus, Patricia M. *Spelling Improvement*. McGraw-Hill, 1978.

Flesch, Rudolf. *Look It Up: A Deskbook of American Spelling and Style*. Harper & Row, 1977.

Furness, Edna. *Spelling for the Millions*. Nelson, 1977.

Gehlmann, John and Eisman, Philip. *Say What You Mean*. Odyssey Press, 1968.

Godshalk, Fred I. *Measurement of Writing Ability*. College Board, 1966.

Gorrell, Robert and Gorrell, Laird. *Modern English Handbook*. Prentice-Hall, 1976.

Graves, Harold F. and Hoffman, L. *Report Writing*. Prentice-Hall, 1965.

Hake, Rosemary. *Mapping the Model: A Basic Rhetoric for the Basic Writer*. Kendall Hall, 1978.

Hook, J. N. *English Today: A Practical Handbook*. Wiley, 1976.

Hubbell, George Shelton. *Writing Term Papers and Reports*. Barnes and Noble, 1958.

Hugon, Paul D. *Modern Word Finder*. Gale, 1974.

Hutchinson, Helene. *Hutchinson Guide to Writing Research Papers*. Glencoe, 1973.

Inglish, Joyce and Jackson, Joan. *Research and Composition*. Prentice-Hall, 1977.

Janis, Jack Harold. *Writing and Communicating in Business*. Macmillan, 1973.

Kearney, Elizabeth I. *How to Write a Composition*. Lucas, 1972.

Knowles, Lyle. *A Guide for Writing Research Papers, Theses, and Dissertations*. Tam's Books, 1973.

Kreirsky, Joseph and Linfield, Jordan. *The Bad Speller's Dictionary*. Random House, 1967.

Lester, James D. *Writing Research Papers: A Complete Guide*. Scott, Foresman, 1976.

Lindblom, P. *Writing the Theme: A Practical Guide*. Winthrop, 1973.

Markman, Roberta H. and Waddell, Marie L. *Ten Steps in Writing the Research Paper*. Barrons, 1971.

Miles, Leland. *Guide to Writing Term Papers*. University of Iowa, 1959.

Mitchell, S. *How to Write Reports*. Watts, 1975.

Mulkerne, Donald J. D. and Kahn, Gilbert. *The Term Paper Step by Step*. Doubleday, 1977.

New York Times. *The New York Times Style Book for Writers and Editors*. The New York Times, 1962.

Perrin, Porter G. *Writer's Guide and Index to English*. Scott, Foresman, 1965.

Pugh, Griffith T. *Guide to Research Writing*. Houghton Mifflin, 1968.

Ranald, Margaret. *A Style Manual for College Students*. Queens College Press, 1975.

Reader's Digest How to Write Better, Speak Better. Norton, 1972.

Roth, Audrey J. *Research Papers: Form and Content*. Wadsworth, 1978.

Schneider, Ben R., Jr., and Tjossem, Herbert. *Theses and Research Papers*. Macmillan, 1962.

Sears, Donald A. *Harbrace Guide to the Library and the Research Paper*. Harcourt Brace Jovanovich, 1973.

Short, Raymond W. and DeMaria, Robert. *Subjects and Sources for Research Writing*. Norton, 1963.

Stegner, Wallace E. *Effective Theme*. Holt, Rinehart & Winston, 1967.

Stein, M. L. *How to Write Better Comompositions, Term Papers and Reports*. Cornerstone, 1978.

Strunk, William, Jr., and White, E. B. *The Elements of Style*. Macmillan, 1959.

Swanson, Richard. *For Your Information: A Guide to Writing Reports*. Prentice-Hall, 1974.

Teitelbaum, Harry. *How to Write Book Reports*. Simon and Schuster, 1975.

Turner, R. P. *Technical Report Writing*. Holt, Rinehart & Winston, 1971.

Index

ca = College Application Autobiography
cs = Complex Subjects
tp = Term Paper
t = Theme